Also by Christopher Buckley

Little Green Men

Thank You For Smoking

Wet Work

The White House Mess

Wry

Martínis

.

Wry
Martinis

Christopher
Buckley

a&b

This edition published in Great Britain in 2004 by
Allison & Busby Limited
Bon Marche Centre
241-251 Ferndale Road
London SW9 8BJ
http://www.allisonandbusby.com

Grateful acknowledgement is made to the US publications
in which many of these essays first appeared.

A catalogue record for this book is available from
the British Library.

ISBN 0 7490 0694 3

Printed and bound in the UK by
Bookmarque, Surrey

For Mum and Pup

No animals were harmed in the making of this book.

Contents

My Title Problem   xv

Aperitifs

Homage to Tom Clancy

Spin Cycle

Want to Buy a Dead Dictator?

Guy Stuff

Hardly Roughing It

Babes

Formative Years

A Few More for the Road

My Title Problem

This is my sixth book, and I've had a hard time coming up with titles for all of them. I thought it would get easier, but it hasn't. I should be better at it, since I'm also a magazine editor and coming up with titles is a big part of that job. When I was a junior editor at *Esquire* in the '70s, I would break out in a sweat trying to come up with clever titles. *Esquire* was famous for them: "Frank Sinatra Has a Cold," "Las Vegas (What?). Las Vegas (Can't Hear You! Too Noisy!). *Las Vegas!!!!*" "Hell Sucks."

One time I spent three days on one headline. I'm not going to tell you what I came up with, because you'd only say, *You spent three days on—that?*

This is mostly a collection of my magazine stuff. Random House doesn't want you to know that. Publishers flaunt the word "collection" on a book cover the way canned soup makers do the words "Tastes best if eaten before the year A.D. 2010."

I wanted to call it *Oeuvre to You. Oeuvre* is a classy French word. No one knows how to pronounce it, but if you make a sound similar to the one you'd make right before throwing up a plateful of *choucroute garni*, you've pretty much got it. I faxed the title to my father, to whom this book is dedicated, along with my mother. He faxed back "NO!!!" which I took to mean NO!!!

Then I came up with *Ruined Weekends,* which sounded stately and grand. For some reason, most of the pieces in here were due on Monday. I tried it out on my editor, Jonathan Karp. With the sensitivity that is his trademark, Jon agreed that it was stately, even grand, but said it was "a kind of a downer." Some people, he said, might have a hard time getting past the word "Ruined."

No comparisons intended, but you wonder if Gibbon today would be able to sell a publisher on *Decline and Fall of the Roman Empire.* They would probably call it *How Kinky Sex, Greed and Lead Goblets Caused the Collapse of the Roman Empire—And How It Can Rise Again!?* Or *Barbarians at the Gate.*

I came back at Karp with *Want to Buy a Dead Dictator?* It's a reference to a hoax we undertook in the pages of the magazine I edit, *Forbes FYI.* We announced with a straight face that the Russians were so strapped for hard currency that they were preparing to auction off the corpse of Lenin. Peter Jennings of ABC's *World News Tonight* went with the story and the Russians went intercontinentally ballistic. It became a big international story. Karp's reaction to my brainstorm was, "We can't have the words 'dead' and 'dictator' in the title. No one will buy it."

The book biz is littered with might-have-been titles. Andre Bernard wrote a fun book a few years ago called *Now All We Need Is a Title,* recounting some of the more resplendent clunkers. *The Great Gatsby* came close to being called *Trimalchio in East Egg* (Trimalchio being the rich patron in Petronius's *Satyricon*). Waugh wanted to call *Brideshead Revisited, The House of the Faith.* On the other hand we might now be saying with equal incredulity, "Can you believe Woodward and Bernstein almost called *At This Point in Time, All the President's Men*?"

I noodled around and suggested *Homage to Tom Clancy.* I liked it. It had a certain *je ne sais quoi,* and there was the chance that five billion Clancy fans might mistake it for the real thing and make me accidentally rich. The background is that I got into a little pissing match with Mr. Clancy after I reviewed one of his books for *The New York Times.* I called him a racist and the most successful bad writer in American since James Fenimore Cooper. The comment was itself an homage to Mark Twain, whose essay "The Literary Crimes of Fenimore Cooper" is still the most hilarious literary evisceration in American letters. Oddly, Mr. Clancy didn't like being called a racist and a bad writer, and my fax machine began humming with incoming missives from him. These were leaked to the press (not—promise—by me). Our pissy fit became gossip page grist for a few days. But in the end Karp and I decided it was a bit of an inside joke and, anyway, did it make economic sense to annoy five billion Tom Clancy readers?

I suggested *Dual Airbags.* At first Karp did not click, being a New Yorker whose only experience with automobiles is riding in the backseat of taxis driven by people with names like Ibrahim Abouhalima (which in Arabic means "America will pay dearly for its support of Israel!"). So I explained that since these days, dual airbags are such a big selling point for car buyers, why shouldn't the concept appeal to book buyers as well? There was, too, the rather nifty, self-deprecating double entendre implying that the author is not just a gasbag, but a *real* gasbag. He liked that, and we would have used it, except everyone else hated it.

Then I came back with a title that I quite liked: *Should I Have Heard of You?* It's taken from a typical airplane conversation:

PERSON NEXT TO ME: And what do you do?

ME: I'm a writer.

PERSON (*Perking up*): Oh? What's your name?

ME: Chris Buckley.

PERSON (*Frowning*): Should I have heard of you?

ME (*Bravely*): Not really.

PERSON: If you're a writer, then you must know John Grisham.

ME (*Seizing the moment*): Who?

PERSON (*After fifteen minutes spent recapitulating the plot to each entry in the Grisham oeuvre*): I have all his books. Hardcover and paperback. I also have them all in audiocassette. I buy his books *before* they come out.

ME (*Pretending to be absorbed in an article called "What's New in Newark?" in the in-flight magazine*): Well, if you like that sort of thing.

PERSON: Do you know, he's got fifty million books in print.

ME: Of course, the real test is, Will you still be in print a hundred years from now? That's more what I'm aiming for. But I'll certainly give this fellow Grashman a try, on your recommendation.

Fans of *One-upmanship* will recognize that exchange for what it is: Homage to Stephen Potter (1900–1965). It is, of course, completely disingenuous on my part. I know all about John Grisham and his fifty million books in print, and I hate him. He probably also has a wonderful sex life, too, damn him. At any rate, *Should I Have Heard of You?* was rejected as too precious.

By now I was getting sullen and resentful, which, being an only child, I frequently tend to get. "Give me my own way exactly in everything," said Thomas Carlyle, "and a sunnier, more pleasant creature does not exist." When I read that quote to my wife, she laughed, bitterly.

Karp manfully suggested that he give the title a go on his own. A few days went by and my fax machine disgorged his suggestion: *The Ten Commandments*. Catchy as it was, I demurred. Let me say for the record: Jon Karp is an excellent editor, smart, funny, eager, hardworking, generous, returns-your-phone-calls, serious. (The man spends his summer vacations in the library at Brown University, rereading Tolstoy and Dostoyevsky. I am not kidding.) And now that we've got that out of the way, let me say that *The Ten Commandments* is, arguably, THE WORST BOOK TITLE SINCE *Trimalchio in East Egg*.

It crossed my mind that it might part of a sinister promotional plan by Random House to turn me into an American version of Salman Rushdie. Publishers strive to get their books turned into news stories.

AUTHOR IN HIDING AMIDST
CONTROVERSY OVER BOOK

There's nothing resembling blasphemy in here. There is a piece about the Pope going on Oprah to promote his book, but it's hardly worth an excommunication. There's also a piece about being an agnostic dad, running my own private Sunday school so my seven-year-old daughter will grow up with the kind of firm grounding in Judeo-Christian tradition that enables you to slam the door in the faces of pesky Jehovah's Witnesses. That *did* get a response, but not quite what I was hoping for. It ran in a Sunday newspaper supplement with a combined circulation of forty million. For one bright, shining moment I had almost as many readers as John Grisham. And they hated me. For months I was deluged with prayer books, Bibles, and letters telling me that unless I repented, I was going to burn in hell for all eternity. I did think it a bit harsh, considering the piece was about trying to raise your kids to know who Moses and Jesus were. In any event, we were still stuck for a title.

We came up with *FedExLax and Other Mergers*. It's a title that needs explaining, and quickly. It's from a Headlines of the Coming Year thing I did for *The New Yorker*. My wife told me she would divorce me if I called it that. And it did occur to me that my parents might not appreciate being the dedicatees of a book named after a famous laxative. Karp loved it, but then he has a very crude and unsophisticated sense of humor. This is why we work so well together. But back to square one.

Bassholes. This too requires some explanation. It's from a *New Yorker* piece in the book, a parody of brief reviews of new books on fly-fishing. One of the books is titled *Bassholes,* a vituperative attack on bass fishermen and -women by a fly-fishing purist professor at the University of Vermont. After it came out, *The New Yorker* got a lot of frustrated phone calls and letters from people who couldn't find the books in stores. One person actually called up the University of Vermont to track down the author of *Bassholes,* and was annoyed to learn that there was no one on the faculty by that name. I wrote them all to explain. I sort of wanted to tell them, "Do you *really* think that Peter Benchley has written a book called *Gills* about a vengeful Dolly Varden trout?" (Having recently caught ten minutes of the TV movie of his book *The Beast,* I'm willing to admit *Gills* is not so far-fetched.) But I took their confusion as a kind of compliment, as I did when the press rose to my Lenin fly. Effective satire doesn't show stretch marks.

On the other hand, it's presumptuous to take credit for living in a world in which pretty much anything is plausible. What *would* surprise you to see on TV? The chief executive officers of the Big Seven American tobacco companies, testifying under oath before the Congress, "I do not believe nicotine is addictive"? Would you believe me if I said that the head of that same congressional committee was replaced a year later by a tobacco-friendly congressman from Richmond, Virginia, who, before he went to Washington, was a mortician? I wrote a comic novel about the tobacco lobby, and I wouldn't have *dared* go that far. But a few days ago, O. J. Simpson said that he never beat up Nicole. No, no. *She* was trying to beat up *him.* See? Those bruises she had in the photographs were makeup. It would take a satirist with balls of stone to come up with that.

On the back page of *FYI* we run a feature called "The Bull Board," a gathering of recent news clippings, a first rough draft of absurdity. I'd count it a good day indeed at the word processor if I came up with any of the following on my own:

"Russian Public Television has cancelled Aleksandr Solzhenitsyn's talk show."

"Everybody knows that I have tougher ethics rules than any previous president." (Clinton.)

"Alert Customs official noticed 'something weird' about a woman's bosom. And on further inspection found 65 baby snakes in her bra."

"A Greenwich, Connecticut, CEO plead guilty to defecating on the food
cart on a flight from Rio to New York. His defense was that he had
been barred from using the first class toilet." If that was the defense, the
plea was wise. (Bonus point: the gentleman's no doubt proud wife runs
a company of her own called The Moving Experience.)

"A Wilmington, North Carolina, neurosurgeon's license was suspended
after he left a patient's brain exposed for 25 minutes while he got lunch."

"An airliner heading to South Africa was forced to turn back and make an
emergency landing in Britain after 72 flatulent pigs triggered its fire
alarms." *Heathrow, we have a problem.*

Some years ago, after watching a forest fire annihilate thousands of
hectares of southern France, the sky buzzing with military airplanes fer-
rying water from a nearby lake, I was told a story utterly harrowing, yet
—forgive me—ineffably comic. After this fire had burned itself out, they
found the remains of a man, snorkel, goggles, and flippers in the upper
branches of a charred tree. One minute, you're looking down at little
brightly colored fishies in the water, the next you're being dumped out
of a plane onto a forest fire. What did they say at this poor guy's funeral?
That God loved him?

"French inventor Yves Renault has fit oysters with pop-open tabs and a
French firm expects 50 million 'ringed' oysters to be sold in France this
winter." My parents call this sort of thing Problems of the Idle Rich.

Finally:

"Three janitors trying to freeze a gopher to death caused an explosion that
injured 19 people." The last paragraph reads, "The gopher survived and
was later released in a field, unharmed." Here one discerns the hand of
God. Wherever you stand on the Problem of Job, you have to admire
the way He intervenes when the least of His creatures are threatened by
cretins armed with freon and lit cigarettes.

You could add to the above items any statement made by any lawyer on
behalf of any Menendez brother since August of 1989. I'm thinking in
particular of that woman—I cannot bring myself to say her name—you

know, the one with the hair, who complained after hanging the first jury that it was an outrage that bail was being denied these two angels who had shotgunned their parents to death, pausing to reload while Mom crawled across the carpet with *her* brain exposed. "These are terrific kids," she said.

Hypocrisy is the night soil of satire. I say, Thank God for defense lawyers, politicians and cigarette lobbyists. They keep people like me in business. I don't flatter myself that my worst shots at them accomplish anything more than a transitory rouging of their cheeks. (If that.) The chairman of Philip Morris, the international tobacco company, was asked by *Business Week* if he had read *Thank You for Smoking*, an "exquisitely vicious" (*Washington Post*) novel about the tobacco industry. He said he'd found it "very amusing." His surname, by the way, is Bible, not that I would have dared to use that, fictionally. But—smart fellow, clever answer. Never complain, never explain. Give Mr. Bible a little legal wiggle room, and he might even quote Claud Cockburn at you: "You cannot satirize a man who says, 'I'm only in it for the money and that's all there is to it.' " If he and his ilk were allowed by their lawyers to say, "What do you take us for, morons? Of course we know cigarettes kill you, but they're legal, people love them, and we can make a killing selling them." Try to distill an "exquisitely vicious" satire out of that.

As for the politicos, here's the stump speech I'm waiting to hear:

"My friends, I've done a lot of rotten things in my life. Cheated on my wife, gotten drunk, fallen down the stairs, hit the kids, kicked the dog, dodged the draft, smoked dope, snorted coke and mainlined crystal meth. I've cut so many deals with shady people it would take ten grand juries working overtime just to keep up with the indictments. As President, I will stand on the White House balcony holding a licked finger up to the air to see which way the wind is blowing. I'll put my friends and cronies, even the ones who should already be in jail, in positions of authority. There will be so many special prosecutors looking into my administration that you will never lack for entertainment. As for the problems facing our nation, I'll do what I can, but, frankly, I don't think there's a hell of a lot anyone can do at this point, things are so screwed up. But I really, really want to be President. I want the limousine and the motorcade and the flashing lights and the big, big airplane."

I'd love to write that guy's inaugural speech.

JONES PLEDGES ERA OF 'SAME GAME, DIFFERENT NAME'; WILL 'MOST LIKELY RAISE TAXES FIRST CHANCE I GET'

Where were we? *Karp!* Oh yeah, titles.

By now I was sort of despairing. I had that thousand-yard-stare of the creatively challenged. I was unresponsive with the kids, the way I am when they remind me that it's time for "us" to swab out their hamster's disgusting cage. (Highlight of my week.) I would sit silently amidst family gaiety, mumbling to myself like one of the inmates in *One Flew Over the Cuckoo's Nest.*

"What about . . ." I would say, biting down on a pathetic pun. One night I looked up from the Mrs. Paul's fish sticks and said, imploringly, "*Crave the Whales?*" You see, there's a piece in the book about—oh, never mind. By now Lucy was sugar-coating her reactions. A bad sign. What fun it must be, being married to a writer.

My dog, Duck, sniffed the aroma of failure about me and no longer went about his game of unplugging my fax machine from the phone jack. It pleases him to do this every couple of days and listen to me on the phone berate my correspondents angrily for *their* defective fax machines.

One day, in the grip of this despondency, I thought about the first piece that I sold to *The New Yorker.* That was a big day for me. It was about Clinton and Bush getting drunk during their presidential debate, and it was called "The Three-Martini Debate." And suddenly there it was, my title.

I know, I know, what a lot of fuss over—nothing. But this time Karp looked up from Dostoyevsky and said, "Hmm. Yeah." Lucy sighed heavily with relief, satisfied she could go back to taking care of only two children instead of three. Duck again took up his pastime of rendering me incommunicado.

The title itself means, of course, absolutely nothing. It's just an excuse to get the word "Martini" onto the cover in the hopes that someone will mistake it for a book on mixology. But it works on at least one level, as a small homage to *The New Yorker,* much owed in my case. I'm grateful to a number of people there, starting with its editor, Tina Brown, who has been more attentive and kind to me than she ever needed to be, which made it all the sweeter. *The New Yorker* still sets the standard for thoughtful editing (to say nothing of the fact-checking). I've been lucky to work with a number of superb editors there: Rick Hertzberg, Chip McGrath, Deborah Garrison, David Kuhn, Chris Knutsen, Henry Finder, Susan Mercandetti and Hal Espen. An all-star team, that.

Thank you, Harry Evans, for publishing yet another book of mine; and thank you, Binky Urban, for making Harry pay for it.

I'm grateful, too—oh god, here it comes, his I'd-like-to-thank-the-Academy-speech—to the editors I've worked with over the twenty years of freelancing covered in this book. Clay Felker gave me my start in magazines and was the kind of editor who leaves you with a lifetime of great stories, and a lifetime of gratitude. I was privileged, and that's not putting it too grandly, to have the chance to work with and learn from some of the other people who made *Esquire* the legend that it was: Byron Dobell, Don Erickson, Rust Hills and Gordon Lish.

The pieces in here originally appeared in a number of publications, including *The New York Times, The Washington Post, The Wall Street Journal, Regardie's, Esquire, Forbes FYI, Conde Nast Traveler, Vogue, Allure, American Health,* and *Architectural Digest.* But there are some pieces in here that have not been published previously. This was Karp's idea; he thought it would let him off having to put the word "collection" on the cover.

I'd be ungrateful, if not downright ungracious, not to thank my boss at *Forbes FYI,* which has been my happy professional home for over five years now. So, Bob Forbes, thanks for the great memories, the support, the friendship and last but hardly least, all the great times on *The Highlander.* A boss shouldn't be this nice, and a day job shouldn't be this much fun. Thanks, too, to his brothers Steve, Tim and Kip for their friendship and support.

Geoffrey Norman has been a buddy and colleague since the old days at *Esquire.* Now he's editor-at-large of *FYI.* I talk with Geoff sometimes three, four times a day, and each time, I come away a little smarter and a lot calmer. For years, Geoff has been the first inflictee of much of the stuff in here, and as such has suffered mightily. There's nothing I can do to repay this debt, except to say, All right, you can have a two-week extension handing in your New Zealand piece.

This book is dedicated to my father and mother. I was going to dedicate my first book to them, but then John Lennon died while I was writing it, and so I dedicated it to his memory. I was going to dedicate the second one to them, but I got married, so I dedicated that one to Lucy. Then I was going to dedicate the third one to them, but my friend Reggie Stoops took ill and I promised him that I would dedicate it to him. Then I was going to dedicate the fourth book to them, only we weren't speaking at the time—happens in the best of families—and anyway my friend John Tierney had been such a help it only seemed right to dedicate it to him. There was also a play I wrote with James MacGuire about Edmund Campion that was published as a book. I was going to dedicate that to them, too, but then seven Jesuit priests were murdered in El Salvador, so we dedicated it to them.

But this time it really is for my parents, with thanks and love, no matter who, between now and publication date, gets shot or comes down with cancer. It was with them that I had my first laughs.

Washington, D.C.
May 15, 1996

POSTSCRIPT: A few hours after I FedExed this book off to the publisher, my good friend Richard M. Clurman died. I've postponed dedicating a book to my parents for too long, so I'll stick to the original plan. But this book would otherwise be dedicated to Dick, and to his wife, Shirley, my extra set of parents.

Aperitifs

House-Guest Hell

Since my wife and I live in Washington, D.C., where summers are bummers, we and the kids and the dog go to Maine. This insures two things: taunts about being idle Republicans, and house guests. This season's triple-digit temperatures have provided a bumper crop of calls from friends old and new, and what I have learned is that, just as the most beautiful words in the English language are "You've lost weight," the most dreaded surely are "We can only stay for a week."

I want to apologize in advance for the hasty quality of this article. I don't have time to make it very good, because I have to leave for the Bangor airport in one hour to pick up the new arrivals, and on the way I have to stop at the laundromat and drop off the twenty pounds of dirty bed linen left by the ones who've just left. Lucy, my wife, would drop them off, except she's already in Ellsworth, shopping for the hypoallergenic foodstuffs required by the incoming house guests. I'm sorry about this. For now, then, here are my notes toward a *Field Guide to the North American House Guest.*

1. The Foreign House Guest from a Non-English-Speaking Country (*Domesticus aeternus helveticus*). A visitation by this variety generally coincides with an entire week of rain and fog, forcing a cancellation of all outdoor activities and necessitating uninterrupted togetherness in one living room. Indications of ennui generally begin toward the end of the fourth day indoors, with conversation taking the form of "How many brothers and sisters does your brother's new wife have?" followed by "And what are their ages?"

Alternatively, "What is the principal industry of Appenzell Inner Rhodes?"

2.   The House Guest Who Injures Him/Herself (*Domesticus aeternus calamitosus*).   This variety is particularly prevalent among the sports-minded house guests. One *calamitosus,* having visited a host we know for a weekend, broke his ankle during a distinctly unvigorous round of Frisbee-catching. Togetherness was extended for eight days. This required a number of adjustments, including turning the master bedroom, on the first floor, into a hospital room, and attending to his every need twenty-four hours a day.

Suggested protocol for coping with *calamitosus:* As you will be providing the injured party with all meals, and most likely in bed, you will have unobserved access to his/her foodstuffs. Halcion .25 mgs. (a.k.a. triazolam or "the blue oval ones") crushed into powder and added to food can significantly reduce the house guest's demands, but hosts are advised to check with doctors for possible contraindications.

3.   The Cash-Challenged House Guest (*Domesticus aeternus britannicus-journalisticus*).   Easily recognized by his distinctive warble "Bloody hell, I must have left my wallet in the city." *Britannicus* is common along the eastern seaboard during the summer months, but is also apt to appear at any time of the year, anywhere, usually with little notice. Another distinctive cry is "Could I ask you to cash a cheque?" However, caution should be exercised, as the "cheques" are often drawn on unrecognizable banks, such as the Second Bank of Aran, or Unión de Crédito Agrícola de Uruguay.

4.   The Telephone-Dependent House Guest (*Domesticus aeternus fiberopticus-praeferrissimus*).   Closely related to *britannicus,* above, *fiberopticus* is identifiable by the telltale question—usually asked within moments of arrival—"Could I use the phone?" and, thereafter, by his habit of cheerfully miming the words "Be off in *two* seconds" as his host approaches, scowling. Tying up the telephone is not the only pitfall associated with this variety. One host reported feeling physically ill upon hearing his guest shout loudly into the telephone, as if

to an overseas operator, "*Vladimir? Da. Da. Yes, I accept collect,*" and on another occasion overhearing a conversation in which occurred the words "Myanmar" and "That's ridiculous, I've only been on for an hour and forty minutes."

5. The Laptopless House Guest (*Domesticus aeternus lotus*). Key identifying phrases are "I didn't feel like lugging mine all the way here" followed by "How many megs does yours have? I'm going to need all you've got." (Important warning: *lotus* has been known to reemerge after an hour with his host's computer, frowning and saying, "I don't understand. Your hard drive seems to be completely empty.")

I should say that we like our house guests. They are good people. So if any of them should read this, do understand that this is not about you. It is about the people who came the week after you did.

—*The New Yorker*, 1995

The Three-Martini Debate

■

"They both come to my house. We serve them a Martini.
And we have an exchange between the two."
—Tom Brokaw in *The New York Times*,
proposing an alternative presidential-debate format

BROKAW: Mr. President, Governor, thank you for coming. I'm sorry Mr. Perot declined, but he's a teetotaler. How do you take your Martinis?

BUSH: Dry as a bone, with fruit, and on the rocks.

CLINTON: I'll just have a beer, thanks.

BUSH: Whoa, what is this, Miller Time? I thought we were going to be hefting Martoonis.

CLINTON: Where I grew up, in a place called Hope, people drank corn liquor. Gin was for country clubs.

BUSH: I wouldn't start in on country clubs if I'd got *my* putter caught in a wringer for belonging to an all-white club. If you see what I'm *driving* at . . . heh–heh.

CLINTON: I was never in that club. OK, maybe I played a little golf there with businessmen, so I could target a few incentives on them. We can't all buy infrastructural investments out of our trust funds, ya know.

BROKAW: How do you want your Martini, Governor?

CLINTON: In a beer glass. Olives on the side. Got any peanuts or crackers?

BUSH: What's the matter? Got the munchies?

CLINTON: Tom, I govern better stoned than he does straight. Not that I ever did get stoned.

BUSH: Hold on. But I'm glad the subject of peanuts came up, because I think everyone in our wonderful country remembers Mr. Peanut, from Plains.

BROKAW: Your point being, sir?

BUSH: Exactly. Mmm. I'll have another. Little less vermouth this time.

CLINTON: Thank you, Tom. First, Al Gore and I happen to believe that there is a place for mixed drinks in today's post–New Deal Democratic Party. So I'll have another, too. Second, I'm proud to have an environmentally aware running mate who's orthographically sensitive to basic tubers. Third, could I get some more olives? In Arkansas we're working closely with the horticultural community on issues of olive-grove deforestation.

BUSH: Thank you. Mmm. Much better. Still a little wet, but getting there. I'd like to ask the Governor what he drank over there while he was learning social engineering at Oxford during the Vietnam War. *Draft* beer? Oh, Bar, Poppy's throwing ringers tonight!

CLINTON: That's been gone into again and again, so I'm not going to go into it. Could I get another, with olives?

BUSH: You know, Tom, after I was shot down by the Japsters while serving my country, which Governor Elvis here wouldn't know about, I was paddling like a wet cocker spaniel in those shark-infested waters down there. Not fun. Know what I couldn't stop thinking about? Aside from that fellow some people don't like to talk about—G-O-D? Wrapping my lips around an ice-cold see-through. How about another? *Thirsty* just thinking about getting shot down.

CLINTON: Tom, it's hard to enjoy getting tanked when so many people in this country can't afford gin. The Germans and the Japanese are way ahead of us in terms of gin availability per capita, and Japan has the highest gin-to-vermouth ratio in the world.

BUSH: Seems to me the last Diberal Lemocrat, capital "D," capital "L," we elected was also anti-Martini.

CLINTON: There you go with that negative stuff. OK, one more. And keep those olives coming, Dan—er, Tom.

BUSH: Just wave the vermouth bottle over the glass. Don't even have to take the cap off. That's how Uncle Herbie used to make 'em. So where were we? Losing track. Out of the looped.

CLINTON: Isaiah Berlin used to say that Hank Williams was like a fox but Elvis was like a badger.

BUSH: Berlin, *great* city. Wall. Down. But didn't see any foxes there and darn sure didn't see any badgers. Ah. *Thank you. Mmm . . .* Now, *that's* a Martini. Just the way Gorbachev liked his. How do you think I got him to give up the Commie thing? That's right, gave him Uncle Herbie's recipe. *Worked.*

CLINTON: The Germans are way ahead of us on walls. For failed Quayle four years of . . . I don't know who's driving home, but it better not be me. That's why I'm proud to have Al Gore for my designated driver.

BUSH: Gotta say, Hillary—a fox. Hair band, love it. Tipper—more of a badger, maybe, but still, *good woman.*

CLINTON: Hey, weren't we supposed to have some TV cameras here?

BUSH: Hold on, *por favor.* That was all worked out ahead of time. So don't cry for me, Bosnia-Herzegovina. But, Tom, gotta say, good format. If you gotta debate, this is how to do it.

—*The New Yorker,* 1992

An Unsentimental Education

TO THE DIRECTOR OF ADMISSIONS, ST. EUTHANASIUS SCHOOL: I am writing on behalf of my godson Lawton, who is applying for admission to your pre-pre-nursery program. At only two and a half, Lawton displays a precocity remarkable for his years, and a noticeable interest in geology. Only yesterday I saw him purposefully at work in his sandbox. I asked him what he was doing, and he held up a fistful of sand and said, without hesitation, "Sand!"

BACK CURSOR DELETE

I have known Lawton literally all his life. From the very first day I met him—the day he came back from the hospital, in fact—I have been tremendously impressed by his intellectual . . . *by the fact that he didn't throw up on me.*

BACK CURSOR DELETE

Lawton, though only two and a half, has packed more into his life than many a three-year-old. Just last summer, he went to Richmond to stay with his grandparents for a week. When I asked him about his observations on the city, he told me . . . *"Rishmond! Gaaa!"* . . . that he only wished he had known it before the war.

BACK CURSOR DELETE

I am godfather to several children, but none of them, by the time they were two and a half, had exhibited quite the grasp—or depth, certainly—of spatial relationships that Lawton so manifestly does. For instance, when I gave him an engraved wooden box, he immediately understood that the lid was hinged and . . . *slammed it down on his fingers, possibly foreclosing a career as a concert pianist.*

BACK CURSOR DELETE

Among his many extraordinary qualities, Lawton, at only two and a half years old, displays a fine musical ear. His favorite afternoon activity, aside from reading . . . *chewing on books, actually* . . . is to sit on the lap of his nanny, who has, I understand, already taught him the rudiments of conversational Lithuanian, which suggests an exceptional language ability on his part, and to play some of his favorite tunes . . . *that is, pound on the piano with his fists until the dog urinates on the carpet* . . . admittedly simple ones, but with a brio that is striking in a child so young.

BACK CURSOR DELETE

Let me tell you about a special young man named Lawton.

DELETE LINE

Lawton is most definitely not your normal two–and–a–half–year–old.

DELETE LINE

What can I tell you about Lawton? That by the time he was two and a half he was already conversant with the work of Stephen Hawking?

DELETE DELETE DELETE

Lawton! Just to hear his name fills me with hope for the future of our country.

DELETE

Look, what do you want from me? He's two and a half, for Chrissake. He's a toddler, an infant. A *kid*. He does what kids do: squirms, spits up on your new silk Hermès tie, sticks his fingers into electrical sockets, hits other kids, tries to set fire to the dog, swallows sharp objects, falls downstairs during dinner parties, crawls into sooty fireplaces and then across the new wall-to-wall carpet. What do you want me to say—he's got a one-man show at the Whitney? You know, schools like you give me a big fat

DELETE

SHUTDOWN

RE–START

I am delighted to be writing on behalf of my godson Lawton. Since he's only two and a half, I'm not sure what to say about him except that he seems pretty happy and normal and smart and clean. He doesn't have lice. I can't see why he shouldn't get along with the other kids in your school. His parents

DELETE

Lawton's parents, as you may already know from their application, have a combined household income of well over $400,000 p.a., with a very attractive projected earnings potential. And I am not even counting bonuses, which, if I'm not speaking here "out of school" (ha-ha), I understand from recent conversations with them should be in the 100–150K range (combined) this year. Additionally, as dedicated Episcopalians, they tithe, and I happen to know that their favorite charities are educational ones.

SAVE PRINT

—*The New Yorker,* 1993

The
Con Channel

■

A group of conservative political operatives is
expected to announce today the launching of the
Conservative TV Network, a 24-hour pay cable-television
channel expected to debut in early 1996.
—*USA Today*

MORNING

5–6: PRAYER (Mandatory).

6–6:30: NIKKEI TODAY—Highlights from the day's trading on the
Tokyo Stock Exchange.

6:30–7: ¿DÓNDE ESTÁ MI CAFÉ? (Educ.)—Communicating with
your servants.

7–8: GRRRR!—Host G. Gordon Liddy lets Camille Paglia shave his
head; N.R.A. chief Wayne LaPierre on why White House shooter
Francisco Martin Duran missed.

8–9: GIRL TALK WITH MAUREEN REAGAN—Does liposuction work?
Also: Is Patti Davis really Ronald Reagan's daughter?

9–11: PHYLLIS! WITH PHYLLIS SCHLAFLY—Pacific tuna fishermen explain how dolphins commit suicide by hurling themselves into the
nets; also: how to tell if your son is queer.

11–11:30: GET A JOB!—Talking back to the homeless.

11:30–12: HOW TO MARRY A MILLIONAIRE (Educ.)—Hostess Arianna
Huffington shows how to find out how much he's really worth;

guest Mercedes Bass talks about her new seven-billion-dollar studio apartment on the Faubourg Saint-Honoré.

AFTERNOON

12–1: PERLES BEFORE SWINE—Strategic thinker and gourmet chef Richard Perle whips up a perfect *soufflé atomique.*

1–2: AS THE WORLD BURNS (Drama)—Kent is forced to reconsider his views on multiculturalism when he learns that Binky is actually Scottish and not Senegalese.

2–4: MIDDAY MATINEE—*Red Dawn* (1984): Communist paratroopers occupy a Colorado high school. With Patrick Swayze. (Violence; Russian profanity.)

4–4:30: MIDDAY MATINEE PANEL (Public affairs)—Michael Medved asks: Could it happen again? A Colorado school principal argues that students today are well armed enough to repel any invasion; N.R.A. chief Wayne LaPierre disagrees.

4:30–6: HOW'D YOU MAKE OUT TODAY?—Stock-market update, with *Wall Street Journal* editor Bob Bartley; guest Malcolm Forbes, Jr., talking about how he did.

EVENING

6–6:30: EVENING NEWS WITH BRIT HUME—American Addenda: Liberals who drive expensive foreign cars.

6:30–7:30: IRV—Irving Kristol demands that Daniel Patrick Moynihan personally apologize for black illegitimacy; guest Hilton Kramer denounces French Impressionism.

7:30–8: CROSSHAIR—R. Emmett Tyrrell calls Donna Shalala a "Druze dwarf"; Florence King goads ACLU head Ira Glasser by repeatedly mispronouncing his name.

8–8:30: DESTINATION: SINGAPORE—Tour guide Margaret Thatcher takes you behind the scenes in the best-run country in the world, where sneezing in public brings a ten-thousand-dollar fine.

8:30–11: BIOGRAPHY: NEWT ("The Gathering Storm," Part 6 of 12)—Despite his anguished pleas that they can "work it out together," Newt's first wife shocks him by serving him with divorce papers as soon as she comes out of the anesthesia after her cancer operation.

11–12: BEDTIME WITH BILL BENNETT—Virtue czar reads from his favorite Brothers Grimm tales and talks about his one date with Janis Joplin.

LATE NIGHT

12–12:30: MARY AND SERPENTHEAD—Mary throws up in a tony restaurant when she accidentally learns that Serpenthead has agreed to manage Clinton's Presidential campaign. (Mild profanity.)

12:30–1: PERSPIRING LINE—Liddy Dole tests the new NordicTrack 2000.

1–2: THE GREAT BOOKS—Tom Clancy talks about how he has grown as a writer.

2–3: OH YEAH, WELL, WHAT ARE YOUR SHOES MADE OF?—Talking back to PETA activists.

3–3:30: CAPITAL GANG—Tonight: Utah's crack firing squad. Also, Florida State Prison's Old Sparky electric chair. Host: Pat Boone. (Mature.)

3:30–4: LETHAL INJECTION—More executions. (Mature.)

4–5: JIM BAKER III

—The New Yorker, 1994

Yowl

For Jay McInerney

I

I saw the best minds of my generation destroyed by stress
    frazzled overtired burnt-out,
jogging through suburban streets at dawn
    as suggested by the late James Fixx,
career-minded yupsters burning for an Amstel Light
    watching Stupid Pet Tricks,
who upwardly mobile and designer'd and bright-eyed and high sat up
    working in the track-lit glow of the Tribeca loft skimming
    through the Day Timer while padding the expense account,
who passed through universities and saved their asses hallucinating Grateful
    Dead posters and eating Sara Lee while watching the war on TV,
who were graduated and went on to law schools burning to save the world,
who brewed decaffeinated coffee doing their yoga in alligator shirts and
    listening to the latest Windham Hill Sampler,
who ate chocolate croissants in outdoor cafés and drank blush
    wine on Columbus Avenue washed down with a little Percodan
    with Dove bars with Diet Coke with Lean Cuisine,
stopping by on the way home for a pound of David's cookies
    telling each other of their fears of intimacy and their need
    for space and inability to commit—for now,
who watched Mary Tyler Moore reruns and wept for Rhoda and worried about
    acid rain and the mercury in the swordfish while strung out on cyclamates

faces flushed with MSG even after specifically making a point of
mentioning to the waiter not to put it in,
who prowled through uncertain money markets chewing Tums and
doing lines with the Hispanics in the mail room
sitting in the gents with baby-laxative runs while the boss buzzes
and the secretary says you're on the phone to Bonn,
who stayed up too late working out their relationships 'n' things feeling
the gnawing rat-fear that they hadn't been communicating lately and
the urgent pounding screaming need to think about their priorities,
yacketayakking analyzing thinking it through making constructive
suggestions as the eastern sky flamed in raw Ralph Lauren pastels,
got to get away for a few days but the Hartmann luggage is being
repaired oh,
who needs this wandering through Needless-Markup wailing (inside) for
the baby seals and the bunnies slaughtered for lipstick
remembering all the unanswered antivivisection junk mail on the
way to the appliances section to beg another blade for the Cuisinart,
who subscribed to *Gourmet* and the *American Lawyer* and after an exhausting
search found Jamaica time-shares in the classifieds for only
$1200 a month coping as best they could with the Negro beach boys
wanting to sell them ganja,
paying outrageous sums for bottled water and having to complain
about the maid service and the warm orange juice knowing they should
have gone to Cape Cod instead where the Peugeot mopeds fart carbon
monoxide and the half-eaten lobster rolls rot in wax paper on the
sidewalks and the Republican men in lime-green corduroys with little
orange elephants bray as their wives buy overpriced scrimshaw,
who nudged and nuzzled over margaritas and dreamed of endless
throbbing hot sticky sex but Not tonite dear I have a yeast infection,
running on spongy Reeboks to sublimate their lust
then plunging into *Bright Lights, Big City*,
who upped their nightly hits of Valium from two to five mgs and
worried if they were going to be groggy in the morning,
who hollow-eyed and febrile read the theater reviews in unread
issues of *The New Yorker* yes *The New Yorker*,
who watched re-reruns of Mary Tyler Moore and decided they hated Rhoda,
who skimmed the Banana Republic catalog with brain-dead gaze

wondering if they really needed Ethiopian saddlebags,
who padded back and forth to the john for endless glasses of water while
worrying about refinancing at ten and an eighth and waited for the
fiendish tweet of birds and the thud of *The Wall Street Journal*
on the porch,
who took a little tootsky after their Yoplait just to get going
and buzzzzzzzzzzzzzzzzzzzzzzzzzzzzzzzzed along in the carpool
yattering to the gray-flannelled bottisatvas in the backseat
about rowing machines and Eddie Murphy's homo jokes,
ah Jay while you are not safe I am not safe and now *Ransom*
is remaindered at Waldenbooks and you're really in a bind—
and who therefore drown in butter-flavored popcorn at the Cineplex as the
answering machines cutely speak to strangers and Discover cards are
mailed to the incorrect addresses while Mohawked clerks at Tower
Records with little crucifixes in their ears play "Pillow Talk" and
everything you want they only have in Beta.

II

Yuck! Gross! Eeewww! Buying crack from the zombies in the
park! Closing out the trust fund! Checking into the rehab!

III

Jay McInerney! I'm with you at Area
    where the shark swims on the wall
I'm with you David Letterman on the tower
    where you drop watermelons and TVs and bowling balls
I'm with you Gary Hart in New Hampshire
    where you stammer and yammer about New Ideas
I'm with you Don Johnson in Miami
    where you don't wear socks
I'm with you Jerry Rubin on Wall Street
    where you only hear yippie when the Dow hits a high
I'm with you Donald Trump on Fifth Avenue
    where Steven Spielberg has an apartment in your building
I'm with you John McEnroe in England

where you appear on world television treating people like scum
I'm with you Maria Shriver in Hyannisport
    where a wedding gift from Kurt Waldheim has arrived
I'm with you John Zaccaro at Middlebury
    where you pursue independent study projects
I'm with you Doctor Ruth on cable
    where you giggle with your guests about orgasm
I'm with you Ron Jr. cavorting
    in your underwear on national television
I'm with you Mike Deaver in Bitburg
    where your mind was on buying a car
I'm with you Billy Crystal in too many places
    where your routines have not aged well
I'm with you Brooke Shields at Princeton
    where you—but who cares?
I'm with you on the Upper East Side
    pricing modems
I'm with you on the Upper East Side
    stopping into the Food Emporium for a quart of lo-fat milk
I'm with you on the Upper East Side
    eating sushi and Ecstasy
I'm with you on the Upper East Side
    looking for myself in *People* magazine

Christopher Buckley
Paul Slansky

—*The New Republic,* 1986

Royal
Eavesdropping

◻

Well-placed observers convincingly argued that the 1989
recording [of Prince Charles and Camilla Parker-Bowles]
must have been made by the national security agency MI5—
the elite service whose duties include state security—and
speculated about other tapes said to exist.
—*People,* February 1, 1993

CHARLES: Gladys?

CAMILLA: Fred! Darling, I've been sitting by the phone all afternoon.

CHARLES: Couldn't get away. They had me—God, if I have to "inspect"
another bloody milk pasteurizing bloody facility again I'm going to
bloody well let Wills *have* the bloody throne.

CAMILLA: Oh darling, it's not fair, the things they make you do.

CHARLES: I'm off milk for a month, that's a bloody fact.

CAMILLA: Don't you want to know what I'm wearing?

CHARLES: "Inspection tour," what am I supposed to be "inspecting"
for? Rogue bacilli? Anthrax spores? Dirt under their bloody finger-
nails?

CAMILLA: I'm lying here in my Wellies, and not a stitch else.

CHARLES: Well, I suppose it's better than what they've got me "inspecting" tomorrow, at seven-bloody-fifteen in the bloody a.m. Bloody
poultry plant.

CAMILLA: I was thinking of our last meeting and—

CHARLES: Have you ever *smelled* a poultry plant? My God, how people can live like that is beyond me. It'll be no chicken for a month after tomorrow and that's another bloody fact.

CAMILLA: Darling, I can't bear to hear you like this. Why don't you just hop into the Range Rover and pop over for a spot of . . . tea.

CHARLES: Tea and strumpet? (Laughs) Sorry. Don't tempt me. They've got me scheduled for another bloody "morale-boosting" pop-in at the bloody Salvation Army in an hour. Won't boost my morale, I can tell you. (Imitates sound of "Now We Gather at the River" being played badly on a Sousaphone)

CAMILLA: But it's so lonely here. Just me and my Wellies.

CHARLES: What, home alone? Where's the Silver Stick in Waiting?

CAMILLA: Here somewhere, I suppose. That's the nice thing about big houses, isn't it? You're not cheek by jowl. What I mean is, it *feels* so empty without you. *I* feel empty when you're not—

CHARLES: I'll tell you what *empty* is. The inside of her skull. Last night I tried to explain to her why modern architecture is so bloody awful. Might as well explain organic farming to one of those bloody heads on bloody Easter Island. "Knock, knock, anyone bloody *home?*"

CAMILLA: Oh darling, how *frustrating* for you.

CHARLES: Then she announced she was going to kill herself—

CAMILLA: What, again? With the lemon peeler?

CHARLES: Oh no, a soup ladle. This time she meant business.

CAMILLA: Well, I never understood what the fascination was in the first place.

CHARLES: Oh, spiffing, rub it in.

CAMILLA: Speaking of which, guess what *I've* got on my bedside table? A jar of Marmite. Family size.

CHARLES: Um. (Sound of lapping)

CAMILLA: Oh stop, you *know* what that does to me.

CHARLES: What time is it? I've got a good mind to tell the Salvation Army to sod off. (Clicking sound, followed by dialing) Is that you?

CAMILLA: I'm on the pho-one.

MAN'S VOICE: Oh, sorry, ducks.

CAMILLA: Andrew, I said I'm on that bloody phone.

ANDREW PARKER-BOWLES: All right, don't get your knickers in a twist. Is that Charles?

HIGH-PITCHED, NASAL VOICE: Neow. It's . . . Wiltshire Telecom.

ANDREW: Who?

HIGH-PITCHED, NASAL VOICE: The phone company. Someone reported a thing with the line. A problem sort of thing.

ANDREW: Oh. How odd.

CAMILLA: Andrew, will you get *off* the phone? (Sound of phone being cradled)

CHARLES: God, that was so close.

CAMILLA: Darling, you were *inspired*.

CHARLES: Well, I—do you think so?

CAMILLA: You were brilliant. He didn't suspect a thing.

CHARLES: Splendid chap. Mum thinks he's a pip.

CAMILLA: A *pimp*?

CHARLES: *Pip*. We really ought to get one of those, what do you call them, cellulite phones. Where were we?

CAMILLA: You were about to spread Marmite all over me and (clicking sound)—*Andrew!* I'm *still on!* Hello? Hello? Well, I don't know what that was.

CHARLES: Bloody country phones.

—*The Washington Post*, 1993

Best Sellers

This Week	Fiction	Last Week	Weeks On List
1	**Wank and File,** by Tom Clancy. President Jack Ryan prevents World War III after a homosexual U.S. Army colonel slaps a North Korean dictator.	2	47
2	**Prophylaxes,** by Anne Rice. Lestat reacts badly at his regular six-month checkup when Dr. Cohen tells him that his incisors will need new crowns.	1	31
3	**The Krupskaya Conundrum,** by Robert Ludlum. A beautiful woman claiming to be Lenin's granddaughter becomes President of Russia, and causes a crisis of manhood in the armed forces.	3	5
4	**Bimbo,** by Danielle Steel. A beautiful woman who starts out in the mail room of a corrupt, powerful businessman becomes his wife and sets out to get her former supervisor fired.		1
5	**Prostate,** by Michael Crichton. A surgeon finds himself on the other end of the scalpel after he discovers that the gland he has just removed from a powerful Japanese businessman has the formula for Coca-Cola tattooed on it.	5	8
6	**Like Mama Thed,** by Winston Groom. America's favorite literary idiot discovers that someone has put a razor blade in one of his chocolates.	6	50
7	**Sump,** by Stephen King. A plumber in a small town in Maine accidentally unleashes hideous forces from the beyond.	9	8
8	*** Baggage Carousel Six,** by Stephen Coonts. Militant Islamic terrorists threaten to blow up a Pan Continental Airlines jumbo jetliner unless documentaries on Ayatollah Khomeini are shown in the in-flight entertainment program.	4	14
9	**Money Isn't Everything,** by Sidney Sheldon. The young widow of a corrupt, powerful businessman must cope with dozens of muscular Mediterranean-style suitors with copious chest hair.	7	11
10	**Dark Duchess,** by Antoinette de Falalo An eighteenth-century English adventurer causes scandal at his ancestral home, Wheaters, when he brings home a beautiful but dusky new wife named De Caf, from the West Indies.	12	16
11	**Money Can Buy,** by Robert Maller Torringford. Defense Attorney Phil (Gut) Cartwright must decide between his integrity and extreme wealth when a rich client reveals that he did in fact kill his wife, children, hamster and sixteen carollers on Christmas Eve.	8	9
12	**Smoola Smelled of Smelt,** by Peter Hoeg. An odd Danish woman has a nervous breakdown while trying to figure out who put rock salt in her galoshes.	11	26

This Week	Nonfiction	Last Week	Weeks On List
1	**Bitch, Bitch,** by Kathleen Gingrich. The mother of the Speaker of the House reiterates her son's opinion of Hillary Clinton.	1	12
2	**I Didn't Do It, Goddammit,** by O. J. Simpson, with Lawrence Schiller. More replies to people who have written to the former Heisman Trophy winner expressing disappointment.	5	15
3	**The Copulation Bomb,** by Brent Goffman, Jr. A demographer argues that too much unlawful carnal knowledge is going on, with dire consequences.	2	16
4	* **101 Uses for a Dead Liberal,** by P. J. O'Rourke. A conservative humorist proposes that Michael Kinsley et al. be clubbed to death like baby seals and turned into hermit-crab food, insulation and golf tees.	3	20
5	**Big Black Book,** by Heidi Fleiss. A Hollywood madam lists the names, phone numbers and Social Security numbers of all her famous and non-famous clients. (CD-ROM included.)	4	57
6	**Adoption by FedEx,** by Mia Farrow. Woody Allen's former mate explains the easy way to keep the nursery jumping.	7	8
7	**Toujours Riche,** by Peter Mayle. More stories about eating too much and dealing with contractors in Provence.	6	17
8	**It's Not the Money, or the Honor,** by Jimmy Carter The former President on his pursuit of the Nobel Peace Prize	8	12
9	**After We Cut It Off and Kill It, We're Going to Let It Go,** by Colin Powell. The General writes about his life, from his childhood in the South Bronx to his and President Bush's decision to let the Iraqi Army escape from Kuwait so that it could save Saddam Hussein and kill more Kurds.	11	46
10	**Billions and Billions and Billions,** by Carl Sagan. The astronomer explains that he doesn't mean to sound funny when he says this.	13	4
11	**Waiter, There's a Prosthetic Limb in My Soup,** by John Amos James A collection of bitter philosophical essays by a man with one arm.	12	14
12	**Charles and Diana: The True Inside Story,** by Robert (Peachy) Bunt. A meticulous former groundskeeper at Highgrove argues that there couldn't have been grass stains on the Prince's pj's.	10	15

This Week	Advice, How-to and Miscellaneous	Last Week	Weeks On List
1	**The Chicken-Fried-Steak, Mashed-Potato, and Two-Martini Diet,** by Duncan Christy, M.D. Losing weight while consuming 8,000 calories a day.	1	39
2	**Becoming God,** by Beepah Doolik. Self-deification in a single afternoon.	2	87
3	**Virtual Sex,** by Thomas Rang, Ph.D. Non-sticky self-gratification.	3	4
4	**How to Kill Yourself,** by Tamara Reem. Self-euthanasia using substances found under most household kitchen sinks.	4	7

Rankings reflect totally unscientific methods of estimating sales figures, for the week ending Feb 17, at something like 3,050 bookstores plus wholesalers serving 28,000 other retailers (gift shops, massage parlors, supermarkets), statistically weighted (whatever that means) to represent sales from Point Darrow, Alaska, to Key Lumbago, Florida An asterisk indicates that we're trying to annoy the author of the book listed above the asterisk

—*The New Yorker,* 1995

Stardate
12:00 12:00 12:00

> "I watch science-fiction movies. . . . I like to watch them on
> tape, so I can examine them closely. There's only one
> problem: I still can't figure out my VCR."
> —William Shatner, in *TV Guide*

CAPTAIN KIRK: Captain's log, stardate 7412.6 . . . hello? The red light
still isn't going on. Testing, 1-2-3-4. Chekov, it's not recording.

CHEKOV: I know, Keptin. Perhaps a negative function with the clock-
timer.

UHURA: Captain, I'm getting indications of a Klingon presence.

KIRK: Mr. Spock?

SPOCK: I confirm at least six Imperial Klingon warships, Captain, and
heading toward our position at Warp 7.

KIRK: No, the Captain's log. Why won't it record?

SPOCK: Might I suggest, Captain, that we first remove ourselves to a
more secure sector and then address the matter of your log? That
would be the . . . logical approach.

KIRK: There's nothing logical about this instruction manual. Chekov?

CHEKOV: Keptin?

KIRK: Try this. "With the Rec-On day flashing, press the 5 key."

CHEKOV: I did already, Keptin. *Still* negative function.

SULU: Captain, I'm having difficulty holding course.

KIRK: Shut down engines. Chekov, "Press the number for the day. For
Sunday, press the 1 key, for Monday, the 2 key, and so on."

CHEKOV: Affirmative, Keptin. Still negative function. Perhaps ve should go back to page 15, vere it said to press Rec-Off time and enter two digits for hour.

SPOCK: Captain, the Klingons are arming their photon torpedoes.

KIRK: Engineering.

SCOTTY: Aye, Captain?

KIRK: Mr. Scott, we've got a malfunction in the log. We're going to need full deflector power while we get it fixed.

SCOTTY: I canna guarantee it, Captain. The systems are overloaded as it is.

CHEKOV: Keptin, the flashing 12:00 disappeared!

KIRK: Good work, Chekov!

CHEKOV: Den it came right back.

KIRK: Damn it. Analysis, Mr. Spock.

SPOCK: It would appear, Captain, that this instruction manual that you and Mr. Chekov have been attempting to decipher was written in Taiwan.

KIRK: Taiwan?

SPOCK: A small island in the Pacific Rim Sector, formerly inhabited by a determined people who believed that the adductor muscles in giant clams, *Tridacna gigas,* conferred sexual potency. In the later twentieth century, they became purveyors of early video equipment to what was then the United States. They were able to successfully emasculate the entire U.S. male population by means of impenetrable instruction manuals. It was this that eventually led to the Great Conflict.

KIRK: But this is 7412.6. How did a Taiwanese instruction manual get aboard the *Enterprise*?

SPOCK: It is possible that a Taiwanese computer virus was able to infiltrate Star Fleet Instruction Manual Command and subtly alter the books so that not even university-trained humans could understand them.

KIRK: It's diabolical.

SPOCK: On the contrary, it is perfectly logical. Their strategy was based on an ancient form of Oriental persuasion known as water torture. In this case, instead of water a digital rendering of the hour of twelve o'clock is flashed repeatedly and will not disappear until the unit is correctly programmed.

KIRK: And for that you need a manual you can understand.

SPOCK: Precisely. Unless . . .

KIRK: Spit it out, Spock.

SPOCK: You have Star Log Plus. A small device that permitted the Americans to bypass the instruction manuals and program their units so that they would not end up with six hours of electronic snow instead of *Masterpiece Theatre* or, more likely, *American Gladiators.*

KIRK: Could you make one of these things, Spock?

SPOCK: It would take more than the one minute and twenty seconds that we have until we are within range of Klingon weapons.

DR. McCOY: Jim, you know I hate to agree with Spock, but he's right. We've got to get out of here. There are hundreds of people on this ship, young people, with homes and families and futures, and pets— little hamsters on treadmills, Jim. You can't sacrifice them just because you can't figure out how to program your damn log!

KIRK: I know my responsibilities, Bones. Spock, would it be possible to beam the flashing 12:00 into the Klingons' control panel?

SPOCK: Theoretically, yes.

KIRK: Do it.

UHURA: Captain, I'm picking up a Klingon transmission.

KIRK: Put it on screen.

KLINGONS: *QI'yaH, majegh!*

KIRK: Translation, Spock.

SPOCK: It appears to have worked, Captain. They are surrendering.

KIRK: Take us home, Mr. Sulu. Mr. Chekov, try pressing the OTR button twice.

—*The New Yorker,* 1993

The
Hemline of
History

■

1,000,000 B.C.: Raquel Welch appears in a movie wearing a micro-loincloth. Rise of *Homo erectus.*

3500 to 3001 B.C.: Linen is produced in the Middle East.

1000 to 901 B.C.: The caftan appears in Israel.

800 to 701 B.C.: The Assyrians, tired of wearing restrictive garments, conquer the Israelites and confiscate all their caftans. Assyrian women start dressing like Assyrian men.

700 to 601 B.C.: Assyrian men, angry and weary of being taunted by Babylonians for dressing like their women, destroy Babylon and, to make sure that they have made their point, divert the Euphrates River and flood the former site of the city.

600 to 501 B.C.: Invention of 501 jeans in what is now San Francisco. Peisistratus usurps democracy in Greece and sets back women's rights. Greek women start wearing the chiton, a short men's garment, as a long dress, creating sexual confusion that will endure to the present.

501 B.C. to A.D. 500: Era of the Sack, a loosely fitting cloth resembling an old sack of grain. Various theories exist as to what exactly was meant by the "sack of Rome" in A.D. 476. One holds that it refers to the city's destruction by the fifth-century social Goth Odoacer; but new evidence suggests it may be a derisive term coined by the Praetorian Guard for the frumpy wife of Romulus Augustulus, last emperor of Rome.

540 to 553: Plague kills off half the population of Europe. Byzantine empress Theodora tries to brighten things up by introducing long white dresses, purple cloaks, gold embroidery, tiaras, and pointed shoes, prefiguring the Reagan era. Byzantine historian and gossip-monger Procopius hints in his lurid *Secret History* that Theodora had been an actress and prostitute before marrying Justinian I, providing encouragement for future generations of society hostesses.

554 to 1000: Black is back! Hems hug ankles as women hedge their fashion bets pending the outcome of a possible Moorish takeover of Europe.

1000: Hems plunge to the floor pending the possible End of the World and Judgment Day.

1250: Hats become the rage. Louis IX is held for ransom by the Saracens, who demand eight hundred thousand gold pieces or the equivalent in French hats.

1253: Linen is manufactured in England for the first time, a mere 4,753 years after its appearance in the Middle East.

1278: The glass mirror is invented, encouraging the end of theocentrism and the rise of secular humanism as people start to think, *If I was made in the image of God, how come I look like this?*

1284: The first sequins are coined in Venice, and ravioli is invented in Rome. Attempts to sew ravioli onto dresses fail, but sequins stay on. First mention of the term *glitterati* appears in the Venetian fashion daily *VD*.

1347: Bubonic plague forces cancellation of Paris shows.

1480: Leonardo da Vinci invents the parachute but then realizes that the airplane, without which parachutes are not much use unless your plan is to jump off the Tower of Pisa, will not be invented for 420 years. Despondent, da Vinci tosses his parachute into his prototype of the dumpster, from which it is retrieved by a Pontine marshes slattern named Vittoria, who fashions a pair of tiny panties out of it, which become known in Rome's red-light district as *Il Segreto di Vittoria,* or "Victoria's Secret."

1514: Pineapples arrive in Europe. They fail as hats but catch on as food.

Mid-1500s: Starched ruff collars appear amid much beheading. One theory holds that the ruff serves as a kind of splash guard to keep blood from spoiling the headsman's pointy slippers. Rigid padding and codpieces also appear, making future generations extremely grateful not to have lived during the Elizabethan era, despite its abundance of good theater and bear-baiting contests.

1600: The Elizabeth R Look is in. Women pull out their hair, rub sandpaper over their faces, and expose themselves to smallpox in an effort to look like her. The queen receives daily facials and massages in a room in Richmond Palace called Elizabeth R's Den, which servants shorten to Elizabeth Arden. Since no one knows what's going to happen when she dies—if she *ever* dies—they cover all bases by letting down their hems even further. Since hems are already at the floor, they are let out laterally, creating the first trains on dresses.

1600 to 1650: Black is back again—did it ever really go away?—this time in Venice. One theory maintains that it flatters everyone's face in portraits; another, that soup stains don't show up as much.

1614: John Rolfe marries Pocahontas and takes her to England, where she is forced radically to rethink her wardrobe. She dies of nervous exhaustion three years later, an early fashion victim.

Late 1600s: *Déshabillé* and *négligée* become the fashion as women strive to make themselves look as though curtains have fallen on top of them.

1700s: The invention of wallpaper frees up millions of square yards of cloth to be hung on women, enabling men to boast about their wealth by showing how much fabric they can afford, again prefiguring the Reagan era.

1746: The British defeat the Stuarts at the Battle of Culloden Moor and forbid the wearing of tartan, giving rise to twentieth-century fashion dictatorships.

Mid-1700s: Fashion à la rhinoceros makes its appearance in Paris after the first rhinos are brought there by a circus. No contemporary fashion plates survive showing what it was, perhaps on purpose.

1789: A French mob storms the Bastille. Royalist-style knee breeches are out. For *le mob*, the sans-culottes look is out, long pants are in. French painter Jacques Louis David, no tool, honors the Revolutionary need to justify political assassination with his painting *Brutus*. Brutus is seen off in the corner shadows in his toga, while the focus is a quartet of grieving women wearing skimpy, clinging gowns.

Neoclassicism becomes all the rage, and women start wearing thin, draped gowns in an attempt to look like Greek statuary. In an effort to *really* look like Greek statuary, women mist each other with water before they go out so that the gowns will stick to them, anticipating the wet T-shirt contests in America during the 1970s.

1792: Fashion frenzy continues as breeches-wearing aristocratic fashion victims are guillotined.

1800s: The concept of comfort is introduced by people who have been uncomfortable for three hundred years.

1830: Barthélemy Thimonnier, a French tailor, devises a prototype of the first sewing machine, making it a lot easier to hem.

1874: While vacationing in Bermuda, Mary E. Outerbridge watches Brits play a newfangled game called tennis and brings it back to the United States, increasing the need to do something to make women's clothing easier and freer.

1890 to 1905: Women play a lot of tennis and start riding bicycles. Something *has* to be done about these skirts.

1908: Hemlines rise, slightly, above the floor.

1912: First parachute jump from an airplane. Da Vinci's reputation is rehabilitated.

1913: Zippers catch on, facilitating the sexual revolution.

1918: Skirts rise above the ankle for the first time since anyone can remember.

1918 to 1920: Influenza kills twenty-two million people. The decision to lift skirts any higher is postponed on the grounds that this is no time to go catching a cold.

1920: The Nineteenth Amendment gives women the vote.

1925 to 1926: Waistlines disappear (along with whalebone corsets), and hems head north above the polar kneecap. Antonio Buzzacchino invents the permanent wave. Polygamy is abolished in Turkey. Tennis "match of the century" between Suzanne Lenglen and American Helen Wills. Year of the Woman.

1927: Long scarves suffer a setback after Isadora Duncan is strangled by hers when it becomes entangled in the spokes of her Bugatti.

1928: The *garçonne*—or "boygirl"—style, named for the novel by Victor Margueritte, is in. Amelia Earhart becomes the first woman to fly across the Atlantic. Long scarves enjoy a comeback after she succeeds in not getting hers caught in the plane's propeller.

October 28, 1929: The stock market crashes, bringing on the Depression. Wives are told, "I hope you like your clothes, because you're going to be wearing them for a long time."

Early 1930s: Hems head south as the world situation sombers, defying Wall Street husbands who told their wives they couldn't afford any more clothes. However, more men are now wearing women's clothes.

1931: Hattie T. Caraway of Arkansas becomes the first woman elected to the U.S. Senate. Her election has no discernible effect on fashion.

1939: Nylon stockings appear, creating desire for more exposed leg area, higher hems.

1941: Start of wartime clothes rationing in Britain. The Utility Look is in, the Unity Mitford Look is out.

1941 to 1945: Women in occupied France thumb their noses at the Germans by fashioning outrageous hats, some made with real fruit; coining of term *pièce de résistance*.

1943: The jitterbug craze creates the need for more leg room.

1947: Dior unveils his controversial New Look: ballerina waists, broad shoulders, and longer skirts. Men howl angrily over "those petticoats," but the fashion catches on and hems remain at midcalf through the 1950s.

1957: Balenciaga sets fashion back fifteen hundred years when he introduces the chemise. It is quickly nicknamed the Sack and bombs. Christian Dior dies. Jack Kerouac publishes *On the Road*, paving the way for the black-turtleneck boom of the 1960s.

January 20, 1961: Jacqueline Bouvier Kennedy becomes the most glamorous woman in the world. Youth is the determinant in fashion for the first time since the 1920s. The hem of Kennedy's inaugural skirt, designed by Oleg Cassini, goes up all the way to midknee, causing inaugural poet Robert Frost to faint.

1962: The restaurant La Grenouille—"The Frog"—opens in New York City and becomes the gastronomic center of the fashion world. *Women's Wear Daily* will refer to it simply with the code letter X. The Frog's stylish, trendsetting clientele will eventually tire of dropping gloppy food on their ten-thousand-dollar dresses and start demanding tiny portions of food without sauce on it, creating the need for *cuisine minceur*, literally, "minuscule portions of astronomically expensive food."

1963: Da Vinci's *Mona Lisa* is exhibited in New York and Washington, D.C. Halston's pink pillbox hat is seen by hundreds of millions following the tragic event in Dallas on November 22.

1964: The watusi, the frug, and other modern dances resembling grand mal seizures cause people to frequent discotheques, where go-go (a corruption of *gaga*) dancers gyrate in cages while wearing *couture minceur*, literally, "next to nothing."

1965 to 1966: London designer Mary Quant invents the miniskirt, changing history forever and not a moment too soon. Parisian designer Courrèges knows a good thing when he sees it and puts women in short white shifts for the space age.

Late 1960s: The microskirt, an abbreviated miniskirt, makes it difficult for women to sit down. Women, tired of standing, revert to the mini.

1967: British fashion model Twiggy becomes a hit in the United States, popularizing the flat-chested look, making many women grateful.

1968: Jacqueline Kennedy, wearing a miniskirt, marries Greek tycoon Aristotle Onassis. Peggy Fleming, wearing the skater's version of the miniskirt, wins an Olympic gold medal.

1971: Hot pants, microshorts for women who want to be able to sit down without having to do things with their legs difficult even for Hindu contortionists, appear and disappear.

1972: Mao jackets, designed to keep you warm and looking exactly like one billion other people, appear in the West after Nixon opens China. After the Mao jacket phenomenon breaks out at home, Nixon tries to close China, but it is too late.

1973: The rise of blue jeans continues as U.S. textile mills produce 482 million square yards of cotton denim (originally *de Nîmes,* or "from Nîmes," a city in France that has not been heard from since).

1974: Heiress Patty Hearst is kidnapped by the Symbionese Liberation Army; she makes a fashion statement in a ransom photograph wearing a striking *militaire* black jumpsuit, prefiguring the rise of The Gap.

1976: Yves Saint Laurent stuns the world with his Ballets Russes collection, designed to make women appealing to defecting Soviet ballet dancers.

Late 1970s: Embarrassed by the male-created Vietnam and Watergate debacles, American women decide they can do better and enter the work force in severe-looking suits.

1980: Franco-Tunisian designer Azzedine Alaïa, taking his cue from women's athletic fabrics, produces stretch wear, in some cases so tight that women cannot even wear panties underneath. Alaïa's fashions emphasize the inherent exquisiteness of the female form and bring about the return of bosoms, or, as it is called, the "full-bodied look."

1981: Ronald Reagan is inaugurated as the fortieth president of the United States, ushering in an era of conspicuous consumption and more sequins than have been seen since thirteenth-century Venice.

Hems take a hike as women exult in showing the results of aerobics. Evening gowns, however, remain long in keeping with the centuries-old tradition of women showing off their husbands' wealth by wearing more expensive fabric than their friends do.

—*Vogue*, 1991

The New Fly-Fishing Books

EXTREME FLY FISHING
By Budd Revill

The author, a former Navy SEAL who used to assassinate Vietcong cadres (he includes a perhaps too-graphic chapter on this period of his life), argues that fly fishing has been "pussified" by an over-reliance on expensive, high-tech equipment, packaged fishing trips, and, especially, "high-priced lodges where you eat off china." His solution is probably not for everyone: he dispenses with waders, preferring to insulate his legs by greasing them with the fat from "whatever animal is handy—a cat will do." He uses only barbless—and hairless—dry flies and, instead of a modern carbon-fiber rod, a four-foot rattan cane of the kind used on American teenagers in Singapore. "It's got a nice feel to it," he observes, "and once the fish is exhausted, you can use it like a club." *First serial,* Esquire.

WHITE BEADS, BROWN TROUT
By J. H. Wells

The title of this collection of somewhat obscure essays on trout fishing by Wells, a lay Zen monk in upstate New York, comes from a saying of Hakuin, the eighteenth-century Japanese Zen master: "Should you desire the great tranquillity, prepare to sweat white beads." One day, while casting for a humongous brown trout in the Beaverkill River, near Roscoe, New York, Wells found himself asking, "What is the point?" (Some readers may ask the same question.) He suddenly flung his rod into the river and "began to bark like a dog." The reaction of the trout is not recorded, but the reader may find himself asking, What is the sound of one trout yawning?

GILLS
By Peter Benchley

The celebrated author of *Jaws* is at the top of his form in this gripping tale of a vengeful Dolly Varden trout that terrorizes a fishing camp in British Columbia. Trouble starts when the fearsome, sixteen-inch monster attacks a female wildlife biologist. The trout will not rise to normal flies, and eventually Game Warden Willie (Mac) Shaughnessy and his half-Jewish sidekick, Hamish Cohen, must engage the trout-battling skills of the grizzled half-Inuit, half-Scots poacher, Angus Nook. The harrowing ending, involving a squadron of Canadian Air Command F-18s and a canoe paddle, is a page-turner that will leave the reader reluctant to go near running water for months. *Book-of-the-Month Club main selection; movie rights to Columbia.*

BASSHOLES
By Ed Weiler

Trout fly fishermen have always thought of themselves as the pure heirs of Izaak Walton, and of spin-casting bass fishermen as Neanderthal throwbacks. This book, by an English professor at the University of Vermont, leaves no doubt as to where the author stands. "Bass fishermen watch Monday Night Football, drink beer, drive pickup trucks, and prefer noisy women with big breasts," he writes. "Trout fishermen watch MacNeil-Lehrer, drink white wine, drive foreign cars with passenger-side air bags, and hardly think about women at all." The last characteristic, he suggests, may have something to do with the fact that trout fishermen spend most of the time immersed up to the thighs in ice-cold water. *First serial,* Atlantic Monthly.

THE APOSTLE AND THE NYMPH
By Elgar Cole, Ph.D.

The author, a biblical archeologist, challenges Norman Maclean's famous asseveration in *A River Runs Through It* that the Apostle John was a dry-fly fisherman. He draws on his excavation of Ut-Ekmek 2, in modern-day Israel, where, he says, John and the other apostles used to go wet-fly fishing during the annual landlocked-salmon run. Cole provides impressive evidence in the form of an almost perfectly preserved No. 6 woolly bugger that closely corresponds with a nymph-type fly made out of chenille which John mentions in a blistering letter to Peter. (Peter had chided John and the other apostles for fishing when they should have been spreading the gospel.) Cole writes about the moment he discovered the woolly bugger with the excitement of Howard Carter peering for the first time into the tomb of King Tut: "When I saw the telltale chenille body, I thought, *Maclean's going to pass bricks when he sees this.*" But before Cole could communicate his discovery to the world he was arrested by Israeli authorities, charged with trespassing on a top-secret military installation, and held incommunicado for more than a year, during which Dr. Maclean died. Cole claims, convincingly, "The Israelis were then trying to improve relations with the Vatican, which didn't want it to get out that John used wet flies. They had too much invested in the dry-fly myth."

—*The New Yorker,* 1994

The Siberian Candidate:
The Hunt for Red
in October

■

LARRY KING: *What do you make of the Clinton Moscow trip thing?*
GEORGE BUSH: *I don't want to tell you what I really think.*
—*Larry King Show,* October 7

KGB Moscow
Topski Secretski
Eyeski Only
File on American Mole W. Clinton
Codename "Elvis"

January 1970: Subject is lured to make visit of Soviet Union by our
Oxford agent who tells him about "exciting" Moscow girls. Subject
extremely eager to make visit but says he has spent all his money on
Elvis records. Tickets and money arranged by Oxford agent as part of
"international youth understanding exchange" program.

Subject arrives Moscow December, 1969, immediately demands to
see exciting Moscow girls. Agent 38–22–36 is assigned to case. Reports
immediate success, says subject will enthusiastically work to undermine
U.S. imperialism and promote World Socialism as long as Agent 38–
22–36 can be his control officer. Is given Deep Cover code-name
"ELVIS" after decadent American singer. Agrees to keep top KGB Directorate regularly supplied with disgusting Elvis record albums.

ELVIS is told to foment anti-U.S. sentiment at Oxford. Unfortunately, he displays tendency to give long speeches, causing anti-U.S. crowds to disperse in direction of nearest pubs. Is insistent that Agent 38-22-36 make regular visits to "debrief" him.

ELVIS is urged to go home, join U.S. military, rise through the ranks and become chairman of Joint Chiefs of Staff. Plan fails when he reveals he has taken elaborate and irreversible steps to avoid any kind of military service, even Coast Guard. Demands to see Agent 38-22-36. She is sent to Oxford. ELVIS tells her that he was careful to retain his "viability within the [American political] system."

1970: Returns to United States. Enrollment in Yale Law School is easily arranged through our many high-level agents at Yale. Is told to foment anti-U.S. sentiment at Yale. Reports that Yale is already extremely anti-U.S., demands meeting with Agent 38-22-36.

1973: Is told to enter government and undermine proletariat's confidence in U.S. government. Reports that proletariat already thoroughly disgusted by U.S. government but will run for Congress anyway—from Arkansas, militarily and otherwise insignificant state west of Mississippi River. Loses.

1979: Becomes governor. Is urged to ignite anger of the proletariat by raising their taxes.

1981: Succeeds too brilliantly in igniting anger of the proletariat and loses reelection. West Mississippi Region KGB resident directed to begin disinformation campaign blaming loss on his wife.

1983: OPERATION PILLORY HILLARY successful. ELVIS reelected. Is instructed to anger proletariat more carefully this time. Also instructed to pollute American watershed by urging local industrialist tools to divert massive amounts of fecal coliform bacteria into Arkansas River.

July 1988: Our many agents within the U.S. Democratic Party arrange for ELVIS to make "keynote" speech at National Convention. A special team of experts from Moscow Institute of Rhetorical Brevity is infiltrated into Little Rock by Soviet submarine to urge him to keep speech short.

Effort fails spectacularly. Prospects for advancement to higher levels of U.S. government in serious doubt. Crew of Soviet infiltration submarine dies from exposure to fecal coliform bacteria. Awarded Order of Lenin posthumously in private ceremony.

March 1992: Prospects improve as American Democratic electorate decides not to nominate another Greek, this one with health problems.

KGB telephone surveillance tape of intimate conversation between ELVIS and unidentified female sex partner is sold by disreputable KGB clerk to U.S. "tabloid paper" for blue jeans and Morgan Fairchild stress-management video. Big problems. Special polygraph-defeating unit is infiltrated into Little Rock by Soviet submarine just in case. Submarine crew mutinies when they discover they are surrounded by toxic chicken excretions in Arkansas River; force submarine commander to turn back.

Americans decide they don't care about female sex partner, only economy. Submarine crew shot.

October 1992: Big Problem: Reactionary Rep. Robert "Mad Bob" Dornan reveals existence of 1970 Elvis trip to Moscow. U.S. press discovers that one of our many agents in the U.S. State Department has removed incriminating pages from ELVIS's passport file with evidence of 1969 Moscow trip. American FBI investigating.

Top KGB Directorate meets to decide whether to "burn" ELVIS before he is "blown" as a Soviet mole. Some say, "We're not communists now. Why do we need a mole anymore in U.S.?" Others say "Are you crazy? I give Yeltsin six months, then—Stalin again. Go for it."

Two decisions are reached: (1) dispatch Special Unit from the Moscow Institute for Rhetorical Brevity to Debates, this time by parachutes from airplane; (2) destroy this file, which a disreputable KGB clerk could sell to the U.S. press for CD players and Madonna books.

—Los Angeles Times, 1992

Poprah

OPRAH: We have a very special guest today, Pope John Paul II. He is the spiritual leader to nine hundred and forty-five million Catholics around the world, but you don't have to be a Catholic to admire Karol Wojtyla— Am I pronouncing that all right? You'd think, living in Chicago all these years, I could pronounce a Polish name. This is a man who has lived life to its fullest. He grew up in Communist Poland, was mentored by Stefan Cardinal Wys-zyn-ski—I'll get it right eventually—made Pope when he was fifty-eight, survived an assassination attempt. He has visited more than sixty countries. This is one pope who loves to travel. And somehow finds time to run the Vatican. And now he's written a book. The name of the book: *Crossing the Threshold of Hope*. We're honored to have him with us today. Welcome, Your Holiness.

POPE: Thank you.

OPRAH: I want to get to the book in a moment, because I'm sure it's fascinating, but I want to ask you something first. You've lost weight, haven't you? [Applause]

POPE: Yes.

OPRAH: You look fantastic. [Applause] How did you do it?

POPE: I was in the hospital for some operations, and so . . .

OPRAH: I think after seeing how good you look a lot of people are going to want to go to the hospital and have some operations. [Applause] I wonder if you could cast some light—and if *you* can't, who can?—on the rumor that you wrote this book because Carl Bernstein, the famous Watergate reporter, is writing a book about you.

POPE: Yes. I have heard of this other book. I respect this man. But, in the spirit of candor, will his book come from the *os equi*?

OPRAH: You're losing me.

POPE: The mouth of the horse. Though I have confidence that he is an honest reporter, I wonder, is he— Well, I don't want to say.

OPRAH: Go on. You're among friends. [Applause]

POPE: Infallible?

OPRAH: *All* men think they're infallible. [Applause]

POPE: As the world approaches the end of the second millennium following the birth of Our Lord Jesus Christ, mankind struggles under the oppressiveness of spiritual hunger, which is the inevitable fruit of solipsism and materialism.

OPRAH: You've got a point there. Even Madonna's talking about getting married and having a baby. Do you think if she does she'll name it Jesus?

POPE: Well, there is the Madonna, and there is Madonna.

OPRAH: Is it lonely being Pope?

POPE: No, it's good to be the Pope.

OPRAH: OK, let's take some questions.

AUDIENCE MEMBER: I'd like to ask His Holiness what advice he has for a young Catholic girl who would like to be a priest.

OPRAH: Oh-oh. I bet you don't get these questions in the Sistine Chapel.

POPE: Very beautiful city, Chicago.

OPRAH: Let's take another one.

AUDIENCE MEMBER: I'm so nervous.

OPRAH: Relax, honey. He's not going to cast you into a herd of swine.

AUDIENCE MEMBER: OK. Do you and the College of Cardinals ever play bingo?

POPE: Yes, often. And I will tell you something that is not in my book. Cardinal Deskur *cheats*. [Laughter]

OPRAH: There go his chances of making Pope. Speaking of which, there's been a lot of speculation lately . . .

POPE: Many Polish people in Chicago.

OPRAH: About who might be the next Pope. You want to handicap some of the front-runners for us?

POPE: Winnetka is a nice suburb of Chicago. I am signing books at The Book Stall in Winnetka.

OPRAH: We're not going to let you off that easy. What about this Cardinal Martini we read about? Do you think that a man named after a cocktail could ever be Pope?

POPE: How is Rostenkowski doing?

OPRAH: OK, we can take a hint. Any more questions for His Holiness?

AUDIENCE MEMBER: What did you want to be growing up?

POPE: My mother wanted me to be a priest. So here I am, you see, just a priest. But with a big church.

OPRAH (Wiping away tears): Thank you for sharing that. [Applause] One final question. It's been reported that you got nine million dollars for the book. What are you going to do with all that money?

POPE: Maybe you should ask Cardinal Deskur what he plans to do with it.

—*The New Yorker*, 1994

Doing the McNamara

■

FLUORIDATION RECONSIDERED
General Jack D. Ripper
Whoops Publishers, $18.95 (192p)

General Ripper is probably best known for destroying the world. In 1964, he ordered a wing of B-52 bombers to attack the Soviet Union, triggering the Soviets' Doomsday Machine, which blanketed the world with fallout. His decision to start the Third World War was prompted by what he now candidly calls his "paranoia" in thinking that fluoridation of drinking water was a Communist plot to make him impotent. Ripper now reveals that he's spent the last thirty-one years undergoing "some pretty hairy counseling," and that the therapy has allowed him to do something he never could before—cry. "I now realize that tears are the most precious bodily fluid of all." *First printing 250,000. Film rights to Stanley Kubrick. Author tour.*

KUWAIT UNTIL DARK
Saddam Hussein
Hussein & Hussein, $20.95 (384p)

On the one hand, Saddam says he feels "immense woefulness" for the families of the thousands of Iraqi soldiers killed during Desert Storm. But then there he is in the next sentence railing against "U.S. devils" doing the "filthy work" of the "International Zionist Cabal." However, he sounds sincere when he says, "I was wrong, terribly wrong, not to have used the chemical-biological weapons. What's the point of hiring all those expensive German consultants if you're just going to sit on your hands while the Satanic Dog Bush fires Tomahawk missiles up your ass?" Crying helps, he writes, but he doesn't like to do it in front of the women. *First serial,* Modern Dictator *magazine. Satellite author tour.*

BEI NOCHMALIGER UBERLEGUNG
(On Second Thought)
Erich Honecker
Schadenfreude, $16.95 (288p)

Whatever your feelings about the man who supervised the construction of the Berlin Wall, and who for thirty years made life miserable and terrifying for everyone in East Germany, it's hard not to feel at least a twinge of sympathy for Erich Honecker when he writes in this posthumously published memoir that "It's a little ironic to find myself in South America, like some Nazi war criminal. I made mistakes. So I'm human. But to devote your entire life to fighting fascism only to end up in mañanaland like Mengele or Eichmann is not my idea of *wunderbar.*" Honecker says he sometimes starts crying while watching his favorite Katarina Witt "Huns of Steel" exercise video, and at one point admits to being, as he puts it, "a total wiener." *First serial,* Der Weltschmerz.

SAUCE FOR UGANDA
Idi Amin Dada
Fatto & Windus, $22.95 (224p)

After years of "prayerful reflection" and "copious weeping" while living in asylum in Saudi Arabia, former self-proclaimed Ugandan President-for-Life Idi Amin writes in this peculiar autobiography that he "may have got a little carried away at times." While he admits that he killed three hundred thousand people and "pulled some stunts that might even have given [his role model Adolf] Hitler the willies," what appears to bother him most is "the canard" about his having sent Richard Nixon a telegram saying, "If you were a woman I would marry you." He writes, "It is true that I wanted to bear his children, but I never asked him to marry me." Doubtless, historians will be grateful for the clarification. *First printing 250. Print advertising. Radio interviews.*

Sometimes a Revolution
Is Just a Revolution
Fidel Castro
Sierra Maestra, $30 (624p)

One of the most enduring, if not endearing, twentieth-century dictators, Fidel Castro seems finally willing to admit a measure of defeat. "My doctor won't let me smoke, the Russians won't take my phone calls, and our engineers have to ride to work on donkeys," he writes. "This morning I asked for sugar in my coffee and the steward said, '*No hay*' ('There is none'). The Minister of Defense says even if we had fuel we wouldn't want to put it in the fighter planes, because the pilots would only defect in them. And now I must freely admit," he adds with a *suspiro* (a sigh), "there are times when I myself feel like defecting." He says he cries a lot, even when ordering his close friends and associates to be shot by the firing squad, "which I *nunca* (never) used to do." Clearly, he finds this troubling. "Maybe I'm getting *flojo* (soft)," he writes, "and a good leader must be *duro* (hard)." The Comandante may not be *duro,* but he's still feisty: "Life in Cuba is no frozen daiquiri, but at least I'm still around, which is more than I can say for the Kennedys." *First serial,* Hola.

—*The New Yorker,* 1995

The Landfill Tour
Is Canceled, but We
Are Offering . . .

⊠

"Mayor Rudolph W. Giuliani said yesterday he had
disposed of a Department of Sanitation proposal to
offer regular tours of the Fresh Kills landfill on Staten
Island, the world's largest garbage dump."
—*The New York Times,* April 3, 1996

ELIZABETH, N. J., UNVEILS "REFINEMENT CITY" PLAN

The City Planning Council today announced that it will offer tours of
the industrial areas along the New Jersey Turnpike.

"A lot of people drive through Elizabeth on their way to somewhere
else," said Harry Bethner, vice president for tourist development. "From
a moving car, it looks like just a lot of pipes in the air with chemicals and
smoke or even fire coming out of them. If we could get people to stop
and smell the roses, we think they might come away more refined themselves. And if they don't like looking at chemical plants, we have nice
rest rooms."

HOUSTON CANAL TO BE "BEST LITTLE VENICE IN TEXAS"

It might take some stretch of the imagination to envision the more than
fifty-mile shipping canal between Houston and Galveston as something
other than a bleak industrial waterway. But the state's Port Authority

thinks that with "a little fixing up and some plumb luck" it can convince tourists that it might be fun to pass the time in pedal boats, observing up close the many varieties of mutant catfish while trying to avoid being shredded by the giant propellers of tankers and cargo vessels.

"We think it's a natural," said Joe (Bob) Gorman, Jr., who is overseeing the plan for the Port Authority. "People could fish, though they might want to check with that center in Atlanta before eating anything they catch. And if you've never paddled to get out of the way of an ultralarge crude carrier, well, shoot, you haven't lived."

In Phoenix, Package Tours of Billboard Ads

Calling Phoenix "the billboard capital of the United States," the city's Department of Cultural Preservation announced today that it will conduct specialized tours of its billboards.

P.D.C.P. Commissioner Faith Quigley said the plan "isn't just to try to show people every billboard in Phoenix. That's like trying to see everything in the Louvre."

Instead, tours will be organized by theme: Colas, Fast-Food Chains, Bail Bondsmen, and Cigarettes are among the first. Future themes will include Muffler Repairs, Topless Bars, Gun Shops, and Immigration Lawyers.

Nevada to Show Tourists Mob Burial Sites in Desert

The Las Vegas Tourist Development Board announced today that, in partnership with La Cosa Nostra Offshore Legitimate Partners Ltd., it would license tour operators to take visitors to the secret final resting places of alleged gangsters.

One concession, Shut Up and Get in the Trunk Tours, will begin operations next month. Owner Frank "Teddy Bear" P., who explained that his last name "ain't nobody's business," says he will "give the customer more than just a look at some—shall we say—real fertile spots in the desert. We're gonna give them the whole nine yards."

Tourists will be "forced" at "gunpoint" to get into the trunks of dark sedans. The "trunks" will be air-conditioned and equipped with comfortable seats, wet bars, and slot machines. "It'll be real nice, I guaran-tee," Mr. P. said.

A tourist board spokesman said the tours should draw a variety of customers, from amateur archeologists to forensic scientists. He called the plan "part of Las Vegas's continuing program to become America's No. One family destination."

—*The New York Times*, 1996

Why I'm Running

⊡

My very fellow Americans: Today, here, on the steps of this historic building, I am announcing my candidacy for President of the United States.

Yes, there are a lot of other people running for President, but I firmly believe I am uniquely qualified for this, the highest office in this great nation of ours, and I intend to explain why.

First, however, let me address a more urgent question, and that is the future facing our children's children's children's children. And their children. When their time comes, our time will have passed. But they will look back and say, "What was all that about?" Someone will have to answer. And that someone is why I am running. My friends, today I say to you, I want to be that someone.

There is a wise saying where I come from. It has been handed down over the ages, and it goes something like this: "Do not give away your socks unless you like going barefoot."

Well, today I am taking off my socks and giving them to the American people.

I do not particularly like going barefoot. But if that is the price of democracy, then I say, "So be it."

I know that people will look at me, in that wonderful American way of ours, and say, "It is cold out, and your toes are turning blue." But I know also that there are larger things at stake than blue, or even brittle, toes.

But that is only part of the reason I stand before you barefoot, ready to run many miles in order to earn your trust. Sure, there will be times when I take an airplane or a car or a train, or even a bus. I will do what I must, just as I must what I will do. And that, my friends, is my pledge to you today.

We live in a time of great challenge. All right, perhaps that is putting it strongly. Perhaps it is old-fashioned to speak bluntly, without vacillation or verbal varnish. So be it. Some have urged me, "Don't be blunt." But if this election is about anything, it is about not hiding one's light of conviction under a bushel of demurral. So to speak. It is about standing up and saying, "Here I am."

Well, friends, *here I am*.

I would not be truthful if I said to you that our problems can be fixed overnight. But, my fellow Americans, today I say to you, if we do not start to fix them, they will fix us. And a fine fix we will be in then.

If I sound urgent, it is not because my feet are cold. Yes, it is early April and I am standing on marble, which gets pretty cold in early April in this great state of ours. But I do not shrink from this numbing sensation in my toes, because I know that it is still warm in America. America is the warmest nation on the face of the earth. To those who say our warmest days are behind us, I say, I have been to many warm countries. And there is no country warmer than the United States of America.

Often, as I have traveled the breadth and depth and width of this great, great land, I have been asked, "Who are you? What do you want?"

Today, I have an answer. Today, I say to you, I want to be that person. They ask, "Do you have it in you to lead this country?"

The answer must be "I think so."

For today I come not to divide but to multiply. Not to criticize but to cauterize. Not to annoy but to alloy. I come, finally, not to naysay but, to quote that great American Willie Mays, to say, "Hey."

Friends—and even if you don't like me, I like you—the time is not yesterday, or even tomorrow. For, as the Founding Parents so wisely said, "The past lies behind, the future lies ahead." The time is now.

Yes, it is true that a stopped watch is right twice a day. But it is also true that it is wrong the rest of the day. My fellow Americans, with your help—and, yes, with your money, for I will need that, lots of it—I will wind the watch of democracy so that it will be right most of the day.

So, as I stand here on the steps of the County Lying-In Hospital for Women, this historic building where I was born, in the days when "illegal aliens" meant little green men from outer space, let the word go forth. And then let it come back. And take a load off, as we Americans say. So that future generations will say, "They ran the good race, fought the good fight. And they knew what time it was, for they kept the watch wound."

Thank you and God bless you.

—*The New Yorker,* 1995

Summer
Blockbusters

∎

Chipper: An evil entrepreneur (Patrick McGoohan) devises a scheme to supply his chain of fast-seafood restaurants with fresh seviche by catching Pacific dolphins and processing them with onboard shredding machines. His plans are complicated by a marine biologist (Kurt Russell) who is convinced that seahorse hooves hold the secret to a cure for prostate cancer, and by a spunky salvage hunter (Jennifer Aniston) who has trained a pod of dolphins to find Amelia Earhart's plane.

Emission Impossible: I.M.F. agents (Charlie Sheen, Courteney Cox) set out to start a war between two ruthless Middle Eastern dictators (Martin Landau, Joe Pesci) by convincing them that they are impotent.

Exterminator: When a pest-control specialist (Arnold Schwarzenegger) is accidentally transported back in time to the fourteenth century by a faulty supermarket checkout scanner, he decides he might as well try to catch the Norway rat that brought the bubonic plague to Europe. After offending the wife (Sandra Bullock) of a Venetian doge (Danny DeVito) by suggesting that the rat might be hiding in her dress, he persuades her to join forces with him against a corrupt ship owner (Alan Rickman) who is transporting the rat to Amsterdam under orders from an evil vizier (Patrick McGoohan) seeking revenge for the defeat of the Muslim hordes at the Battle of Tours.

Plight of the Osprey: A Marine test pilot (Brad Pitt) is told not to worry when the control stick of his tilt rotor plane keeps coming off in his hands, but after a Defense Department procurement officer (Demi

Moore) tells him that the aircraft's engines are powered by slave labor they decide to take matters into their own hands and Osterize the evil defense contractor (Patrick McGoohan) and his chief designer (John Turturro).

Maya: A pre-Columbian archeologist (Ed Harris) discovers a runic horoscope predicting that the New York Stock Exchange will crash in seventy-two hours unless five hundred virgins are sacrificed to the god Chachacha. When he and the N.Y.S.E. president (Meg Ryan) realize they have little hope of locating five hundred virgins in Manhattan before the deadline—or, indeed, ever—they enlist the help of a legless computer hacker (Elijah Wood) and a Guatemalan shaman (Jimmy Smits) to outwit the deity and in the process make a tidy profit by shorting the market. Written and directed by Michael Crichton.

S.W.A.K.: An orthographically challenged philatelist (Johnny Depp) advertises in the personals for someone of similar interests and finds himself mixed up with a stockbroker (Maria de Medeiros) with a penchant for oral sex.

No, Houston, You Have a Problem: The crew of a U.S. space shuttle (Denzel Washington, Helen Hunt, William Baldwin), tasked with performing experiments to determine the effects of weightlessness on the mating habits of fruit bats, detects an asteroid the size of Liechtenstein on a collision course with the earth. A heated argument breaks out when Mission Control orders them to deflect the asteroid by ramming it with their craft.

Dwagonheart: A tenth-century knight with a speech impediment (Keanu Reeves) must slay a mythical half kangaroo, half garden slug before a beautiful princess (Patsy Kensit) will make merry with him. But just as he is about to behead the repulsive creature it reveals (voice by Dick Cavett) that the beautiful princess has already made merry with all the other knights in the fiefdom.

Baywatch, the Movie: A Chinese military satellite containing plutonium lands in the bay and starts turning beach babes and dudes into gnarly mutants. Local authorities clash with the military over who has jurisdiction. As bureaucrats argue, it becomes clear that the lifeguards must remove the toxic debris themselves, using their bare hands and those orange lozenge lifesaver things. Lt. Hank Hunk (David Hasselhoff) and Tiffany Topps (Pamela Anderson Lee) find themselves in a race against time with a band of renegade Australian lifeguards, who plan to recover the satellite themselves and sell it to the Russian mafia so they can afford to buy imported beer.

—*The New Yorker,* 1996

Introducing Yourself
to the Waiter

(From the Introduction to the Second Edition)

■

"Hello, my name is Ralph, and I will be your server this evening."
Americans were surprised when waiters began introducing themselves to their customers a few years back. While the custom has long been in practice overseas, it was late coming to our own country, and as with Pearl Harbor, we were taken by surprise.

Clearly some guidance on this New Familiarity was in order, and it was for that reason that I published my ground-breaking—indeed, seminal—book, *And My Name Is: Getting Acquainted With Your Waiter* (Dove Press; $22). The response was extraordinary. Since its publication five years ago it has been translated into sixteen languages, including British. The immense volume of mail, not all of it complimentary, prompted the publishers to ask me to undertake a second, revised edition, which will appear this fall.

Perhaps a bit of historical background is in order first. Waiters did not always introduce themselves, even in Europe. Hard though it may be to believe, it was virtually unheard of before the seventeenth century. Not surprisingly, the practice seems to have begun in that most civilized of countries, France.

The first recorded instance of it happening occurred in Paris in the year 1684. As soon as the Duc de Pentheville had been shown to his seat at the fashionable boite, *Haricot Vert,* a young man by the name of Ralphe de Villiers strode up purposefully to the nobleman and said, *"Je suis Ralphe de Villiers. Je suis votre garçon ce soir."* Unfortunately, the old Duc was not progressively minded, and the wretched Ralphe was hanged in front of the *Haricot Vert* as the Duc and his guests were finishing their *pâte de lapin a la façon Suedois.*

Ralphe's body was left hanging as a warning to other waiters. Indeed, the incident seems to have discouraged further social experiments by waiters, since the next recorded instance of the phenomenon did not take place for nearly a century, until a bold would-be sommelier from Nantes named Jean de Nantes said to the Baron de Boudin, "*Moi, je m'appelle Jean. Et vous?*" Jean was summarily burned at the stake with the Baron looking on and declaring to the executioner that he wanted the impetuous young man "*Bien cuit*" (well done). But Jean's death was not in vain. It was his death that sparked the riots that lead to the Second Edict of Nantes, and eventually to the French Revolution.

These are, of course, only two historical instances in a long line of gastronomic martyrs. The atrocities committed by the Turks, the Arabs and—sad to say—the English against waiters who dared to introduce themselves are, alas, as numerous as they are deplorable.

As I wrote in *And My Name Is*, the first and most obvious dilemma is whether to shake the waiter's hand from the left or the right.* But of the thousands and thousands of letters I received from readers of the first edition, most concerned the question of asking the waiter to sit down and join in the dinner.

The culinary world remains sharply divided on the issue, but I remain firm, maintaining as I do that it is just plain bad manners not to invite the waiter to sit down for a brief get-acquainted chat before ordering. It is true that in certain parts of France, notably the Camargue and the Dordogne, the practice is to invite the waiter to sit down for coffee or an *anis* or cognac *after the meal*. But the fashion of following the French in waiter etiquette is, to my way of thinking, overdone, given France's deplorable history in the matter.

In an attempt to calm the waters that I have roiled with my advice in the first edition, I have slightly amended this section of the book to say that after the preliminary round of introductions, go ahead and ask the waiter to join you—*but only for a brief chat*. Simply make it clear that if the service is good, he will be invited back for coffee.

Many of the letters I've received ask the question, "What if the service is lousy?"

---

* When introducing oneself, always shake hands to your right When bidding the waiter good-bye, to your left In some Middle Eastern countries, it may be advisable to forgo the handshake altogether in favor of a simple denunciation of United States policy toward Israel

This is perhaps The Problem in social relations with waiters. There is no one answer, but as a general rule: if the waiter seems to be the sort of person one wants as a lifelong friend, then does it matter if the osso bucco ever arrives? Or that when it finally does arrive, it tastes like wet cardboard?

(One solution: if rotten service makes you agitated, bring along some Valium. One person I know always eats a full meal *before* going to the restaurant leaving him free to concentrate on developing a personal relationship with the server.)

On the other hand, if the waiter seems not at all the sort of person we want to associate with outside the restaurant, then I recommend being absolutely forthright. I.e., "Now look here, Giancarlo, or whatever your name is"—*that* gets them where it hurts—"if that osso bucco isn't on the table by the time I count to *tre,* I'm going to beat you to death with this [obscenity] peppermill."

One correspondent of ours says that's how he introduces *himself* to the waiters. The downside is that many of them forget to introduce themselves to him. But service, he reports, is usually quite brisk.

That said, *Bon appétit,* and remember: developing a relationship with the person who brings you your food lessens the chance that he or she will spit on it in the kitchen.

—*Key West Restaurant,* 1986

You,
the Jury!

⌘

Interactive TV Movie of the Week: *Beauty and the Juice*. Menu of Alternative Endings. Make Selection, Then Press Number of Desired Ending.

1.   O. J. pretends to have a heart attack in the courtroom. In the ambulance on the way to the hospital, he overpowers his guards and leads the LAPD, the National Guard, the United States Air Force, the Border Patrol, and the Coast Guard on a harrowing chase into Mexico, where he claims political asylum. The Mexican government, still angry with the United States for stealing California in 1848, refuses to extradite him. In retaliation, the United States withdraws from the North American Free Trade Agreement. O. J. becomes a greeter at the El Conquistador Hotel in Acapulco. Business there quadruples.

2.   After pleading their client not guilty by reason of insanity, the defense attorneys Robert Shapiro, F. Lee Bailey, and Alan Dershowitz argue that the "admittedly unfortunate events" were actually all the fault of Nicole Simpson. "Who paid for that house?" Shapiro asks movingly in his summation. "Who paid for that Ferrari? I put it to you—if you came home and found your ex-wife thanking a man who had appeared on the television show *Studs* for returning a pair of her mother's eyeglasses, wouldn't you go a little nuts?"

3.   O. J. is found guilty on two counts of murder in the first degree and sentenced to death. But as the cyanide pellets drop inside the San Quentin gas chamber, the phone rings. It's the governor, ordering a

halt to the execution. The police have just found a suicide note on the Golden Gate Bridge, signed by Al Cowlings, Simpson's long-time friend and sometime chauffeur. After thanking a hundred and twenty-four golfing buddies, Cowlings says that it was he who committed the murders, in an attempt to frame O. J. in revenge for O. J.'s having married his girlfriend many years ago. L.A. District Attorney Gil Garcetti sends O. J. a handwritten letter of apology, saying, "I never thought you did it, man." O. J., through a spokesman, replies, "Hey, no sweat," and asks Garcetti to be his partner in the Pebble Beach National Pro Am.

4. As word of O. J. Simpson's acquittal spreads throughout Beverly Hills, angry crowds of expensively dressed white people overturn gelato venders' carts and set fire to Cartier. The fire spreads to Tiffany and Chanel. People without lunch reservations storm the front door of Morton's and threaten the maître d' with physical violence if they are not immediately seated. Governor Wilson appeals for manners. Letitia Baldrige is brought in by armored riot vehicle and exhorts the crowds with a bullhorn, "Remember where you are!"

5. At the conclusion of the fourteen-month-long "preliminary hearing," Judge Kennedy-Powell determines that it would be impossible to impanel a jury that hasn't already arrived at a verdict, and orders that the trial be held in Guam. Prosecutor Marcia Clark vociferously objects to the change of venue, saying that she looks "ridiculous" in a *mestiza,* the traditional Guamanian attire. The judge sternly informs her that she is under no obligation whatsoever to wear Guamanian garb. O. J., extremely popular with Guamanians, is acquitted by an all-male jury after a two-hour-long trial. The jury foreman tells the press afterward that the jury might have voted to convict if Clark had worn a *mestiza.*

6. The legal battle of the century heads for the highest court in the land: Bailey v. Dershowitz. Bailey is livid with Dershowitz for calling him, in his best-selling book, *Can't Get Enough of Me,* a "washed-up, publicity-mongering limousine-chaser who couldn't get Mother

Teresa off on a shoplifting charge." Bailey has retaliated in *his* book, *The "F" Stands for Fabulous,* by calling Dershowitz a "short, four-eyed Harvard hairball who cares about only one thing—gross participation in movie deals." After many exciting motions and countermotions, the Supreme Court decides not to hear the case. In a joint press conference brokered by superagent Michael Ovitz, Bailey and Dershowitz declare, "Sadly, brilliant lawyers can no longer get justice in America," and announce plans for a miniseries about their reconciliation.

—*The New Yorker,* 1994

Apartment
Hunter

□

O. J. Simpson is considering moving from his posh estate in
the Brentwood section of Los Angeles to New York City.
—*New York Post*

I am pleased to write in support of Mr. Simpson's application to become a member of your cooperative.

I have known Mr. Simpson for many years. I would describe him as a
devoted family man. As you may be aware, he has recently suffered the
devastating loss of his former wife, to whom he was very close. But he is
strong and his attitude is "Life must go on."

Initially, his plan was to return to his home and raise his children according to his own strong sense of family values. But the crime problem
in Brentwood persuades him that it is time to look elsewhere, and so he
has decided to move with the children to New York, where they can
have a "normal" upbringing.

Sincerely,
Robert Kardashian

Ladies and gentlemen, good morning!
O. J. Simpson will make an *excellent* tenant in your building. I can
truthfully say I know him intimately, having spent a lot of time with him

recently. He is a godly man who has suffered bitterly at the hands of the unrighteous. His only desire right now, apart from seeing that the Colombian drug dealers who slew his ex-wife and her companion are brought to justice, is to raise his children in an atmosphere of serenity and security.

I understand that the late Mrs. Jacqueline Kennedy Onassis, another parent of two young children left bereft by a senseless act of violence, lived in your building, so you are familiar with these tragedies, and the need to be sensitive and sympathetic to the victims.

In the matter of finances, I can say without fear of contradiction that Mr. Simpson will be more than able to meet the necessary requirements. His financial future shines brightly indeed!

Sincerely,
Johnnie Cochran

To the board:

O. J. Simpson will make an ideal tenant, and you should move expeditiously to approve his application.

Aside from the reflected glory that all your tenants would share in having a tenant of his stature, there is an additional benefit—my own occasional presence in the building. As you know, it was I who masterminded his entire defense strategy, despite the fact that my esteemed colleague Mr. Cochran seems to be crowding the limelight. My only point is that I am the most brilliant legal mind in the United States, and my occasional visits to the Simpson duplex at 1040 would lend great respectability to all of you.

Another of my clients, Mr. Claus von Bülow, lived on Fifth Avenue, and my visits to his apartment brought considerable social stature to his cotenants.

I should add that in the event you turn down Mr. Simpson's application I will be handling the appeal. The upside for you would be spending many, many hours in my presence. The downside would be legal fees that will force you to send your children to public schools.

Sincerely,
Alan Dershowitz

THIS IS A. C.:

He's got a gun to his head. You better let him come live in your building. Be cool with this. He just wants to chill out. Everyone needs to chill out here.

Do you have a parking garage? Also, what is the freeway situation in New York in case we need to go for a quick cruise?

Sincerely,
Al (A. C.) Cowlings

DEAR MR. SIMPSON:

The Cooperative Association has met to discuss your application. We reviewed the many strong letters of recommendation submitted by your friends and associates.

After almost four hours of deliberation, the board unanimously voted "Not Approved." Let me hasten to say that this decision had nothing whatsoever to do with race, or the notoriety surrounding the recent unfortunate events. It was simply that the board, recalling your statements regarding your activities on the night of June 12, 1994, took note of your predilection for nocturnal golfing on the premises.

The board felt rather strongly that nocturnal golfing is inappropriate in a Fifth Avenue duplex, and therefore decided to pass on your application, with the keenest regret.

Sincerely,
1040 Fifth Avenue
Cooperative Association

—*The New Yorker*, 1995

Hillary Pilloried

February 2: Barbara Feinman is called to testify before the Senate Whitewater Committee as to whether she saw the Rose Law Firm documents on the third floor of the White House. Feinman collaborated with Hillary Rodham Clinton on her book, *It Takes a Village,* but received no acknowledgment from the First Lady. She tells the senators that she did not see the subpoenaed billing records but "did find Mrs. Clinton's habit of chewing computer printouts into little balls and swallowing them a bit peculiar." Mrs. Clinton explained to her, she said, that it was "a new high-fiber diet" she was trying.

February 13: The *Washington Times* prints a leaked extract from Hillary Clinton's January 26th grand-jury testimony:

> MR. STARR: When did you last see the documents?
> MRS. CLINTON: I have no recollection of that.
> MR. STARR: Is your name Hillary Rodham Clinton?
> MRS. CLINTON: I have no recollection of that.
> MR. STARR: Do you live in the White House?
> MRS. CLINTON: You'll have to be more specific. I've lived in a number of white houses.

March 12: FBI experts report that Mrs. Clinton's fingerprints are on the documents. However, the revelation is complicated by the fact that so are O. J. Simpson's.

March 14: Hillary Clinton hires Johnnie Cochran.

March 18: Cochran demands full DNA testing of documents.

April 15: Senator Alfonse D'Amato, Whitewater Committee chairman, asks for six billion dollars to continue his investigation until the year A.D. 2021.

May 17: While vacuuming under the First Couple's bed, White House janitor Manuel García finds a deed to a choice waterfront plot in the name of Hillary Rodham, witnessed by Vincent Foster. Attached to the deed is a Post-it note bearing Foster's handwriting: "If this gets out, we're in *major* doo-doo."

May 20: Mrs. Clinton's lawyer, Johnnie Cochran, says of the new controversial document, "If it's just a Post-it, we aren't toasted."

August 25: On the eve of the Democratic National Convention, the White House announces that Mrs. Clinton will immediately embark on a weeklong goodwill tour of mutton ranches in New Zealand.

August 26: *Times* columnist William Safire writes that Mrs. Clinton should not be permitted to leave the country.

August 28: President Clinton issues a statement saying that if he weren't President he'd "chop off Safire's chestnuts and feed them to the hogs." White House spokesman Mike McCurry later says Clinton was merely using a "colorful Southern expression indicating honest disagreement."

September 5: In an interview with *Newsweek*'s Eleanor Clift, Hillary Clinton suggests that the Rose Law Firm documents were put there "by Richard Nixon." In a somewhat rambling explanation, she ventures that "Carolyn [Huber] first found the documents in August. The same month Nixon resigned." Nixon's own secretary was Rose Mary Woods. "Rose Mary Woods, Rose Law Firm, see?" "Finally," the First Lady says, "Nixon's never forgiven me for working on the impeachment committee back in '74. So it all fits. I mean, right? Right?"

September 12: First Cat Socks wanders into the East Room of the White House during a Presidential press conference and in full view of TV cameras coughs up a hairball. Upon closer examination by ABC's Brit Hume, the hairball turns out to be a length of dictation tape. When it is played, Mrs. Clinton's voice is heard saying to her chief of staff, Margaret Williams, "Where are the [expletive deleted] billing records you got out of Vince's office? I had them right here. We don't want Carolyn to find them."

September 13: Mrs. Clinton denies that it is her voice on the tape. Her lawyer, Johnnie Cochran, says of the evidence, "If there's feline spit, you must acquit."

—*The New Yorker,* 1996

Unaclíent

■

Lawyers from around the nation are trying to hawk their
services directly to Unabomber suspect Theodore Kaczynski.
—*USA Today*

DEAR MR. KACZYNSKI,

I won't pussyfoot around: I'm the best there is, and you, my friend,
are knee-deep in kimchi. Here's how we handle it: The FBI had dozens
of agents staked out around your cabin for weeks. We put each and
every one of them on the stand and ask him if in the last twenty years
he ever used the word "weirdo." Let them deny it! We'll put their fifth-
grade teachers on the stand, then nail them for perjury and move to dis-
miss.

I would have come up there personally, except that urgent business on
behalf of a very fine client is detaining me here. But my jet is fueled and
ready.

Sincerely,
F. Lee Bailey
Tallahassee, Fla.

P.S. It turns out my jet won't be available after all. Do they have commercial flights into Helena?

DEAR MR. KACZYNSKI,

Greetings! Perhaps I can be of some assistance. Most important, we need to get this case moved out of Buffalo Dung, Montana, to Berkeley where we'll get a jury of peers who won't sit up all night drinking beers. Those people up there look as if they'd all been swimming in the same gene pool too long and someone forgot to add chlorine. Also, my Rolls-Royce would not take kindly to driving over cattle guards. As for those so-called bombs in your cabin, we'll tell the jury "if they did not detonate, you must exonerate."

> Sincerely,
> Johnnie Cochran
> Los Angeles, Calif.

DEAR MR. KACZYNSKI,

I practice law here in Wyoming and I have experience with men such as yourself, who want only to live in harmony among the elk and bear and antelope, but who wake up one morning to find that Big Brother has descended from the Big Sky.

My client Randy Weaver went through a similar infringement of his rights in Ruby Ridge, Idaho. Before I took over his case, he was looking at spending the rest of his life in a federal dungeon, cursing the darkness.

> *Now he is a free man,*
> *And FBI Director Freeh*
> *Fears to arrest the Freemen.*

I wrote that. I also do some painting.

I'm not saying it will be easy. Westerners don't make easy promises. What they do is spit on their hands and go to work. The FBI has found material in your cabin that might lead a jury to suspect you weren't just tinkering with new recipes for jackrabbit: specifically, bombs, trigger devices, saltpeter, sulfur, and ammonium nitrate, and also what appears to be the original draft of that manifesto they printed in the newspapers and this here piece of paper they found with the words "hit list" written above "airline industry," "computer industry," and "geneticists."

As we say in these parts, "If you got a rope around your neck, it's no time to goose the horse." We'll want to be very deliberate about this and pick our own hunting ground.

Sincerely,
Gerry Spence
Jackson, Wyo.

DEAR MR. KACZYNSKI,

I'm in the middle of the tour for my book on the O. J. Simpson case, *Reasonable Doubts*—it's really excellent. Have you read it? It's getting great reviews. I don't want to sound defeatist, but in my opinion you're going to need the best appeals lawyer in the country. And, since I'm already halfway through the manuscript for the book about your appeal, you might as well hire me, right?

Let me set you at ease. First, I would take you on without charge. The deal for the book and movie about your case, which I've already signed, will cover my costs.

Second, I am not the kind of lawyer who asks his client improper questions, like "Did you try to decapitate your wife?" or "Did you pump your wife so full of insulin in the eighties that she's still asleep in the nineties?" That's not my role. My role is to uphold the Bill of Rights by establishing that a bailiff picked his nose during the voir dire and tainted the entire proceeding. Call me.

Sincerely,
Alan Dershowitz
Cambridge, Mass.

P.S. If you have any casting ideas for who should play you—Eastwood? Van Damme?—let me know right away. They want to move on this quickly.

—*The New Yorker,* 1996

Répondez,
Sí Vous
Payez

▪

THE HONOR OF YOUR PRESENCE
IS REQUESTED AT A
SALUTE
TO THE CUTICLE INSTITUTE
UNDER THE GRACIOUS PATRONAGE OF
HIS ROYAL HIGHNESS
PRINCE BEGIN LE BEGUINE

Ticket Prices:

$50,000—*Gala Benefactor*

1.   One Table, Very Near the Prince's. Includes a Confusing Array of Forks and Knives, and Eight Inches of Elbow Room (on Each Side).

2.   Ten Private Cocktail Reception Tickets. Includes Photo Opportunity with H.R.H. Prince Begin; Cameras Graciously Provided by Disposable Cameras, Inc.

3.   A Warm Embrace of Your Person by H.R.H. Prince Begin, Including a Hearty Pretense That He Has Met You Before.

4.   Cocktails of Your Choice Made with Liquors with Recognizable Brand Names. Glasses Graciously Provided by Baccarat.

5. Dinner: Beluga Caviar with Blinis; Fugu (Potentially Poisonous Japanese Blowfish, Prepared by Chefs Skilled at Removing the Toxins); Chocolate Leveraged Buyout. Catering Courtesy of Phabulous Phoods, Served by Trained Actors, Superbly Resentful at Finding Themselves in This Line of Work.

6. Your Name Included in All Press Releases and Media Promotions.

7. Keepsake Bag. Contents: New Cologne "Joxx" (Perfect for Chauffeur's Christmas Present); Gold-Plated Cuticle Remover. Both Wrapped in an Abundance of Crinkly Colored Tissue (Perfect for Maid's Christmas Present).

———

$25,000—*Patron*

1. Twelve-Foot-High Dried-Flower Arrangement on Table, Courtesy of Fleurs du Mel.

2. Brief Acknowledgment of Your Existence by H.R.H. Prince Begin During Cocktail Hour. Champagne Graciously Provided by Château X-ellente, Napa; Glasses Courtesy of Pierre One.

3. The Imperial Portion of Sevruga Caviar (Two Full Grams); Crackers Courtesy of Ritz.

———

$10,000—*Host*

1. Photo Opportunity with H.R.H. (Extreme-Wide-Angle Lens Graciously Provided by Maxiflex.)

2. Two Glasses of Sonoma Sogood '95. Glasses Provided by Party Rite Plastix.

3. Capellini Alla Lumpfish. Plates Courtesy of Paperware.

$5,000—*Friend*

1. Table Near Speakers. Earplugs Courtesy of Bleeding Ear Corporation.

2. A Selection of Locally Brewed Beer, Served *en Bouteille*.

3. Fleeting Glimpse of H.R.H. Prince Begin.

4. *Le Diner sur l'Herbe:* A Medley of Recently Mown Grasses from the Sheep Meadow; Dandelion Salad; *Tarte de Boue* (Mud Pie).

$1,000—*Acquaintance*

1. *Le Mariage de Brun et de Violet* (Peanut Butter and Grape Jelly).

2. *Eau de Tap à la Façon Paysanne.* Served in Your Own Cupped Hands with One Full Cube of Ice (Hole Included).

3. Full Coat-Check Privileges (Tipping Extra).

$500—*Do We Know You?*

1. Ropeside Tickets Outside Main Entrance to Grand Foyer, Ideal for Viewing the Arrival of the Less Economically Challenged Invitees.

2. Loan of Umbrellas (in Event of Rain).

3. *Vol de Pigeons.* (Magnificent Aerial Display of Pigeons as They Gambol Delightfully Above the Assembled.)

4. *Venin de Fugu à la Mort.* Canapés Made from Removed Blowfish Toxins. Transportation Courtesy of Emergency Medical Services.

—*The New Yorker,* 1996

Moodest
Proposals

NEW DELHI, April 2 (Reuters)—A Hindu group in
India offered today to shelter British cows threatened
with slaughter because of mad cow disease.
—*The Times*

"Surely the solution to Cambodia's mine problem is
here before our very eyes in black and white."
—A Cambodian newspaper, quoted in *The
Times,* on using British cows to detonate
unexploded land mines

BERLIN, N.H.—Republican Presidential candidate Patrick J. Buchanan
today proposed that the United States import the 4.7 million British
cows affected by mad-cow disease and deploy them across the U.S.–
Mexican border to deter illegal immigrants.

DALLAS—Ross Perot today attacked the idea of deploying cows along
the U.S.–Mexican border, saying that hungry illegal immigrants would
be likely to "take a bite out of 'em on the way over and then we'd end
up with tens of thousands of crazy Mexicans running around. I ask you,"
he told a crowd, "is that the America we want to leave for our grandchildren?"

FAIRFAX, VA.—The National Rifle Association today announced that
it has offered to send its entire 3.3-million membership over to England

to assist with its massive cow-culling effort. N.R.A. executive Wayne LaPierre said that if Britain did not have such stringent gun-control laws "they'd have been able to nip this problem at the start." He called on Congress to immediately repeal the ban on some types of assault rifles, including the .50-caliber Elsie Eliminator, so that the membership can "do the job right."

BOGOTA—Luis Alfonso Maquilon Amaya, a head trafficker for the Cali cocaine cartel, is reportedly trying to buy up all 4.7 million mad British cows on the black market. According to sources here, the plan is to stuff the cows full of cocaine and ship them to the United States. "Normally we have problems with customs when the bags break inside and the animals make a big scene," a source said. "But a *vaca loca* isn't bothered too much by even a couple of kilos in its bloodstream."

CANBERRA—The Australian government has said it will take delivery of all British mad cows. Trade Minister Tim Fischer said that the plan is to "float the cows off beaches so the sharks will eat them instead of tourists and the odd Prime Minister."

LOS ANGELES—Entertainer Michael Jackson and Saudi Prince Al Waleed Bin Talal announced today that they will create a theme-park home for all British cows afflicted with mad cow disease. Stroking a cow's forelock as he spoke at the press conference in a barely audible whisper, the singer would not provide details of the amusement park or venture to explain why people would pay to be with millions of mad cows other than to say it would be "really, really wonderful."

WASHINGTON—Mayor Marion Barry today offered to use Britain's mad cows to fill District of Columbia potholes. The one problem, he said, is that there are only 4.7 million cows, and the District has 7.8 million potholes.

JORDAN, MONT.—The FBI plans to stampede more than four million mad British cows in an effort to force the Montana Freemen to end their standoff, it has been learned. FBI director Louis Freeh declined to comment on reports that British C-130 Hercules cargo planes have been observed dropping large numbers of cows by parachute near the standoff area.

BEIJING—China announced today that it plans to conduct "amphibious mad-cow exercises" in the Taiwan Strait. Secretary of State Warren Christopher warned China's leadership that the U.S. viewed the development "seriously."

NEW YORK—The Council of Fashion Designers of America said today that it would use British mad cows in runway shows. "Fashion recognizes its responsibility to help," said C.F.D.A. director Fern Mallis. "The cows are very contemporary, they look great in leather, and their eyes have the look."

HOLLYWOOD—A group of actors and actresses has called on Prime Minister John Major to "stop the slaughter" of British mad cows and "do something positive instead, like vaccinate them or whatever."

"We feel the government hasn't done enough," said Liam Neeson. Neeson said he has felt sympathetic toward British cows ever since the filming of the movie *Rob Roy,* in which he escaped from soldiers by hiding inside the carcass of a large, decomposing Hereford. The group, Creativity United to Denounce the Slaughter (CUDS), plans to distribute lapel udders with ribbons.

OAK BROOK, ILL.—The McDonald's Corporation announced today its plans to introduce a new line of sandwiches next month called Mad Macs.

—*The New Yorker,* 1996

Homage

to Tom Clancy

The Ego
Has Landed

The office of the O. F. Bowen insurance agency is about a forty-five-minute drive from Washington, in Owings, Maryland, opposite a corn-field and just up the road from the Dash-In food store. The decor is Hartford Drab: gray steel desks, beat-up filing cabinets, wooden chairs, and veneer paneling. Near the door is a picture of the Sacred Heart of Jesus. Books and folders with such titles as *Reliance Auto, CAMP Risk Management Series,* and *The World's Missile Systems* line a bookshelf. An-other photo shows President Reagan, in black tie, introducing the owner of the O. F. Bowen agency to President Raúl Alfonsín of Argentina.

The phone rings; it's the William Morris agency in New York.

"Yeah," says the man behind the steel desk, lighting a cigarette. He is in his early forties and wears very thick, tinted glasses. "Number eight hardcover and three soft. We're on *both* sides." He listens, inhales, um-hums. "We may have one more week, then it'll die. But it's been one hell of a ride."

Indeed it has. A year ago no one had ever heard of Thomas L. Clancy, Jr. Then along came *The Hunt For Red October,* his book about the So-viet Union's hottest new submarine and its captain, who decides to take the sub and defect to the United States. All hell breaks loose, and it falls to a bookish CIA analyst named Jack Ryan to tell the President whether *Red October* is the Trojan horse of World War III or the vehicle for a le-gitimate high-stakes dash to freedom.

In a business in which the average free-lance writer makes less than five thousand dollars a year, Clancy accomplished the equivalent of hit-ting a grand-slam home run in his first at bat.

Red October sold about 330,000 hardcover copies during twenty-nine weeks on *The New York Times*'s best-seller list and moved onto the paperback best-seller list, where it had risen to the number-three slot by December. He sold the book to Hollywood for "pretty serious money" if the cameras actually roll. And he has a six-figure advance for his next book, which will appear simultaneously in thirteen countries. "We missed Greece, but that's no great loss," Clancy says.

It should also be noted that Clancy has become Writer of Sea Thrillers to the President of the United States. The job is without portfolio, but it does have its advantages.

There's a fat note of irony to all this, since Clancy, who started selling insurance fourteen years ago because it was the first "decent" job offer he got, had always wanted to be a writer. But as a level-headed, Jesuit-educated Baltimore boy, the son of a mailman, he knew the truth—that "writers die poor." So he went to work selling policies and raising a family.

Eventually he and his wife were able to buy the business and make a "decent living." They insured country things: barns, oats, the odd restaurant, tobacco (while it hung out to cure), and horses. They stayed away from life insurance, says Cheryl Terry, their assistant, "because it's too morbid." It was a nice, quiet, no-fireworks kind of life.

In many ways it still is, apparently, since much of what Clancy has to say is about how success has not changed him. Clancy is, in fact, so self-deprecating about his sea thriller and so generous in talking about the talents of others that he often uses the pronoun "we" rather than "I." While he has the aw-shucks down pretty good, we—I, that is—suspect he is getting more of a kick out of all this than he is letting on.

The saga of *Red October* actually began on a winter morning in 1976, when Clancy was reading his *Washington Post* and saw a story about the *Storozhevoy* incident. The *Storozhevoy* was a Soviet frigate whose crew mutinied and tried to take the ship and defect to Sweden. They got within about thirty miles of Swedish waters before the Soviets stopped them. The mutineers were shot. Clancy clipped the story and filed it away, thinking there might be a book in it.

Seven years later he found himself listening to sea stories being told by one of his clients, a former sub driver (as they call themselves). "All of a sudden a light bulb went off and I said, 'Hey, submariners are pretty much the same as fighter pilots. They just do it a little slower.' " The Wet Stuff!

He started writing, and by late October 1983 had two chapters to show Marty Callahan, an editor at the Naval Institute Press in Annapolis. Clancy had worked for Callahan once before, writing an article on the MX missile for *Proceedings,* the NIP's magazine. Other than that, NIP publishes mostly naval textbooks and had never published a novel. But Callahan liked the two chapters and told Clancy to keep going. So he went home and started over at page one.

He wrote in his spare time, sticking a piece of paper into his IBM Selectric whenever he got a chance. He had no outline and didn't even know how it was going to end. "I let my characters do all the work. Sounds crazy, but it works."

Clancy thought it was more "fun" to write that way, anyway. "It's a discovery process for the writer as well as the reader," he says, "and I think that's really the enjoyable part of writing—that everything you write is actually new, and you don't know what's going to happen until it does."

He banged out the pulse-quickening last two chapters—almost one hundred manuscript pages—in *two days.* Then, on February 28, just four months after his initial meeting with Callahan, he showed up at the NIP's offices with a 720-page manuscript.

Clancy says he waited three weeks "to find out if it was worth fooling with, or something to be used for starting a fire." (We ourselves think he is pulling our leg here.) Finally an NIP editor called and said, in so many words, *don't* use it to start a fire. He doesn't remember exactly what she did say.

"It was kind of a euphoric day for me. . . . It was nice, but I didn't go out and get drunk that night. I had three kids at the time. That tends to keep you down to earth."

The NIP's editors then asked some naval officers for an opinion of the manuscript and, according to Clancy, one of them "really freaked." He wrote a letter to the Press saying the story was so full of classified stuff that there was no way the firm could publish it.

Clancy chuckles as he pulls out a copy of the letter, which says that *Red October* "is no *Run Silent, Run Deep*" (the classic submarine novel and film of World War II). "He's right there," says Clancy. "Ned [Edward L.] Beach is a much better writer than I am."

Clancy even disclaims the title of writer; he calls himself a storyteller. "I may never make the transition. I'm gonna try. I wrote a fairly decent thriller, okay? It's not *King Lear.* And it kind of embarrasses me sometimes when people make so much of it." (We don't remember anyone calling it *King Lear,* but it is a fine sentiment.)

Nonetheless, the navy was genuinely alarmed by the depth of Clancy's knowledge of its top, top secrets. All of a sudden Clancy found himself being swarmed over by the Naval Investigative Service and a commander at the Pentagon who wanted to know how he had found out so much about the world of nuclear subs—and from whom.

Clancy obliged the commander by telling him where he'd gotten it all, without mentioning the names of any of the active-duty naval officers who had talked to him. Not that they'd given him classified material, but Clancy didn't trust the brass to believe that they hadn't. Finally Clancy said, "Look, if you'll tell me what sensitive stuff you want removed, I'll remove it."

This put the commander in a bit of a pickle. "Well, I can't tell you," he answered. "Then I would be confirming some stuff that I can't confirm."

"The thing that *really* bent 'em out of shape is I knew what 'Crazy Ivan' meant," Clancy says, referring to the navy's term for a maneuver used by Russian subs to detect if they're being followed. "I picked that up from one of my clients. They were really torched that I knew what that meant."

When Clancy finally met John Lehman, the secretary of the navy, Lehman told him that his first reaction on reading the book had been to say, "Who the hell cleared this?"

Red October was published in October 1984 and sold twenty thousand copies in the first six weeks. "For a first novel, that's not bad at all," Clancy says in a classic bit of understatement; most first novels sell about one-tenth that number, total. By the end of the year it looked as if the book was going to top out at fifty thousand. "Which," Clancy deadpans, "for a first novel is all right."

That might have been the end of it, but for a chance series of events. Jeremiah O'Leary, a *Washington Times* reporter who had served as the National Security Council's spokesman under Reagan, gave a copy of the book to Nancy Reynolds, a friend of the Reagans and a partner in the Washington lobbying firm Wexler Reynolds Harrison and Schule. Reynolds was on her way to Buenos Aires, and O'Leary wanted her to pass the book on to the U.S. ambassador there, who is a mutual friend of theirs. Reynolds read it on the plane and was so taken with it that she ordered a case of *Red Octobers* for Christmas presents. One of them ended up under the president's tree.

Not long afterward, *Time* printed a story on Reagan in which he mentioned that he'd read the book. He pronounced it "the perfect yarn."

The folks at the Naval Institute Press may have been new at publishing novels, but they weren't dumb. They ran the presidential imprimatur in huge type in a *New York Times* ad. "That quote," says Clancy, "put us on the national [best-seller] list. And we've been there ever since."

Red October peaked at number two on the hardcover list. "It would have been number one if it hadn't been for Stephen King, the dirty guy," says Clancy, attempting a scowl. "If he'd waited one more week before bringing out *Skeleton Crew,* I would have been number one. Well, who ever said the world was fair?"

The book was helped by the fact that it was a curiosity in the publishing world. That it came out of left field, from a company that publishes naval textbooks, "made people sit up and notice it," says Daisy Maryles, the executive editor of the industry's bible, *Publishers Weekly.* "It was unusual, and that made it easier to promote; there was an automatic angle. Obviously, it helped that behind all this there was a good book. But there was a serendipity to it all."

And so it was that in March 1985, the insurance agent from Owings found himself being invited to the White House—three times in two weeks.

"The first [time] was meeting the president in the Oval Office," Clancy says. "That was the day Chernenko was buried." (So *that's* why he declined to attend.) "Henry Kissinger was there. We had lunch in the Roosevelt Room with some relatively important folks: Secretary Lehman, Senator [Mark] Hatfield, General Brent Scowcroft, Nancy Reynolds, of course. The president told me he liked the book and asked me what the next one was about, and I told him. He asked me, 'Who wins?' And I said, 'The good guys.'

"It was a great experience," Clancy says with a smile, "and the next week we were back for the welcoming ceremony and the state dinner for the president of Argentina. So that was quite a week." He adds, "I'm glad I voted for the guy."

Clancy shakes his head. "If I had his charm, I'd be the richest insurance hustler in the world. I'd just stand there on the corner and say, 'Bring me your insurance.' And they would!

"It's like walking into a spotlight. The only thing that's missing in the Oval Office is a burning bush."

Though it's not a political book, *Red October* has a strong anti-Communist point of view that's somewhat atypical of the genre, where normally there isn't much moral difference between the Soviet Union and America.

The anticommunism was not part of any thought-out marketing strategy. The NIP's editorial board didn't sit around a table wondering what political tone the book should have. At the same time, the NIP, by its nature, isn't the sort of outfit that would set out to make the boys in the Kremlin seem to be honest guys who are just trying to keep their heads above water.

Red October hit because it *is* a darn good yarn. But it is a fair guess that Jimmy Carter might not have found it so, and that the book might not have fallen on such a sympathetic audience in Jimmy Carter's America.

Clancy looks surprised when he's asked what influences his view of the Soviet Union. "The truth," he says. He is skeptical about people who get arrested while demonstrating outside the South African embassy when, as he sees it, no one seems to care that the Soviets are committing genocide in Afghanistan, doing things like dropping mines specifically designed to kill and maim children.

"Everything in the book is drawn from a real incident, one way or another," he says. The commander of *Red October* decides to defect after his wife dies while being operated on for a burst appendix by a drunken physician. Clancy got the appendix idea from hearing an American doctor talk on a radio show about an incident in which an American tourist in Russia died from the same thing.

"In the real world, that just doesn't happen. But it did there. Soviet medicine is a joke. The Soviet Union is the only industrialized country in the world where life expectancy is decreasing. Very few things in that book are completely made up."

. . .

Clancy went on to do the things best-selling authors do—although live television made him nervous: "It's actually the nearest thing to death." He preferred Larry King's late-night radio call-in show.

He sold the paperback rights to *Red October* for $50,000. Putnam signed him to write another novel for an advance of $325,000. (His advance for *Red October* was $5,000.) The producer of the movie *The Omen* optioned *Red October.*

Clancy became a free-lance expert, giving speeches "at every place you can shake a stick at." Now when high-ranking KGB officers defect, CBS calls him to appear on morning television. On one trip to the studio, he was relieved to find someone there who knew more about defecting Soviets than himself—William Stevenson, the author of *The Man Called Intrepid.*

"Success," Clancy says as if he was talking about an amusing nuisance, "has complicated my life enormously." Yes, we can see that.

He seems surprised to find himself in such demand. "The transition from insurance agent to best-seller author is kind of like being cured of leprosy," he says. "All of a sudden everybody wants to meet you and talk to you and ask your opinion on things. And hell, I'm the same guy I was two or three years ago. I was just as smart then as I am now—or just as dumb, depending on your point of view. So all it's done, really, is open doors for me to a remarkable degree. If I want to ride on a submarine, it's just a matter of picking up the phone."

The navy has adopted Clancy. For someone with Coke-bottle-thick glasses whose only previous experience in the military was army ROTC during college, it's pure Walter Mitty. Last summer he spent a week on a Perry-class fast frigate doing research for his next book, *Red Storm Rising.* ("World War III at sea," as he tersely describes it.)

"They put me in officer country. I got treated like an officer, and I'm just a dumb landlubber. In many ways, that's embarrassing." He found himself in great demand aboard the FFG-7, with admirals wanting to know how he wrote *Red October*—and, of course, where he got his information.

"They treated me like some kind of damn hero, and I'm not. I'm just a writer. All I do is write about the stuff they really do. They're the heroes, not me. They're the guys who go out there and work eighteen-hour days under fairly unpalatable situations.

"The crew age on any ship is twenty-one, twenty-two. These are kids, and they're awfully good at what they do. And nobody appreciates it. All the crap you see in the media is about the toilet seats and the wrenches and the gadgets that don't work. And that's not what it's about. It's about people, and they're good people. Especially sub drivers. I don't know how they do it." We think we see his eyes misting up behind the glasses. "I'm a hopeless romantic," he adds.

So far the only subs Clancy has been on were securely tied to the dock—which is fine by him. "The first [submarine] I was on was the USS *Whale*. Before we went into the forward torpedo room, they took us into the auxiliary machine space, and I looked around—90 percent of the space is occupied by the machines themselves—and I thought, 'My God, what if you're in there and the lights go out and you hear water coming in?' What do you do, other than say, 'Get me out of this one, God. I'll never chase women again.'

"At that point I decided, no, I do not want to do this for a living. No thanks. It's a special breed of cat, and I'm not that kind of cat."

Aboard the British nuclear ballistic-missile submarine HMS *Resolution* he got a chance to hoist a few beers in the control room. "They showed me around the missile control room," he remembers. "That's one thing I really got right"—a reference to the scene in *Red October* where his hero finds himself in the "boom boom room" of the Russian sub.

The phone rings, and Clancy picks it up. He listens, puts the call on hold and says to his secretary across the room, "It's a guy who wants a car quote. You wanna wing it?" She takes the call, and we return to best-sellerdom.

"I wrote the kind of book I like to read," he says, lighting another cigarette. "I like thrillers. I read Forsyth, Richard Cox, A. J. Quinnell, Jack Higgins. I didn't think politics, I didn't think philosophy; I just wrote the kind of book I like to read.

"My two objectives were, first, to have fun; I wrote the book entirely for fun. I never really thought about the money. The other thing I wanted to do was portray the people and machinery we have out there as accurately as I could. And I've succeeded. I've had too many people tell me that I hit it pretty much on the head. I've had sub skippers tell me, 'I gave this book to my wife and said, "Here's the stuff I can't tell you." ' And that's very satisfying."

Clancy is writing his second book with a coauthor, Larry Bond, his son's godfather and the creator of Harpoon, a naval-strategy game that sells in hobby stores for $9.95. Clancy says it was his best source for *Red October.* "It explains how weapons and sensors work. It's played with miniatures. Mainly you do it on pencil and paper."

Though reviewers praised Clancy for his extraordinary facility in explaining Cold War technology, he almost dismisses it. "Everybody makes a big deal about the technical stuff. When I was researching the book, actually, that was the easy part. Simple. The hard part was getting into their heads. What kind of guy goes to sea in a ship that's supposed to sink?"

He reaches into an American Tourister briefcase and pulls out about three pounds of *Red Storm Rising* manuscript. He's working on a Macintosh now, and told his paperback publisher he didn't have the time to do a promotion tour, what with a February book deadline, a move into a new house, and the expected arrival of a new baby. (Anticipating a question we do not ask, he says, "Yes, if it's a boy we'll call him Red.") After that he's planning three more novels in which Jack Ryan, the hero of *Red October,* will figure. He says he has "only just gotten to the point where I understand the guy." After some hesitation, he also admits that Ryan is in part modeled after himself.

Given how busy Clancy has become, is it safe to assume that his secretary will be winging it a lot this fall? Will he even stay in the insurance business?

He ponders this. "Probably. Almost certainly. It's a family business. I'm not going to walk away from it. I've got over one thousand clients. A lot of them are my friends; I'm not going to walk away from them." Besides, he adds, "That's where I get a lot of my stories."

Leaving the office to pick up the mail at the post office, he remembers a poster he saw in one of the subs he visited. It showed a gigantic, flaming orange mushroom cloud. Beneath it the caption read: "Twenty-Four Missiles Away. Target Destroyed. It's Miller Time . . ."

—Regardie's, 1986

Tíred Gun

"Let's assume I get struck by lightnıng and I end up in the
U.S. Senate. I'm there for six years. What's the
worst thing that could happen to me? I serve out my six years
and I come back . . . and I wrıte a book about it.
And the book will sell!"
—Tom Clancy, in *The Washington Post Magazine*

Senator Jack Ryan stared at the papers on hıs desk. They were from the
Government Printing Office, on North Capitol Street, between G and
H Streets, and bore the characteristic "eagle" watermark. Ryan decided
that the eagle was more like a turkey these days. This document made
Ryan's stomach juices churn, and he yearned for a cigarette, but the
pantywaists who made the laws had outlawed smoking, along with
school prayer, so he would have to wait until he got to the cloakroom,
where he liked to blow smoke in the faces of the women senators. Ryan
liked women. His mother was a woman, and his wife was one, too, but
it was madness that they were allowed to serve in combat or in the
Senate.

The document was a second-degree amendment to a first-degree
amendment closing the last military base in the United States. It man-
dated the confiscation of every last one of the two hundred million privately owned guns in the United States, even assault weapons used for
shooting deer. He had filibustered against it for seventy-six hours. He

was tired. He thought of Vietnam. Not that he had ever been to Vietnam, but he knew lots of people who had. Now another battle loomed, and Ryan had to summon every joule of energy in his weary musculature if it was to be won.

He cleared his throat and shouted, "Mr. President!"

All heads turned. A murmur of groans went up in the chamber. He was used to it. Ryan had been a thorn in their side for the past six years, and they could not wait for him to retire at the end of this term. He was not seeking reelection. He was going to become a novelist and write manly sagas about big guns that could vaporize the human heart in milliseconds. Who needed *this*?

"Chair recognizes the gentleman from Maryland," said the president of the Senate, who, according to the Constitution, was also the Vice President of the United States. He was a tree-hugging liberal who had smoked pot in his youth, but he had gone to Vietnam, so Ryan hated him a little less than he hated the others.

"I move for a quorum call," Ryan said. More groans.

"With respect to the distinguished gentleman," Senator Joe (Stalin) Biden, of Delaware, one of the most liberal men ever to sit in the United States Senate, said. He had had a hair transplant. Ryan had information from sources deep within the National Security Agency that the Soviets had implanted a microchip in Biden's skull while he was having the hair plugs put in, and so could now control virtually every piece of legislation that went through the Judiciary and Foreign Relations Committees. It didn't matter that the Soviet Union was now defunct, its heirs rattling the tin cup. Ryan knew that the Bear would be back. "Can we please just get *on* with it?" Biden said.

Ten more seconds. If only Ryan could hold on. He stood up again. "Mr. President, I move for a brief recess."

Still more groans. What did they know of stamina, these people who had never met a payroll, or written fat beach books about expensive weapons systems that worked 100 percent of the time?

Eight seconds . . . seven seconds . . .

Suddenly, men in cool black uniforms, with blackened faces, carrying CAR-15s, M16s with M203 grenade launchers, and Belgian-made SAWs, swarmed into the Senate. It was the Army's elite Ninja Seven company, a group of such efficient, highly trained killers that they scared even Ryan, and, Lord knows, he did not scare easily. They shot every liberal-wimp member of the Senate. When it was over, only Ryan and a handful of senators remained.

"Sometimes democracy is messy," Ryan said as he opened his desk and removed a Heckler & Koch MP-5 SD2 submachine gun, and administered the coup de grace with a few crisp bursts into a heap of twitching bodies. "But it's still the best system we've got."

—*The New Yorker*, 1993

Megabashing Japan

Somewhere, if memory serves, Mark Twain said of one of Henry James's books, "Once you put it down, you can't pick it up." *Debt of Honor,* the eighth novel in Tom Clancy's oeuvre, is, at 766 pages, a herniating experience. Things don't really start to happen until about halfway through this book, by which time most authors, including even some turgid Russian novelists, are finished with theirs. But Tom Clancy must be understood in a broader context, not as a mere writer of gizmo-thrillers, destroyer of forests, but as an economic phenomenon. What are his editors—assuming they even exist; his books feel as if they go by modem from Mr. Clancy's computer directly to the printers—supposed to do? Tell him to cut? "You tell him it's too long." "No, *you* tell him."

Someone, on the other hand—friend, relative, spiritual adviser, I don't know—really ought to have taken him aside and said, "Uh, Tom, isn't this book kind of racist?" I bow to no one in my disapproval of certain Japanese trade practices, and I worked for a man who once conspicuously barfed into the lap of the Japanese Prime Minister, but this book is as subtle as a World War II anti-Japanese poster showing a mustachioed Tojo bayoneting Caucasian babies. If you thought Michael Crichton was a bit paranoid, *Rising Sun*-wise, well then, to quote Mr. Clancy's favorite President and original literary booster, Ronald Reagan, "You ain't seen nothing yet." His Japanese aren't one-dimensional, they're half-dimensional. They spend most of their time grunting in bathhouses. And yet, to echo *Dr. Strangelove*'s Group Captain Lionel Mandrake, "the strange thing is, they make such bloody good cameras."

The plot: Japan craftily sabotages the United States financial markets, occupies the Mariana Islands, sinks two American submarines, killing two hundred and fifty sailors, and threatens us with nuclear weapons. Why, you ask, don't we just throw up on their laps and give them a countdown to a few toasty reruns of Hiroshima and Nagasaki? Because, fools that we are, we have got rid of all our nukes in a mad disarmament pact with the Russkies. (Plausible? Never mind.)

For a while it looks like sayonara for Western civ, until Jack Ryan, now White House national security adviser, masterminds such a brilliant response to the crisis that he ends up vice president. To make way, the current V.P. must resign because of charges of—sexual harassment. I won't be ruining it for you by saying that Ryan's ascendancy does not stop there; the President and the entire Congress must be eliminated in an inadvertently comic deus ex machina piloted by a sullen Japanese airman who miraculously does not grunt "Banzai!" as he plows his Boeing 747 into the Capitol. Former Secretary of the Navy John Lehman has recently had the arguable taste to remark, apropos this episode in *Debt of Honor,* that this particular fantasy has long been his own. I don't like Congress either, but Abraham Lincoln, Lehman's fellow Republican and mine, did go to some pains to keep the Capitol's construction going during the Civil War as a symbol of the Union's continuity. Oh, well.

To be sure, the war enacted here is not the fruit of national Japanese will, but rather a manipulation of events by a *zaibatsu* businessman whose mother, father and siblings had jumped off a cliff in Saipan back in 1944 rather than be captured by evil American marines, and by a corrupt, America-hating politician. But that hardly lets Mr. Clancy off the hook, for the nasty characteristics ascribed to Yamata (the former) and Goto (the latter) are straightforwardly racial. To heat our blood further, Goto keeps a lovely American blonde as his geisha and does unspeakable naughties to her. When she threatens to become a political hot tomato, Yamata has the poor thing killed. It all plays into the crudest kind of cultural paranoia, namely, that what these beastly yellow inscrutables are really after is—*our women.* (A similar crime, recall, was at the heart of Mr. Crichton's novel *Rising Sun.* Well, archetypes *do* do the job.) Her name, for these purposes, is perfect: Kimberly Norton. "Yamata had seen breasts before, even large Caucasian breasts." To judge from the number of mentions of them, it is fair to conclude that Caucasian breasts are at the very heart of Goto-san's *Weltanschauung*. Farther down that same page, he expresses his carnal delight to Yamata "coarsely" (naturally) in—shall we say—cavorting with American girls. Jack Ryan is therefore striking a blow for more than the American way of life: he is knight-defender of nothing less than American bimbohood.

It must be said that the hapless Kimberly Norton is a glaring exception among Clancy women: so much so that you wonder if he's been reading Susan Faludi under the covers at night. With this book, Mr. Clancy stakes his claim to being the most politically correct popular author in America, which is somewhat remarkable in such an outspoken, if not fire-breathing, right winger as himself. Practically everyone is either black, Hispanic, a woman or, at a minimum, ethnic. The Vice President is hauled off on charges of sexual harassment; the Japanese Prime Minister is a rapist; the deputy director of operations at the CIA is a woman; there is Comdr. Roberta Peach (Peach? honestly) of the Navy; Ryan's wife receives a Lasker Award for her breakthroughs in ophthalmic surgery; one of the CIA assassins is informed, practically in the middle of dispatching slanty-eyed despoilers of American women, that his own daughter has made dean's list and will probably get into medical school; secretaries, we are told again and again, are the real heroes, etc., etc.

All this would be more convincing were it not for the superseding macho that permeates each page like dried sweat. Ryan's Secret Service code name is, I kid you not, "Swordsman." And there's something a bit gamey about this description of the CIA's deputy director of operations: "Mary Pat entered the room, looking about normal for an American female on a Sunday morning." His feminism, if it can be called that, is pretty smarmy, like a big guy getting a woman in a choke hold and giving her a knuckly noogie on the top of her head by way of showing her she's "O.K." (Preferable, I admit, to the entertainments offered by the officers and gentlemen of the Tailhook Association.) And there is this hilarious description of Ryan's saintly wife saving someone's sight with laser surgery: "She lined up the crosshairs as carefully as a man taking down a Rocky Mountain sheep from half a mile, and thumbed the control." You've got to admire a man who can find the sheep-hunting metaphor in retinal surgery.

Tom Clancy is the James Fenimore Cooper of his day, which is to say, the most successful bad writer of his generation. This is no mean feat, for there are many, many more rich bad writers today than there were in Cooper's time. If Twain were alive now, he would surely be writing an essay entitled, "The Literary Crimes of Clancy." He would have loved *Debt of Honor,* the culmination, thus far, of Mr. Clancy's almost endearing *Hardy Boys–Jane's Fighting Ships* prose style:

"The Indians were indeed getting frisky."

"More surprisingly, people made way for him, especially women, and children positively shrank from his presence as though Godzilla had returned to crush their city."

" 'I will not become Prime Minister of my country,' Hiroshi Goto announced in a manner worthy of a stage actor, 'in order to become executor of its economic ruin.' "

"The captain, Commander Tamaki Ugaki, was known as a stickler for readiness, and though he drilled his men hard, his was a happy ship because she was always a smart ship."

" 'This is better than the Concorde!' Cathy gushed at the Air Force corporal who served dinner."

"Damn, how much crazier would this world get?"

"But what kind of evil synergy was this?"

"Night at sea is supposed to be a beautiful thing, but it was not so this time."

"*But I'm not a symbol,* Jack wanted to tell him. *I'm a man, with doubts.*"

"The dawn came up like thunder in this part of the world, or so the poem went."

" 'I knew Goto was a fool, but I didn't think him a madman.' "

" 'Gentlemen: this *will* work. It's just so damned outrageous, but maybe that works in our favor.' "

" 'Bloody clever,' the head of the Bank of England observed to his German counterpart. '*Jawohl,*' was the whispered reply."

And finally, this: "The man knew how to think on his feet, and though often a guy at the bottom of the food chain, he tended to see the big picture very clearly from down there."

—*The New York Times,* 1994

Fax Fire

■

TOM CLANCY TAKES ON BUCKLEY
OVER PAN OF BOOK

By Stephanie Mansfield
Special to *The Washington Post*

Tom Clancy, former suburban Maryland car insurance salesman turned best-selling techno scribbler, learned this week that the pen may be mightier than a full squadron of F-14 Tomcats with AS-6 Kingfish missiles hanging under each wing.

A sizzling review by Christopher Buckley of Clancy's latest novel, *Debt of Honor,* which appeared in Sunday's *New York Times Book Review* section apparently sent the author into orbit, sparking what passes for a literary feud these days. Conducted by fax no less.

The wickedly funny review will long be remembered by anti-Clancy forces as a direct hit, concluding, among other gibes, that Clancy is "the James Fenimore Cooper of his day, which is to say the most successful bad writer of his generation."

Upon reading an advance copy, Clancy immediately fired off a fax to Buckley, a Washington writer and son of William F. Buckley, Jr., whose literary sparring partners have been more along the lines of Gore Vidal.

On a letterhead inscribed with the name of Clancy's hero and alter ego, "JACK RYAN ENT.," the typed, single-spaced missive read:

"DEAR CHRIS,

Thanks for the review. You seem to have inherited your father's hauteur, but, alas, not his talent or noblesse. Revealing a surprise ending for a novel is bad form, lad.

For the body of your review, Dr. Johnson said it best:

'A fly, sir, may sting a stately horse and make him wince, but one is but an insect, and the other a horse still.'

> Regards,
> Tom Clancy."

"I don't know how he got the fax number," says Buckley. "He must have gotten it from the CIA." He faxed back:

"DEAR TOM,

I may be the insect, but you're still the horse's arse.

> Regards,
> Christopher Buckley."

Clancy again:

"Sonny, when your paperback sales begin to approach my hardcover sales in, say, England, do let me know.

Until then, at least learn how to do a professional review.

Your dad knows how. Ask him.

> TC."

But the younger Buckley had needed no help from daddy in crafting a withering notice.

"I've always loved Chris's writing," says *Book Review* Editor Rich Nicholls. "And he approached this assignment with *such zest*."

The review opens by quoting Mark Twain, who once said of one of Henry James's books, "Once you put it down you can't pick it up."

Buckley, whose most recent novel, *Thank You for Smoking*, was well reviewed but not mega-selling, calls Clancy's eighth novel, at 766 pages, "a herniating experience." What's more, its anti-Japanese theme is "racist" and "as subtle as a World War II anti-Japanese poster showing a mustachioed Tojo bayoneting Caucasian babies."

Referring to Clancy as a "fire-breathing right winger," he describes the prose style as "superseding macho that permeates each page like dried sweat. [Hero Jack] Ryan's Secret Service code name is, I kid you not, 'Swordsman.' " And although Clancy took great pains to include more female characters, "his feminism is pretty smarmy," observes Buckley, "like a big guy getting a woman in a choke hold and giving her a knuckly noogie on top of her head by way of showing her she's 'O.K.' "

Of course, *Debt of Honor* is No. 1 on *The New York Times* best-seller list and, like all of Clancy's books, is likely to stay there awhile with or without Buckley's review.

Perhaps that's why Clancy was playing meek yesterday when he said in a telephone interview that his faxes were meant as a joke. "I'm sorry he didn't take it that way. I goofed. I'm sorry."

Sadly then, this skirmish seemed destined not to rise to the mythical level of, say, Lillian Hellman and Mary McCarthy, Stephen Spender and David Leavett or even Kitty Kelley and Barbara Howar. But it at least has the novelty of being fought with a modern communications tool. "This must be the first feud to be fought over faxes," says Nicholls.

But there was hope. As Buckley was preparing to make a train to New York yesterday, the familiar high-pitched whine of an incoming fax could be heard over the telephone.

"Must dash," Buckley laughed, in best faux hauteur voice. "More hate coming!"

—*The Washington Post,* 1994;
reprinted with permission of the
author and the Washington Writers
Group

Spin Cycle

How I Learned to (Almost) Love the Sin Lobbyists

■

A couple of years ago, while wondering with some desperation what to write about, I turned on the TV and there was a nice-looking talking-head lady from the Tobacco Institute, manfully (as it were) denying that there was any scientific link between smoking and cancer, heart disease, respiratory disease, or athlete's foot. She was attractive, well-spoken, intelligent, and as persuasive as she could be, given the deplorably disingenuous data she was pitching. I thought: *What an interesting job that must be. Get up in the morning, brush your teeth, and go and sell death for a living.*

A few days later I was reading in the paper about some teenage kid who, to judge from his blood alcohol content, had drunk two kegs of beer single-handedly, then got in his pickup truck and careened over the yellow line into a minivan, annihilating an entire Boy Scout troop. And there at the bottom of the story was a quote from a spokesman for the beer-keg industry saying what an awful tragedy it was, but that no one was more concerned about teenage drunk driving than the beer-keg industry. I thought: *Boy, I bet that guy trembles every time his beeper goes off.*

A few days after that, a "disgruntled postal worker" went bonkers and blew away his supervisor and a half dozen others with a gun with a name like Hamburger-Maker .44 Triple-Magnum. And sure enough, the National Rifle Association was right on the case, worrying out loud that if we start outlawing Hamburger-Maker .44s, how long before we outlaw the Swiss Army knife? I thought: *There's another interesting job.*

The idea formed of writing a major, thick, serious, nonfiction study of institutional hypocrisy in America. It would be grandiose and groundbreaking, but with an *accessible* title: *I'm Shocked—Shocked!* (said, of course, by Captain Renaud in *Casablanca*, on being handed his gambling winnings moments after closing down Rick's Café for gambling). The book—no, the *volume*—would cover government, business, society. It would be comprehensive, exhaustive, thorough. And boring.

But I kept coming back to these three yuppie Horsemen of the Apocalypse. Another title came to me: *Thank You for Smoking*. And then the mortgage bill arrived, so that settled it.

I wrote to the Tobacco Institute, the various liquor lobbies, and to the National Rifle Association. These were artfully worded letters announcing that I had had enough of the neo-Puritanism that was sweeping America and was embarking on a book about it. True enough. They may now complain that they were deceived, but if they look at those letters, they'll see that they really weren't—and anyway, people who make their living pushing cigarettes, liquor, and guns ought not to claim the high moral ground. And they shouldn't look a gift novel in the mouth: The trio of characters who make up the book's Mod Squad—it's an acronym for "Merchants of Death"—are sort of likable. Or at least sympathetic.

Likable? Yuppie mass murderers? Or mass enablers? *Sympathetic?*

I went to see the attractive lady from the Tobacco Institute. She was very nice and . . . tall. I don't want to get into amateur psychology here, but my guess is that it's not all that easy being a six-foot-one-inch-tall woman, especially as she had no doubt reached this height in her teens; and maybe, just possibly, there's some anger inside that she's still, uh, working out. (But it wasn't my business, and I didn't ask.) I was surprised, however, to learn that her previous job had been at the Department of Health and Human Services. "At my going-away party, they were going to give me signed copies of the Surgeon General's report," she said, smiling, "but thought better of it."

I wanted to know what it's like, being a merchant of death. I didn't use that exact phrase. Well, she said, it's not easy. No, I said, I imagine it's not. You get threats, she said. What do you do about them?, I said. You throw 'em away, she said.

Once she was at a health symposium—that's part of her job, attending *health* symposiums; what a warm welcome she must get—standing next to Everett Koop, the formidable former Surgeon General who looks like

Captain Ahab. And someone mentioned that she used to work at HHS. And he said, "I wish she'd gone to be a prostitute on Fourteenth Street instead." Don't think that didn't hurt.

I said, How do you introduce yourself to strangers? "Well," she said, "you never come straight out and say, 'I work for the Tobacco Institute.' " First she'll say, "I work in public relations." If they press, she'll say, "I work for a trade association." If they still press, she says a trade association "for a major manufacturer." She added, "You never know if this guy's mother has just died of cancer." By now I'm shaking my head in sympathy, thinking: *Gosh, it must be just awful.*

But why, I fumbled diffidently, what's—

"A nice girl like me doing in a place like this?" she finished my sentence.

"Yes!" I cry. "Why?"

She exhales her smoke—like Lauren Bacall. "I'm paying the mortgage."

Of course: the Yuppie Nuremberg defense: *I vas only paying ze mortgage!* I admire this woman. In the kingdom of the morally blind, she has the echolocation of a bat. On the way out, she points to a booklet on her credenza. Next to it is a packet of "Death" brand cigarettes, an actual brand of cigarettes, no name on the front of the pack, just a white-on-black skull. As tchotchkes, the Tobacco Institute could do no better than a pack of Death cigarettes.

But the booklet. It says, "Helping Youth to Say No to Tobacco." She says, "That's what I'm proudest of."

This *was* an impressive statement. My admiration for her faculties of cognitive dissonance, already large, swelled to even greater proportions. Goebbels might as well have produced a booklet entitled "The Führer and the Jews—A Love Story."

Oh dear. I promised that I wouldn't moralize. It's not my job as a novelist. It's just that I have kids myself and . . . well, no, back to the story.

Much in the news at the time was the controversy about Old Joe, Camel cigarettes' famous dromedary with the nose that seems to remind some people of a penis. Camel started a new campaign with Old Joe at its center, wearing sunglasses and playing the saxophone, shooting pool, coolly eyeing the chicks. RJR Nabisco was putting out about seventy-five million dollars' worth of Old Joe ads a year. The cigarette companies say that they are not—repeat, *not*—trying to get new business. They say they seek only to reinforce brand loyalty—and brand disloyalty, trying to get a *teeny, tiny* percentage of smokers to switch brands.

In the wake of the Old Joe campaign, Camel's share of the illegal children's cigarette market climbed from .5 percent to 32 percent. Outraged mothers howled. Even *Advertising Age,* Mammon's own trade journal, editorialized against the Old Joe campaign, to little avail. Old Joe is still among us, playing his saxophone.

Meanwhile, overseas, the U.S. trade representative had begun to bully Pacific Rim countries—Taiwan, Japan, South Korea, and others—into opening their markets to U.S. tobacco. Up till then, those countries hadn't allowed cigarette advertising. Then comes the U.S. trade rep threatening something called a 301 action, named for a section in the 1974 Trade Act that allows the president to slap retaliatory tariffs on foreign products if their country of origin is seen to be discriminating against Marlboro et al. by not allowing Marlboro et al. to advertise—never mind that *no* cigarette advertising has been allowed.

Inevitably, the countries buckled to U.S. government pressure. The happy result? In just the first year that South Korea allowed U.S. tobacco advertising, the smoking rate for male teenagers rose from 18 percent to 30 percent. For female teenagers, it rose from 2 percent to 9. The trends were similar in the other countries. The World Health Organization estimates that between now and the end of the century, smoking will kill 250 million people in the industrialized world. That's one in five, roughly the population of the United States.

So it's clear that the tobacco industry is doing its level best to help youth to say no to smoking. I left the Tobacco Institute lady's office feeling warm and fuzzy.

My next new friend works for the Beer Institute. The *Beer* Institute! I come to him straight from a visit with the head of the hard-liquor lobby: the Distilled Spirits Council of the United States. They hate each other, the beer and the booze people. Why? Because of a tax issue called "equivalency." If one beer and one highball contain the same amount of ethanol, well then, say the DISCUS people to the government, you should tax beer at the same rate you tax us. This makes the beer people—Augie Coors, especially—very unhappy. So I do not tell my beer people that I am bellying up to the booze people.

My beer guy—what a guy! Good-looking, jockly, hail-fellow-well-met. He is calling me "guy" and we have only known each other for ten minutes. On his desk is a recent copy of *Fatal Accident Reporting System,* a Department of Transportation publication. On the bookshelf: beer steins, empty bottles of exotic beer. On the wall: his diploma from the Summer School of Alcohol Studies. I yearn to ask, Do they know how to party at the Summer School of Alcohol Studies, or what? There is also an autographed photo of him and his wife and President Bush.

He works hard. And with a handicap. He hates to fly, and yet he used to have to fly one million miles a year. Once, he was on a plane that got struck by lightning. He drank fifteen drinks to calm down. After that he got so nervous that he had to get himself drunk to fly. "Which sometimes leads to trouble," he allows.

He gives me a *tour d'horizon* of the beer world. It is not a pretty picture. Sales have been basically flat for ten years: Neo-Prohibitionism is on the rise. Hypocrisy is rampant. Congressman Joe Kennedy II is demanding yet more warning labels on beer bottles. You know it's bad when a Kennedy is staking out the moral high ground on alcohol.

"We pour *millions* into traffic safety issues each year," he says. And what thanks do they get? None, *nada, rien,* zip, zilch. Ingrates. We discuss the government's "Controlled Availability Theory," the idea that if you tax something, people will buy less of it. He quotes Himmler: "We must get rid of the alcohol." He adds, "That's not an exact quote."

I follow him to a health symposium called Healthy People/Healthy Environments 2000. My beer guy says that he sort of "relishes" being at the conference. He says it's "like being black in the Old South." I will hear variants of this as I shuttle between my alcohol, tobacco, and firearms people: They are the new pariahs, the niggers of postmodern morality—the *victims.* The DISCUS person, gray-haired, grandfatherly, and aggrieved, will crack the faintest smile when asked about the effects of neo-Puritanism on his social standing and will shrug, "It's not *quite* as bad as being a Colombian drug baron."

My beer guy gets up and speaks to the healthy fifteen hundred. They sense the presence of the enemy. Fifteen hundred bottoms—three thousand buttocks—shift warily in their seats. You can hear them clenching.

It is called buttlock—gridlock of the indignant. They do not like him. He is . . . unwanted.

He looks like an Eagle Scout up there. He pleads earnestly, "All we're looking for is some input." Can't they see that? It's all he wants, input. Just a little input. "We're not saying we in the industry should control alcohol policy in this country, but for Christ's sake"—he smiles when he says this—"give us some input!"

At the National Beer Wholesalers' Convention in a few weeks their banners and lapel buttons will say it loudly: "WE'RE PART OF THE SOLUTION!" And they are! Drunk driving is down 40 percent since 1982, but you don't hear that from the Healthy People. "It interferes with their funding needs."

He is finished. The applause defines politeness: over in less than a nanosecond. The next speaker, from Mothers Against Drunk Driving, receives applause befitting Schwarzkopf ticker-taping up Broadway. I begin to appreciate what my beer guy is up against: a massive, tectonic moral shift, spearheaded by a phalanx of pissed-off acronyms: MADD, SADD— Mothers Against Drunk Driving, Students Against Drunk Driving. P. J. O'Rourke, booze muse of the open road, wants to form an organization called DAMM: Drunks Against Mad Mothers. My beer guy loves P. J. O'Rourke. So does my cigarette girl, so does my gun guy. So do I.

We descend the hotel escalators into the exhibit rooms, where the individual groups that form the body Healthy have set up their booths. It is just like any trade fair. My beer guy says, "We're sort of shocked that they're even allowing us to exhibit here. They were very specific that we could not give away free products. It was a real interesting discussion," he chuckles, "about what we could and couldn't do with that booth. It was their worst nightmare that we'd have a couple of kegs tapped and some trashy trinkets like bottle openers." He laughs. Animal House. A toga party. *To-ga, to-ga!* He is hearty, my beer guy. Which is really what you want in a beer guy.

Together we walk down the aisle between the booths. It is to walk a gauntlet. I keep my reporter's notepad well in view, like a shield, so that they will not mistake me for a beer lobbyist. You would not want to be mistaken for one yourself, walking past displays from Mothers Against Drunk Driving, Trauma Systems Associates, the Mid-Western States Substance Abuse Committee: Facing Alcohol Concerns Through Education. Their display shows the Coors ad girl altered so that she's pouring a pitcher of beer down the toilet. He shakes his head and says, "What a waste."

There is the National Head Injury Foundation booth. He says they're "okay" but adds winkily, "We usually define the good guys by who'll take our money." We then come face to face with another of the enemy, and here is more evidence that God is a bad novelist. She is a nice lady, in charge of Washington D.C.'s anti-drunk-driving initiative. Her name is Pam Beers.

On we go past the National Highway Safety Administration, the New Hampshire Concerned Citizens Against Drunk Driving. They have caught on to the quilt thing: Theirs is inscribed with the names of all the kids killed in drunk-driving incidents. "Chipper, We'll Always Love You."

Does this crack my beer guy's heart? Not. In truth, he didn't even see it. We have arrived at the Beer Institute's booth—no Spuds Mackenzie, no Swedish bikini team, instead a model of sobriety and educational material. Signs proclaim the 39 percent decline in drunk-driving fatalities between 1982 and 1990. A slogan urges, THINK WHEN YOU DRINK. A lonely color poster proclaims the photographic glories: a frosty mug surrounded by mountains and valleys of fried chicken, burgers, ham, and pizza.

But what's this? The booth next to the Beer Institute's is . . . the National Coalition to Prevent Impaired Driving. My beer guy grins wickedly, "They're going to be *sooo* pissed."

What does the novelist make of all this? As much as he can, I suppose, while straining—straining—not to turn his director's chair into a seat of judgment. Anyway, who's to escape whipping in *this* crazy, mixed-up world? An ethical man, said Twain, is a Christian holding four aces. While in the midst of my research, I was somewhat surprised to find on the back cover of the magazine I edit an ad for cigarettes. My indignation, expressed to my superiors, was duly noted. What goes around karmically comes around: Several weeks ago an excerpt from my novel, eagerly desired by the literary editor of a national magazine of reputation, was turned down by the magazine's editor in chief on the grounds that it would imperil advertising. "Yes, yes," I said, "I understand."

—Adapted from a talk given to
The Century Association, 1994

Blubber

DEFIANT JAPAN TO PROMOTE EATING WHALE MEAT
—*The New York Times*

CONFIDENTIAL MEMORANDUM
To: FISHERIES AGENCY, TOKYO
FROM: ZEIT, GEIST, WELT, SCHMERZ
   & SCHAUUNG, NEW YORK
RE: WHALE MEAT

THE PROBLEM:

While consumption of whale meat among older Japanese has remained at satisfactory levels, consumption among the younger generation, susceptible to international whale-lobby disinformation about alleged "endangerment" of world whale stocks, has fallen off drastically. Groups of young Japanese are even being lured to Hawaii, where instead of playing golf they participate in offshore whale-watching parties, and they return home to disseminate pro-whale sentiment and dissuade their peers from eating whale meat.

THE SOLUTION:

An immediate and all-out information campaign targeting the under-thirty Japanese, to show the new generation that eating whale meat is not only nutritious and healthful but also "cool."

THE STRATEGY:

To bypass ordinary advertising methods, which the media-savvy younger generation regards with suspicion, and to develop dramatic and documentary television programs and specials that will bring about a real "sea change" in attitudes toward the true nature of whales. Specifically:

Situation Comedy:

The Harpooneers, a hilarious series about the antics of the wacky but brave crew of the whale ship *Minke Business.* Sample episode: After a grueling six-month whale-gathering mission, the good ship *M.B.* is on its way back to Yokohama in time for the big dance, but the young crew members have all broken out in pimples and are ashamed of showing themselves to the pretty young port girls. Fortunately, the wise, fatherly Bos'n Kikkoman knows that whale meat is an ancient cure for unsightly acne. He advises the youngsters to eat plenty of whale meat. They receive this advice respectfully and, sure enough, their pimples disappear just as the ship pulls into Yokohama. As the crew files down the gangplank, the girls cry out, "What fine skin they all have! We cannot wait to have sex with them!"

Public Affairs:

Devils of the Deep! Narrated by Leonard Nimoy (if we cannot get him, we will get someone who looks like him), this series will expose the whale for what it is: a large, ugly nuisance that only a *gaijin* could love.

Who Cries for the Krill? A shocking, heartrending documentary about the alarming depletion of the world krill supply caused by the irresponsible eco-gluttony of the blue whale, which has enjoyed "protected status" since 1966. The krill, the most gentle of the creatures of the sea, faces virtual extinction, with dire consequences for the world's food. Using a special new underwater "krill-cam" developed expressly for this investigation, the documentary will feature twenty-four hours in the harrowing life of a krill as it is pursued across the South Pacific by a so-called "gentle giant of the sea."

Ahab's Children. Real-life interviews with people who have lost limbs to whales.

Exxon Valdez: The Untold Story. This fresh look at the 1989 tanker "grounding" uncovers shocking new evidence suggesting that the fateful Alaska oil spill was not the work of a drunken captain and a submerged rock but, rather, a whale's coolly calculated revenge upon the sea otters of Prince William Sound.

Mega-Waste: The Coming Crisis. A frightening documentary that demonstrates what scientists have long suspected: if present whale excretions continue unchecked, the world's oceans will rise twenty-five feet by the year 2000, causing unimaginable global havoc. A family in low-lying Bangladesh expresses its hope that the international whaling community will not stand idly by as this tragedy gathers critical mass.

Mammals, Schmammals. A controversial cetologist (to be determined) reveals that these so-called ocean monarchs are really fish after all, and feel absolutely no pain when harpooned.

—*The New Yorker,* 1993

Ayes Only

⊡

AUGUST 1, 1994
TO: THE PRESIDENT
FROM: STROBE TALBOTT, DEPUTY
   SECRETARY OF STATE
RE: TURNING AROUND PUBLIC PERCEPTION
   OF HAITIAN "LIBERATION"

It is imperative that we move swiftly to correct the growing public misperception that the *liberation*, as opposed to invasion, of Haiti is anything less than an *urgent national-security priority of the United States government*. In the face of national complacency about the Caribbean powder keg, we must demonstrate that Haiti represents a threat to *every American citizen*.

The following proposals ought to be immediately implemented so as to insure that public opinion is squarely behind you when Operation Daydream becomes operational and the troops hit the beaches.

> 1. National Security Adviser Lake should hold a strictly off-the-record meeting with the press and reveal that the government has determined that the pilot of the Cessna that crashed into the White House last week was in fact a *former member of the Tontons Macoutes*, working on behalf of General Cédras, to decapitate the U.S. leadership. Though it is admittedly unusual for a middle-class white man from suburban Maryland to be a Tonton Macoute, strange things happen in time of *war*.

Your measured response would be along the lines of: "I can't really comment on an ongoing national-security investigation. I'm just grateful that Hillary and Chelsea and Socks are safe. Meanwhile, I would stress that I do not hold the *fine Haitian people* responsible for the vile, cowardly actions of their military dictator."

2.   Director of Central Intelligence Woolsey should hold an urgent press conference to assert that "at this point we can't say for sure one way or the other" whether *Haiti has nuclear weapons capable of reaching Miami, Atlanta, and Mobile.* He should stammer, avoid eye contact, and, if possible, sweat freely. (Surely CIA technical people can accomplish that much.) The briefing should be conducted against a backdrop of blown-up satellite photographs of Haiti, with a detail of the interior labeled "LASCAHOBAS HEAVY WATER FACILITY" and another labeled "PETITE RIVIÈRE DE L'ARTIBONITE ICBM SITE."

3.   Secretary Christopher should publish an Op-Ed piece revealing that, based on our interrogation of Haitian detainees at Guantánamo, the tide of so-called Haitian "boat people" is in fact the vanguard of a Haitian invasion of the American mainland. SecState can assert that, despite their scruffy and half-starved appearance, these are the highly trained élite of the Haitian Special Forces—so deadly, indeed, that they don't even need conventional weapons to carry out their instructions to *sabotage vital U.S. military and civilian installations.*

4.   U.N. Ambassador Albright should convene a plenary session of the Security Council and reveal the existence of a document entitled *Plan Vraiment Secret et Extraordinaire pour l'Overthrow des États-Unis et du Canada par les Dictateurs d'Haiti.* The Haitian ambassador will of course denounce the document as a forgery. Let him. Ambassador Albright's position should be: "*Je suis prête à attendre votre réponse jusqu' à ce que gèle l'enfer.*" ("I am prepared to wait for your reply until hell freezes over"—a nice Stevensonian echo, which will connect this crisis with the Cuban Missile Crisis, when Americans faced down another Caribbean threat to the security of the United States.)

5.   American tourists who had unpleasant pre-embargo experiences in Haiti should be urged to come forward with their *horror sto-*

ries of lost luggage, stolen purses, turista, misplaced reservations, indifferent service, and beach boys urging them to buy marijuana. Your average American basically does not care one whit what happens in the Caribbean as long as it doesn't interfere with his vacation. This aspect of the plan would therefore strike at the very heart, so to speak, of America's soul, Caribbean-wise.

6.   Delta Force, our most secret and élite military element, should immediately, and under cover of night, establish a third-rate medical college deep in the Haitian interior. The "students" would consist of short, young, gender-mixed, and, if possible, pimply Delta Force personnel. The Haitian military will of course attack the facility. The students, equipped with a state-of-the-art satellite telecommunications uplink, can tearfully appeal for U.S. military assistance, paving the way for thorough and enthusiastic public acclaim of your bold leadership.

—The New Yorker, 1994

Whitherwater?

⌑

LOGON
WELCOME TO TIMELINE AMERICA
PLEASE ENTER THE PASSWORD
ENTER DATABASE NAME
WHITEWATER CHRONOLOGY
AUGUST 1994—MARCH 1995
ACCESSING . . .

August 5, 1994: Special independent counsel Robert Fiske denies report in *The Washington Post* that he is "bored out of his gourd" with the Whitewater investigation.

September 7, 1994: Congressman Jim Leach, ranking minority member of the House Banking Committee, announces that his investigators have discovered "something really, really interesting" on the Whitewater case but that he cannot reveal what it is for fear that once he does, people will stop paying attention to him.

September 28, 1994: *The Washington Times* runs a story saying that former U.S. assistant attorney general Webster Hubbell received collagen injections to enlarge his lips. The story notes, "While so far there is no direct link between Whitewater and Hubbell's lip injections, federal investigators are said to be 'very interested' in the fact that Hubbell discussed having his lips enlarged with White House counsel Vince Foster, who subsequently committed suicide."

September 29, 1994: Hubbell strenuously denies having had cosmetic lip enlargements. "Lotta people in Arkansas got lips like this. And I wouldn't even know how to spell *collagen.*"

October 16, 1994: White House adviser David Gergen denies telling Maureen Dowd of *The New York Times* that Whitewater was "a dumb, Dogpatch-type thing between a couple of bubbas and a woman obsessed with making an easy buck despite trying to make herself into the second coming of Eleanor Roosevelt"; furthermore, he denies saying, "This is starting to make me look bad."

October 17, 1994: Hillary Clinton tells *Newsweek* that it was White House adviser David Gergen who, during the 1978 Renaissance New Year's weekend at Hilton Head, suggested to the Clintons that they invest in the Whitewater Development Corporation.

October 18, 1994: President Clinton announces that he is nominating David Gergen to be U.S. ambassador to Rwanda. "As much as I need him here," the President says in a written statement announcing the appointment, "I need him more there."

November 8, 1994: Senate minority leader Robert Dole demands that outgoing Senate majority leader George Mitchell "stop thinking about girls and baseball the whole time" and start holding Senate hearings on Whitewater. Mitchell says Dole is "just jealous" over the fact that his fiancée is younger than Dole's wife.

November 21, 1994: *A Current Affair* airs an interview with a man identified only as "Fred," who says that on the afternoon of July 20, 1993, the day Vince Foster committed suicide, he saw a large man with "humongous lips" lurking on the grounds of Fort Marcy, the Civil War–era fort where Foster's body was found.

December 4, 1994: Clinton political strategist James Carville tells reporters at the Godfrey Sperling breakfast that Whitewater independent counsel Robert Fiske is a "motherf- - - - -." Carville later confirms that he did call Fiske that but not in reference to Whitewater.

January 16, 1995: An ABC/*Washington Post* poll shows that 78 percent of the American people no longer give "a rat's ass" about the Whitewater scandal, and that an overwhelming 94 percent are "much more interested" by the fact that more than a dozen female Arkansas state employees have now filed lawsuits against President Clinton, alleging that he asked them to perform oral sex on him.

February 2, 1995: Hillary Clinton, in an East Room press conference, says that she wishes the media would stop asking her husband about oral sex and concentrate on Whitewater, which, the First Lady says, "is much more interesting."

February 10, 1995: In his first interview since his resignation more than a year ago, former White House counsel Bernard Nussbaum tells Sidney Blumenthal of *The New Yorker* that the reason he wouldn't let Park Police investigators into Vince Foster's office after Foster's 1993 suicide was that he was afraid they would discover the bills for Webster Hubbell's collagen treatments in Foster's safe. "That's what this whole miserable thing has been about from the start," Nussbaum bitterly tells Blumenthal. "Webster Hubbell's secret obsession with bigger lips."

March 15, 1995: Independent counsel Robert Fiske releases his final report on the Whitewater affair. While absolving President and Mrs. Clinton of any legal wrongdoing, it says that there was "still something kind of fishy about the whole arrangement between whatsisname, McDougal, the Madison Guaranty guy, and the Clintons." It adds that the President probably exercised "questionable" judgment in asking so many female state employees to perform oral sex on him, even if he was governor at the time.

—Esquire, 1994

Please
Refrain from
Breathing

To save money, airlines in the United States are circulating
less fresh air into the cabins of many airplanes.
—*The New York Times*

CONFIDENTIAL MEMORANDUM
TO: CHIEF EXECUTIVE OFFICER,
     AEROAMERICA AIRLINES
FROM: SENIOR V.P., REVENUE
     ENHANCEMENT DIVISION (RED)
RE: FURTHER SAVINGS

1.   FOOD/BEVERAGE. Nutritional Research (N.R.) informs us that by
adding a mixture of sawdust and polyethylene foam to the food—most
of which is going uneaten anyway—we could cut costs *significantly.*

After extensive testing on focus groups, in which "passengers" were
served "beef" and "fish" selections consisting of equal parts of real beef
or fish and the sawdust-polyethylene mixture, it was determined that
only 3 percent noticed they were eating wood and plastic instead of our
standard fare.

First and Business Class pose a challenge, as these are more sensitive
palates, but N.R. feels that the problem can be solved by heavily spicing
the dishes with inexpensive cumin and calling them, respectively, "Beef
Bangalore" and "Fiery Fish."

Bonus: Once the sawdust-polyethylene mixture reaches the stomach, it expands to five times its normal volume, greatly reducing passenger desire for expensive complimentary beverages. (See Tab A—Flight Surgeon's Report on Effects of High-Altitude Consumption of Wood and Plastic.)

2. SAFETY EQUIPMENT. Studies have shown that a statistically insignificant number of seat-cushion PFDs (Personal Flotation Devices) are ever actually deployed. Their primary value is psychological, providing passengers with the illusion that they might survive in the event that the aircraft plunges into the ocean at five hundred miles per hour. Additionally, since 85 percent of our flight routes are over land, it might logically be asked: Why bother with flotation devices at all?

RED suggests that it makes prudent, even urgent, economic sense to remove the polyethylene foam from inside the seat cushions and put it where it can be more profitably used—namely, in the passengers' food. (See Tab B—Polyethylene Foam: Tofu of the 1990s?)

As for the inflatable life rafts, these items are both bulky and heavy. They take up space that could be more profitably used for passenger seating (see below), and they increase drag and reduce lift, putting strain on the engines and requiring more fuel. RED recommends that these be sold, and replaced with smaller and lighter substitutes—yellow bags filled with shredded in-flight magazines.

3. THE COCKPIT. While employing pilots, copilots, and flight engineers was once desirable, even necessary, sophisticated computers and flight systems can now do their work far more efficiently. (How many times has the NTSB attributed a crash to "computer error"? Not many.) Additionally, computers do not demand raises, require medical or pension plans, go on strike, or participate in profit sharing. (See Tab C—Rethinking Profit Sharing: Whose Airline Is It, Anyway?)

A possible solution: As you are only too well aware, AeroAmerica's policy of terminating female flight attendants over the age of fifty has met with stiff—and very costly—legal resistance from their union, and has resulted in unfortunate (and grossly unfair) publicity. Would it therefore not make sense to take these troublesome flight attendants, pay them half or a third of their former salaries, put them in pilot, copilot, and flight-engineer uniforms, and stick them in the cockpit? This would kill many birds with one stone: (a) passengers peeping into the cockpit on entering and leaving would not become agitated on finding no one there; (b) the aging flight attendants would be grateful to have jobs, even at reduced salaries; and (c) AeroAmerica would be seen to be in the forefront of women's rights.

4.   SEATING. Though passenger-satisfaction questionnaires often reflect dissatisfaction with existing seating configurations, our research has determined that seventeen inches is more than generous for the average passenger's posterior, and that ten inches of legroom is probably adequate in most cases. Over the centuries, the human body has shown itself to be almost infinitely adaptable. RED recommends reducing current posterior allotments to fourteen inches and legroom to six inches. (See Tab D—Coffins, Tiger Cages, and Cattle Cars: Masterpieces of Ergonomic Design.)

5.   EMERGENCY MASKS. Does it not strike management as odd that as we are reducing passengers' air supply we continue to supply them, gratis, with *oxygen*?

—*The New Yorker*, 1993

Confidential
Memorandum

□

To: MERCEDES BASS
FROM: ZEIT & GEIST PUBLIC RELATIONS, INC.
RE: RECENT ARTICLE IN *W* ABOUT YOUR NEW $75-MILLION RESIDENCES
  IN FORT WORTH AND NEW YORK CITY

Given homelessness, recession, blah blah, short-term fallout admittedly may be damaging. But medium/long-term we recommend an aggressive spin strategy to reverse perceptions stemming from the piece. Goal: insuring that portrait of you that ultimately emerges is neither "Marie Antoinette" (page 12) nor "Madame de Pompadour" (*ibid.*) but, rather, concerned fighter for the country's economic welfare. Talking points (key buzz words in CAPS) for future media hits:

1.   Re cost of Fort Worth house: $3-million wall, $12-million landscaping, helipad, lake-size fountain, etc. Complacent Easterners may not understand this, but Texas is hurting. Oil prices down, unemployment soaring, lives ruined. We (that is, you and Mr. Bass) choose the SOCIALLY RESPONSIBLE course of plowing money back into the Texas economy as LABOR INTENSIVELY as possible. The *W* article teemed with inaccuracies, but at least got it right in saying that the Crestline Road PROJECT involved "an army of workmen . . . one-hundred-strong." Assuming a normal family of four per workman, that makes four hundred people who directly benefit (clothing, food, tuition, etc.). Sid (that is, Mr. Bass) and I have always felt that trickle-down begins at home.

2a.   Re $9-million co-op on Fifth Avenue, plus $26-million renovations and furnishings. At a time when people are fleeing New York in droves and eroding its tax base, is it wrong for others to register a strong yes vote for the city by making a HOME there? Yes, the apartment needed work. Most 1920s-era apartments do. We were happy to be able to PROVIDE EMPLOYMENT for so many talented UNION craftsmen. Also French and other craftsmen, many of them BILINGUAL.

2b.   Imported art and furnishings, including $1.7-million pair of Louis XVI commodes, $825,000 pair of Louis XVI planters, $1.21-million Louis XIV carpet. Also $30k worth of dried topiary for the Aspen lodge. Yes, we have spent a lot of money. The whole POINT OF THE PROJECT was to insure worthy GIFTS when we DONATE BOTH THESE RESIDENCES to New York City and Fort Worth as HOMELESS SHELTERS. Sid and I had been planning to announce the GIFTS upon completion of the work, but *W,* by RUSHING INTO PRINT, has imputed to us less selfless motives. (Obviously, you will want to discuss this approach beforehand with Mr. Bass, but you could emerge as the modern Eleanor Roosevelt—minus the frumpy frocks. Important: remain vague as to the precise timing of the gift.)

—*The New Yorker,* 1992

Want to Buy a Dead Dictator?

Lenín
for Sale

It has come to our attention through private channels
that the Soviet government is preparing to make a
very unusual, indeed unprecedented, offering:
the embalmed remains of V. I. Lenin.

With its ruined economy fast approaching crisis point, and a severe winter food shortage looming, the Russian government is being forced to
undertake some very drastic measures in an attempt to bring in desperately needed hard currency. Last summer, cosmonauts aboard the Soviet
space station *Mir*, circling 240 miles above the earth, were reduced to
earning money for the ailing national space effort by sipping Coca-Cola
in an experiment for the company.

Last April, the Soviet Interior Ministry was tasked with coming up
with a list of patrimonial items, such as icons, Fabergé eggs, and other
treasures that the government could sell off. The Deputy Minister, Mr.
Viktor Komplectov, first proposed selling Lenin's remains last April,
pointing to the enormous profits earned by the British government when
it sold London Bridge to an Arizona developer in 1962. At the time, according to one source at the Ministry, the proposal was considered "sacri-
legious," but after last August's coup attempt by Communist hard-liners,
the citizenry reacted with vengeance against all vestiges of bolshevism.
The government announced that it was considering burying Lenin beside
his mother in his Russian hometown of Ulyanovsk. It reconsidered that

proposal when, according to a high-ranking Ministry official, "a significant number of threats were received stating that the body would be dug up and indecent things done upon it." At that point, the Ministry decided that it might be safer to remove the corpse from the country. Mr. Komplectov's proposal was thus unshelved and submitted for study in a new light. Russian President Boris Yeltsin is said to have given his final approval in late October, in the wake of the tumultuous summer upheaval.

In an attempt to save the significant commission that an auction house such as Christie's or Sotheby's would charge—as well as to discourage an extraordinary, and to the Russians, unseemly, public spectacle—the Ministry has decided to hold a closed, sealed bid auction. Bids must be received by the Ministry no later than midnight (Moscow time) on December 31st of this year. The reserve is set at $15 million, U.S. The winning bidder will be contacted within three days.

A condition of the sale is that the Lenin corpse not be used for any "commercial, or improper" purpose, the deed of purchase to be administered by the International Court of Justice at The Hague, in the Netherlands, making the conditions of sale enforceable by that international legal community.

Description: Mr. Lenin's body was embalmed at his death in 1924, and stored in a sealed, climate-controlled glass casket. (Shades of Sleeping Beauty!) It has been periodically re-embalmed. Every five to ten years the skin, somewhat yellowish but by no means jaundiced-looking, requires a special application of preservative, or "waxing." Under the terms of sale, maintenance is to be provided only by qualified Russian mortuary specialists from the Interior Ministry, expenses to be paid for by the purchaser. (Estimated annual upkeep: $10,000–$15,000; varies with climate.)

Obviously, the Lenin corpse is not for everyone. But as a conversation piece, it would certainly have no equal. You might have some explaining to do to the lady of the home, but the item is fairly compact and could be accommodated to fit in most large dens.

Bids should be addressed to:

Viktor Barannikov, Minister of the Interior
Ministry of the Interior
UL Ogaryova #6
Moscow 103009

—*Forbes FYI*, 1991

Premier Kissoff Is on the Line and He's Hopping Mad

"You know what they *really* ought to sell," Geoffrey Norman said one day in the fall of 1991, after the news reported that in order to raise desperately needed hard currency, the former Soviet Union was selling items from its space program and KGB Cold War archives, "is Lenin."

"Hm," I said.

Thus was born OPERATION RED BOD, the code name we adopted around the office. At 4:30 on the afternoon of November 5 we faxed a galley page of the article—minus the accompanying photo illustration showing Lenin under a glass coffee table in the midst of a cocktail party—to dozens of news organizations, which were by then starting to close their evening broadcasts and next day's editions. And went home.

Two hours later I was exercising on my cross-country ski machine in front of (my favorite) evening news show, ABC's *World News Tonight,* when on came Lenin's waxy face on the screen next to Peter Jennings's bemused own. This was the last time Jennings would smile for several days.

Early the next morning my phone rang, for the first of many times that day. It was *Forbes* Chairman Steve Forbes, my boss.

"The Russians have gone ballistic," he said. "We're going to refer all calls to *you.*"

The fiftieth, or perhaps fifty-first call (before noon) was from the BBC, informing me that Minister Barannikov had been forced to break into regular Moscow TV programming to assure an anxious nation that he was not, in fact, secretly planning to auction off their former dictator, even if he was a god that failed. Moreover, said the BBC, Minister Barannikov had some strong words for *FYI*'s editor. The phrases "international incident," "brazen lie," and "serious provocation" occurred. I suggested to the BBC that Minister Barannikov "chill out." This caused some confusion but was eventually translated into English as "relax." I then received a number of subsequent phone calls from persons with thick Russian accents suggesting that relaxing was not a viable option.

Peter Jennings was very gracious, under the circumstances. He called personally, without an intervening secretary, "to get your exact title." That night, with the expression of a headmaster informing assembly that one of the students had let down not only the school, but himself, he retracted the story. To the quite numerous reporters who called him for comment, he said that he had believed the story because it had come from *Forbes,* which he regarded "up to now, as a responsible news organization." Paramedics were summoned to the offices of *Forbes* editor Jim Michaels, who had devoted a lifetime of hard work to establishing *Forbes*'s reputation as a paragon of reputability.

Reactions of other news organizations ran the gamut from bemused to outraged. One newspaper called for me to be "drummed out of the international press corps."

Postscript: Half a year later I picked up *The Washington Post* to a large story that the Kremlin had been "inundated" with bids "ranging from $10,000 to $27 million for the pickled corpse of Vladimir Ilyich Lenin."

One letter, from the director of a Virginia printing company, read, "We are in the final planning stages of our new corporate headquarters. We were recently discussing the new lobby and saw the need for an appropriate centerpiece. Our interior designer has agreed with us, and feels that suitable arrangements can be made to house Mr. Lenin's body here."

A Merrill Lynch broker in Houston who submitted the $10,000 bid said, "I don't think my wife would allow me to keep Lenin at home. It wouldn't go with the furniture. If my bid is accepted, I will probably donate it to our Museum of Fine Arts. There is quite an interest here in culture."

Minister Barannikov's sense of humor had by now been restored. His spokesman told the *Post* that everyone who submitted a bid would receive a polite letter declining their offer, but thanking them for their interest.

Mr. Lenin was last reported still resting comfortably on Red Square; the dead mouse, as it were, on the floor of Russia's living room.

—Forbes FYI, 1995

Guy Stuff

Driving Through the Apocalypse

"You'd be surprised," said Andy, surveilling a row of smashed-up cars, "at how few people know how to properly ram a vehicle."

It had been an interesting morning so far. It started off with a slide show featuring the last mortal remains of various German executives, Italian politicians and U.S. diplomats. The classroom was a windowless room hung with the sayings of PLO Party Animal George Habash, quotes from the Baader–Meinhof training manual, autographed photos of FBI agents duded up in Ninja outfits, bomb diagrams and a "DEFEND FIREARMS DEFEAT DUKAKIS" bumper sticker.

Next came the lecture on how to steer and brake properly—chances are you are doing it all wrong—how to "swerve to avoid," and drive off the road without requiring surgery. Very useful stuff, this.

You don't have to be an exec who's just gotten the happy news that you're being sent to head up the Lima, Peru, office to appreciate the three-day Executive Security Training course they give out at BSR in Summit Point, W.Va., two hours down the road from Washington, D.C. Suppose, as one of the instructors put it, you have a loved one who is going to die unless you get her to the hospital in ten minutes, and the hospital is 20 minutes away? You *will* learn how to do that. That's how they talk, the instructors, most of them former military sergeants: "I will give the first lecture tomorrow on surveillance detection, and you *will* find it compelling."

Right now we *were* about to get into a Buick LeSabre and ram a Volvo station wagon, and I *did* have a burbly sensation in my stomach. Angel, a 150-pound knot of muscle with a Zapata mustache, two tours in Vietnam with the 101st, and he won't say how many with Delta Force, was our ramming instructor. Here's the situation, he said: you round the curve, and there's a car blocking the road and two guys standing in front of it with guns pointed at you. "You can try to turn around, do a boot-leg or a J-turn. Or," he added, insinuating his preference with just a crease of a smile, "you might just decide you want to put a little Goodyear on 'em."

What you will find out about ramming is that it is counter-reflexive. All your life you've been hitting the brakes when you see a car stopped in front of you. Here they tell you to align either your right or left front wheel with the center of the other car's rear (usually) axle, to downshift into first gear one-and-a-half car lengths away, then to hit the accelera-tor and to *stay on the accelerator* so that the other car absorbs the energy of the crash, not yours. You will do this twice during your three days at BSR. You *will* like it better the second time. The first, you're too busy concentrating on keeping your head from going through the windshield, which Angel assures you it won't, but you do not entirely believe him.

My classmates were natural rammers. They got the hang of it right away. One was with the Department of Labor's Inspector General's of-fice, here so he would be able to drive the Secretary of Labor through harm's way. I could not for the life of me remember when an attempt had last been made on a Secretary of Labor, but who am I to begrudge the lovely Lynn Martin and her successors this consolation?

The others did not pass out business cards, or even last names. They were lean, fit, had short haircuts and Berettas. They were not in the least put out by the photographs of German industrialist roadkill, and when it came my turn to be ambushed, they shot me upside the head easy as pie, though they were considerate enough to say afterwards, "Sorry about killing you. Shoulda seen your face." Yuk, yuk.

I was not able to get a straight answer from Calvin Frye, who at the time was director of training programs at BSR, as to just who these cheery killers were, but I was able to determine that BSR is where they all send their people for special driver's ed: all branches of the military and government agencies, CIA, et cetera, et cetera. American executives come here as well, especially the ones who get those plum overseas post-ings that come with the name tags saying, "HELLO MY NAME IS JIM. MY COMPANY WILL GLADLY PAY MANY U.S. DOLLARS IN RANSOM."

There are other executive training schools. The advantage of BSR—aside from the fact that it comes with a two-mile, ten-turn racetrack upon which you *will* have a gas—is that this is where all the feds go to train. The instructors have security clearances, meaning that they get state-of-the-art antiterrorism input from the agencies whose people they train. They don't pass along classified information to noncleared clients, but the expertise they impart is based on it.

The key theme of the course is: *force the bad guys to pick on someone else.* The way to do that, of course, is to make yourself a difficult target. Vary your route to the office every day, never set patterns, spend the five to six minutes every morning to see if they've wired a mercury switch and C-4 to your windshield wiper, phone in fake restaurant and airline reservations, change your plans constantly, and at the last minute, reschedule, cancel again. "If you can get them to pick another victim," said Cal during the Attack Recognition class, "then you've been 100 percent successful. Once you're attacked, your chances of survival are about 10 percent."

"All right, suppose I throw you in the trunk," said Bruce during the Vehicle Security exercise, showing us how to detect car bombs. "What do you do?" Damn good question there, Bruce, and hell if I knew. Suffocate? Wet my pants? Bruce reached into the side of the trunk, pulled out the two wires leading to the electric hood latch. With a pocketknife, he cut through the insulation and then pressed the wires together, shorting the circuit. The latch popped open. What if you don't have a knife? "Use your teeth," said Bruce. Better yet, carry a penknife.

We found a half-dozen bombs in the car, under the hood, on the exhaust, attached to the windshield wipers, underneath the seat, in the headrest. They kept going off before we found them, too. The bombs consisted of ten-inch-long sections of dowel painted red to simulate sticks of TNT, and Play-Doh to signify C-4, attached to mercury switches, heat sensors and plain old plastic traveling alarm clocks. Angel gave the lecture on bombs, demonstrating some seventeen different kinds. Once you learn how, it only takes five to six minutes to safety-check a car, using just a small 40,000-candlepower Maglite and a plastic tie as a probe.

Every time Angel introduced a different bomb, he'd say, "Now this one's my favorite." See that can of Coke on the backseat floor? "Pick it up, and next thing we'll be reading about you in the newspaper, in orbit up there with Sputnik." Ever heard of a "Firefly"? I'll refrain from divulging the precise recipe here, but it's pathetically simple to make:

you fill a gelatin capsule with a certain household chemical and drop it down the gas tank. The water in the bottom of the tank will melt the gelatin, the chemical will make contact with the metal, causing a spark, causing the car to turn you into ground chuck. This seemed to me a darn good argument for locking gas caps, but Angel said no, no, "Those only keep honest guys out of your gas tank." What you do is dust the cap—as well as the door handles—with talcum powder. If that dust looks disturbed the next morning, take a cab.

Angel said he plays "the dumb American" when he picks up his rent-a-car at foreign airports: makes them drive it up to him at the curb, then asks the guy to open the hood, show him the spare, the dipstick, battery. If the guy won't open the hood, "get the hell away from the car." (I wonder how this is going to play at the Budget Rent A Car counter at LAX.)

Rental cars are an inside joke here. The BSR fleet consists of second-hand Chevy Caprice police cruisers, specially fitted with 350-horse V-8 engines, Rochester Quadrajet carburetors, Bilstein gas shocks, NASCAR-grade stock-car wheels, sway bars and chrome moly axles. It is possible that the family car is not so neatly equipped, so we were advised to think twice before we went home and started pulling bootlegs and J-turns in the driveway. (Respectively, forward and reverse 180-degree turns, done at about 40 mph. The name comes from the inventors of the techniques.) At this point, Bruce grinned and, with a twinkle in his steely blues, said, "Why do you think God invented rent-a-cars?"

After a thoroughly enjoyable hour of doing bootlegs and Js, spreading rubber on the track like so much soft butter, it was time for the Barricade Confrontations. These were ambushes, basically. On us they used .22 caliber blanks; on advanced students they use 12-gauge shotgun blanks, which, Bruce said, "tends to increase the stress factor." After getting shot twice in the head, my stress factor did not need increasing. What it needed was a stiff drink. Before that could be achieved, though, there was the High Speed Pursuit, in which we drove around the track at 100 mph with instructors following close behind, blowing their horns, swerving, and bumping into our rear fenders. Contrary to the movies, they tell you here, most high-speed chases end with the pursued person crashing within two minutes or two miles. After the exercise, this did not come as a surprise to me. But there are things you can learn to make yourself faster. A car race, Bruce said, is won by the person who comes out of the turns fastest. It is also essential not to go into the turn too fast, and to come off your brake as you start your turn. "That's the difference," said Bruce, "between a mechanic and an artist."

The lecture the next morning on Surveillance Detection was given by Andy, twenty-seven years old, affable and boyish looking, with ten years in the Marines, including tours at the JFK Special Warfare Center and, I think, with Delta Force, the elite of the elite antiterrorists. (BSR, I got the feeling, is fairly thick with Delta grads.) He was determinedly close-lipped about his experiences, except to allow as how they had been "practical."

Predictability, he emphasized, is the cardinal sin. Two people, he said, were snatched in Beirut during their routine golf game. (Is nothing sacred?) He was critical of Brig. Gen. Dozier, the U.S. Army general who got nabbed by the Red Brigades in Verona in 1981. "He was not the prime target," he said. "He was not even the secondary target. He was the tertiary target. He was the easiest. He PT'd (Physical Training) every morning on the dot at six."

He brought up an assassination attempt on General Trujillo. The gunmen struck while he was on his way to his regular assignation with his mistress. "Your principal," said Andy, "may try to hide this aspect of his life from you." Unwise, definitely. If no man is a hero to his valet, he sure as hell should not try to be one to his bodyguard. I thought back to a misty night in Washington when my wife and I saw a cabinet official walking up a side street toward a hotel. Here was a man with a security detail nearly the size of the president's, and he was completely alone. He kept his head down, avoiding eye contact, and the collar of his raincoat pulled up. What a nifty challenge it would have been for his press secretary to explain why he was found full of holes, naked and covered with Dom Pérignon in a suite at the Four Seasons.

The portion of Andy's lecture that dealt with Route Analysis was for the benefit of chauffeurs and bodyguards. Eighty percent of all terrorist incidents occur at the "chokepoints"—and almost always on the way to the office. The human element fails us once again: we're always running a little late, no time to vary the route this morning.

Fleeing the ambush is indeed heartily recommended, but only twice in the history of attacks have the bad guys given up the chase. (Tenacious little pricks, these terrorists.) And since your chances, as the pursued, of eluding them for more than two minutes or two miles are not favorable, you will want to have a preplanned response. This basically means preselecting whither precisely you will flee.

Should the unpleasantness be occurring in an Arab country, Andy counsels against running to the nearest mosque. "Those places have a higher meaning," he said in his Georgia drawl. "You want to get *away* from that." He did advise driving your car into the nearest bank—literally, that is, through the front door. The drawback being that "the guard might shoot you, and the police might be pissed off at you." You could also throw a rock through a jewelry store, a definite attention-getter. Or run to a "high-density environment," like "an elementary school." ("U.S. EXECUTIVE HIDES FROM ATTACKERS IN KINDERGARTEN; 17 CHILDREN SLAIN!") As to shouting for help, he said it's better to yell "Fire!" than "Help!" Why? "Because it involves them."

The last day of the course was spent driving in a van through the streets of nearby Winchester, Va., while we tried to figure out who was "surveilling" us. Everyone, we paranoiacally assumed: mothers in Volvo station wagons, old ladies—surely they didn't think we were so dumb as to think those things in their ears were hearing aids?—tattooed biker types leaning against fences, a father and his three-year-old daughter parked outside a pediatrician's office—ha! did they think we were *fools*?—and everyone in every phone booth we passed. We wrote down their physical descriptions and the time of sighting, just as Andy had instructed us, to determine any patterns.

There are some tricks to Surveillance Detection. One is to wait until the light turns red, then go through and see who follows (other than annoyed cops, that is). If you're on foot, go into a restaurant, order a meal, prepay and pretip the waiter, then bolt, leaving the "surveillant" stuck with his tab. Oh, and if it's a Latin country, be sure to try this one: head for the nearest gay bar, leaving your macho surveillant too embarrassed to follow you in, presumably after fighting off a half-dozen Carmen Miranda wannabes.

Most of the people we were convinced were tailing us turned out to be "ghosts," which is to say, they weren't. On the third and final run through town, Andy dropped hints about where the ambush would occur. Being a surveillant is the most boring job in the world, definitely entry-level terrorism. But that doesn't mean they're asleep. On the contrary, these people are looking to move up the terrorist career ladder. They're on the ball. General Haig was under surveillance for a month before the cranky Euro-terrorists blew up his motorcade outside Mons, Belgium, in 1979. The Basque separatists spent three years planning Spanish Premier Carrero Blanco's 1973 assassination. (Based, incidentally, on the 1881 assassination of Czar Alexander II by the Narodnaya Volya.) The Uruguayan Tupamaros who nabbed Sir Geoffrey Jackson in 1971 actually practiced on his car. The surveillance of the two U.S. Air Force colonels killed in Tehran in 1975 was so painstaking that the planners painted footprints for themselves on the ground at the attack site.

The diligence has to cut both ways. Following its bloody but unsuccessful attack on Maggie Thatcher in 1984, the IRA passed this message to the British government: "You have to be lucky every time. We only have to be lucky once." Probably the most conspicuously unsuccessful graduate of the BSR course was U.S. Marine Lt. Col. William Higgins, who while serving with the U.N. observer force in Lebanon was kidnapped, tortured and, probably, hanged. His captors, driving a brown Volvo, forced his Jeep Cherokee off the road with a basic blocking maneuver. The terrorists confused pursuing Israeli troops by deploying five brown Volvos in the area.

The most conspicuously successful BSR graduate is probably a certain U.S. diplomat who was stationed at the U.S. Embassy in Cairo in 1988. He and another man were driving through town one day when a Peugeot sedan started to pull up beside them. Three things were not right about the Peugeot. First, everyone inside was sitting on the left. Second, all the windows were down (in an air-conditioned car, in Cairo?). Third—this was the clincher—the driver was wearing mufflers over his ears. (No sense in losing your hearing over a couple of American diplomats.)

The diplomat and his passenger ducked and gunned their car forward. The attackers opened fire with submachine guns. The diplomat was shot in the neck, but he kept control. He drove up onto a sidewalk, where another gunman was waiting. He did what they train you to do here: not to reach for your gun, but to use the car as a 4,000-pound bullet. It works. The gunman jumped out of the way rather than end up as tread jam. The diplomat and his companion got away from their pursuers, members of a group that had specialized in killing Israeli diplomats in Cairo.

"We call that incident a failure," said Cal, "because the whole point is to avoid being attacked." Andy mentioned another instance in which a woman graduate "drove into her attacker and cut him in half, then did a J-turn and got out of there." Sounded like a success to me, but "No," he said, "she should have kept right on going through him." They're tough graders here.

As we approached the chokepoint, we saw it pull out behind us, a brown Volvo, oddly enough. And there, up the street in a phone booth was the same guy in the Hawaiian shirt whom we'd seen earlier, standing on a corner. And there, pulling out in front of us was the same, white four-door sedan. It turned to block us. The Volvo had us boxed from the rear.

"Okay, what do I do?" Andy asked.

"Ram," said one of the guys in the back.

"Which end?"

"Front."

"Nope. The trailing end. Always go for the trailing end, unless you have no other choice."

Suddenly a nice-looking woman, maybe the wife of one of the BSR instructors, and a cute little seven-year-old girl popped out of the shadows. They aimed sticks at us and went *bang bang*. The guys in the back knew exactly how it would all play out. They just smiled at the mom and little girl and went *bang bang* with their fingers.

"You figured it out," said Andy to his soldier-students, "and that's the difference between someone who's going to live and someone who won't."

—*Forbes FYI*, 1992

I Visitz
the Nimitz

■

It is hunched and hot inside the Grumman Trader, nickname: "Blue Ghost." I'm wearing my cranial, an abbreviated helmet with goggles, and my Mae West. Deflated, it looks more like a Twiggy. The crew chief passes a cup of coffee. Below, the Gulf Stream is gray-green and flecked with chop.

Our seats face backward. At the far end of the cabin the sign on the door is not inviting: a European-style traffic sign showing a man peeing in silhouette. The pee, traced by a broken line, arcs onto the floor short of the toilet. A red diagonal slash is superimposed over the silhouette. It is not clear what is going on.

"WHAT DOES THAT SIGN MEAN?"

To talk you have to pull on the ear cups and shout.

The crew chief shouts back that the plane is usually bouncing around and most people miss the toilet. So they have an attachment.

"KIND OF LIKE A FUNNEL."

"I SEE."

"WE HAD A HARD TIME COMING UP WITH A SIGN."

A few minutes later he gives us the prelanding prep, an attention getter beginning with, "IF WE DITCH—" The possibility seems more remote when stewardesses explain it.

The pilot banks left and I catch my first glimpse of CVN-68, aircraft carrier *Nimitz*. We think of aircraft carriers as immense, and they are. This one is a fifth-of-a-mile long, almost as long as the Empire State Building is tall. There's a Ripley's Believe-It-or-Not quality to nuclear aircraft carrier statistics. She only needs refueling every thirteen years. Her last fill-up cost $100 million. (Comes out to something like $133 per mile.) She sleeps 6,100 people. A single link of her anchor chain weights 365 pounds. What we have here is 95,000 tons of U.S. airpower projection. We are talking Big Floating Stick. Carrier aviation has come a long way since Eugene B. Ely took off in a biplane from an eighty-five-foot boardwalk built onto the bow of the U.S.S. *Pennsylvania* in 1911. But from 800 feet up, that four-and-a-half-acre flight deck looks awfully small.

I was told to press my body against the seat. The water got closer and closer. Then suddenly it became flight deck. Bump. The hook grabbed the cable and we went from ninety knots to zero in less than two seconds. All very smooth.

The flight deck of a carrier is, as one officer puts it, "the most dangerous place on earth." There is an interesting variety of ways to die. One is having 50,000 pounds of F-14 or A-6 land on you. Men have been blown off the deck; sucked whole into the inlet ducts of jet engines. (Pity the poor swabbos who have to clean up after that.) The most gaping of these maws belongs to the A-7E Corsair light attack bomber. It looks like the mouth of a great white shark that's had all its teeth pulled.

A few years ago on this same flight deck an EA-6B Prowler veered to the right at the last minute and rammed into a row of parked aircraft, creating a fireball that killed fourteen men. (The autopsies of the deck crew revealed traces of marijuana; ever since Navy crews have been subject to random, on the spot urinalyses. OK, but it wasn't the deck crew that crashed; why not just make the pilots pee in a cup? Never mind.) During a similar accident aboard the *Midway* some years ago, about a dozen deck crew were knocked unconscious and asphyxiated on spilled jet fuel fumes. Sometimes the inch-and-a-half arresting-gear cables snap and slice through torsos and legs. For exposing themselves to all this twelve hours a day, the men who work the deck earn ninety dollars extra per month. But then it's an adventure, not a job.

As I was stepping out of the Trader into the furnace heat of the deck, a crewman checked to see that no pens or eyeglasses were protruding from pockets. These items do not agree with delicate million-dollar jet engines.

We are shown an orientation film. At Pensacola, Navy officer candidates are shown a film in which a drill instructor is screaming himself blue in the face at a trainee who has not quite mastered the art of folding his boxer shorts into little neat squares. (At moments like this, I am grateful to my Maker for endowing me with 4-F asthmatic lungs.) "There's this emphasis on attention to detail," says one of the *Nimitz's* lieutenants. "If you've ever tried to fold boxer shorts into little tight squares you'd appreciate how difficult it is." The next scene in the film is a close-up of a plane just before a carrier takeoff. The camera goes in for a close-up of the wheel well and you see a bolt sticking out. It's loose.

I ask if the next scenes show a plane plowing into the flight deck.

"No," he says. "They've already made their point."

There's a certain élan aboard these ships. A skull and bones adorns the tail of an F-14; a business card affixed to a pilot's cabin says MARAUDERS, and beneath, SOMETHING TO OFFEND EVERYONE. The antisubmarine helicopter guys wear patches showing a mythological griffin standing astride the carrier, snapping a sub in two.

We meet Capt. Eugene Conner and RAdm. Roger Box. They have this after-you-Gaston number: the admiral earnestly defers to the captain ("This is his ship. I don't tell him anything.") and the captain earnestly defers to the admiral ("Let me tell you, we're glad to have the admiral aboard. We sure can use his guidance."). Between them they have about four hundred combat missions over Vietnam.

We scarf up finger sandwiches as Captain Conner excuses himself. He needs to get back to the bridge. They are in the midst of CQ—carrier qualification. Right now there are pilots circling up there who've never landed aboard a carrier. Poor bastards.

In the Combat Information Center, the Tactical Air Officer rules over a dark domain of martial blips and colored lights. This is the nerve center of the ship's defense system, where threats to the carrier are identified and assessed. Once the captain has given permission, the TAO orders planes into the air to intercept fighters or missiles or to sink submarines. He can also launch missiles and fire gatling guns at such things as incoming Exocet missiles.

He and his watch officers wear leather jackets with a quiltwork of squadron insignias. Amid these manly motifs is a Planned Parenthood lapel pin. I'm wondering about that when I notice a CRT screen that looks interesting. Looking closer, I see that it shows every Soviet ship on the face of the earth. Cool! The young black seaman sitting in front of it maneuvers the control ball with his palm. The cursor zips about, from the Bering Strait to the Caribbean, down to Tierra del Fuego. He centers the cursor over a Soviet sub off the Isle of Pines, south of Cuba, punches a button and the sub's characteristics flash up on the screen: name, speed, course, and symbols I can't begin to figure out, probably the captain's mother's maiden name and favorite brand of scotch. The TAO appears and discreetly tells the seaman to stop revealing military secrets to visiting journalists.

I ask a theoretical question. Suppose someone decided to try to land a Cessna aboard the *Nimitz*. How far would he get? The TAO fields it, but it's one of those military answers: "Well, I don't think it'd be a good idea." I persist. Wondering, no doubt, why this bozo is trying to get him to say "Guess I'd blow the goddam thing into pieces smaller'n a bee's pecker," he creases a grin and says, "I'm trying to avoid giving you a straight answer."

Up in the Pri–Fly (Primary Flight Control) bridge, the man who controls flight operations looks out with fixed grimness on his quarter-of-a-million square feet of flight deck. He wears a yellow T-shirt over his uniform. It's stenciled, AIR BOSS. He is, basically, God, in that whatever he says, goes. Below on the flight deck, everyone is also color-coded. Red shirts for ordnance handlers; green shirts for men who hook the planes up to the catapults; brown shirts for those charged with plane maintenance; and so on. They all wear a "Mickey Mouse" radio. Every few seconds a pulse called a "confidence tone" goes off inside the mouse, letting the wearer know his set is working.

When things are hot, the *Nimitz* can launch a plane every thirty seconds and "trap"—land—one every forty. Today things are considerably slower because of the CQing. I know you've seen *Top Gun*, but let me tell you, watching in person 58,000 pounds of F-14 being catapulted screaming and smoking off the flight deck into a horizonless black night, one after another, is a fairly amazing spectacle.

The thrill of which wears off as soon as you go to bed in your cabin right under the flight deck. This is roughly like having a 12-gauge shotgun fired off in your ear during a significant seismic disturbance. Human beings apparently get accustomed to this.

The catapult on a carrier, combined with the thrust of the plane's engines, shoots thirty tons of aircraft from zero to 140 miles per hour in two seconds. Admiral Box says the catapult is powerful enough to propel an elephant one mile. With all the animal rights groups around, I hope someone looks into this barbarous practice.

Launching is a piece of cake compared with "trapping," or landing. An F-14 is going more than 150 miles an hour when it hits the deck. By the time a pilot tries this for the first time, the Navy has invested about $1.2 million of training in him. His plane costs anywhere from $25 to $35 million. As Admiral Box puts it, staring out into the night as an F-14 "bolters"—misses the arresting gear and keeps on going—off the deck, its hook trailing a fierce shower of sparks, "By the time you add it all up, you're talking about a national asset."

Before landing on a carrier, planes dump their excess fuel. If the launch and recovery clockwork breaks down, and a plane has to be waved off, the stress on the pilot is considerable. If he doesn't trap on the next attempt, he has to refuel in midair before trying again.

Peering out through binoculars at approaching planes is the Landing Signal Officer. In the old days, the LSO stood precariously on the deck of carriers and held the colored paddles with which he guided planes in. LSOs are still called "paddlemen," but they use something else these days.

When the plane is a mile out, the LSO tells the pilot to "Call the ball." That's the Light Landing Device, a vertical arrangement of Fresnel lenses. It's also called the "meatball." If the pilot is high of the glide path, he sees the top Fresnel lens; low, the bottom ones. If he's right on, he sees the middle one. If the pilot can't see the meatball, he says, for reasons no one seems to understand, "Clara." ("Susan" or "Alison" apparently will not work. At this point, I myself would be whimpering "Mama.") At the last moment, if the LSO doesn't like the approach, he presses a button on his "pickle switch" that activates a bunch of red lights around the meatball. That's the wave-off signal.

The LSO is a veteran pilot. He grades each trap, and critiques it with the pilot afterward. There are four grades: OK with a line underneath (awarded to about one in every thousand traps); OK; Fair; and Cut. A Cut is given when the pilot has endangered not only his own life but others'.

Then there is "hitting the spud locker." This is not a form of KP duty. Otherwise known as a "ramp strike," this happens when a plane comes in too low and hits the rounddown, or threshold. This is an especially unpleasant occurrence. The plane explodes and breaks into ton-sized pieces of flaming wreckage and ordnance that roll down the flight deck like amok bowling balls. Asked to describe the carnage and horror, one pilot said with proper sangfroid, "Ruin your whole day."

The whole trick here is knowing when to "punch out." It takes less than a second for both Radar Intercept Officer and pilot to eject out of an F-14; the former is gone in four-tenths of a second, the latter one-half second later. Since F-14s have something called "zero-zero" ejection seats, you can eject while sitting on the ground and not kill yourself. (Thanks anyway.) Trouble is if you eject too soon before a ramp strike, there's a good chance you'll land in the middle of your own fireball. Eject too late and you won't eject.

One former F-14 backseater I talked to once came very close to punching out. The pilot was using Direct Lift Control spoilers. Those take explaining, but the gist of it was that as the plane was a hundred yards from the spud locker a little thingamabob jiggled loose off the pilot's joystick, causing loss of control. The F-14 dropped like a rock toward the ramp. The RIO had his hand on the eject handle, ready to go when the wheels *just* greased over the ramp. The hook grabbed the number one wire. "It was *close*," he said. This is as close as fighter jocks get to expressing actual fear.

There are four arresting cables stretched across the deck at intervals. The one wire is the closest to the ramp, the four wire is the farthest. Trapping the number one is dangerous; it means you almost hit the spud locker. A pilot aims for the three wire. Two is all right, but still too close to the ramp for comfort. Four does the job, but means you were high of the glide path. The wires are thrown over the side after one hundred traps.

Just before touching down, the pilot throttles up to full power. By now he has less than four hundred feet of deck, and if he doesn't trap one of those wires, his brakes aren't going to do him any good. So he bolters. If a pilot can't get it right and the carrier is within range of shore, he's sent to land onshore, at a "Bingo Field." Oh, ignominy.

To CQ, a pilot must make ten day traps and six night traps. If he goes more than thirty days without a carrier landing, even if he's a veteran, he has to requalify. Even Admiral Box tries to fly his F-14 two or three times a week.

I stayed up late in the island—the carrier's superstructure—watching the planes come and go. Most had already been repainted with the drab camouflage gray that will soon cover all Navy planes. It looks as if someone has taken sandpaper to a high gloss finish. The pilots don't like it. It has a certain advantage, like hiding them from the enemy; but it's the end of the fighter plane's cool aesthetic. No more screaming eagles, unsheathed swords, aces of spades, and coiled vipers on all those Tomcats, Corsairs, Intruders, Prowlers, Vikings, Hawkeyes. No more skulls and bones.

The night is warm off Key West. The view from the admiral's chair of the *Nimitz* is OK, underlined. (He's turned in; his aide said I could sit in it.) It's moonless black. The F-14s and A-6s are alternately trapping and roaring off the bow cats in almost metronomic regularity. Off the stern of the *Nimitz* some twenty-two-year old is approaching a critical moment in his life. G. K. Chesterton said courage is almost a contradiction in terms—a strong desire to live taking the form of a readiness to die.

At the end of *The Bridges at Toko-Ri*, after William Holden has been shot down and killed by the North Koreans, Fredric March sits in his admiral's chair and looks out to sea and asks, "Where do we get such men? *Where do we get such men?"*

A carrier pilot watching that movie would probably pop his chewing gum and say, "Denver, Seattle, Bridgeport . . ." But it is still a good question, even in peacetime. What I wonder is, where do we get such elephants?

—1983

How I Went Nine Gs in an F-16 and Only Threw Up Five Times

"Can you have it ready by Monday morning?" is a hard question. "Would you like to fly with the U.S. Air Force Thunderbirds?" is not. I gave my answer (you bet), and went on with life, not daring to hope that my intermediaries, an aviation buff and a retired three-star U.S. Air Force general, would be able to deliver. Slowly the request worked its way through the Air Force channels, from Thunderbirds headquarters at Nellis Air Force Base in Nevada, to the one-star general of the 57th Wing, then to the two-star commander of the Air Weapons and Tactics Center at Nellis; then to the two-star general for Operations at headquarters of the Air Combat Command at Langley AFB in Virginia, and finally all the way up to his four-star commander. It's not all that routine to go for a ride in a $30 million fighter plane, when those planes are more profitably employed teaching real macho to Cessna-shooting Cuban MiGs or strafing people named Ratko. But the answer was yes, and so I found myself in the midst of the second improbability, Las Vegas on Ash Wednesday. "There isn't a free room in town," said the front desk clerk at Caesars Palace. So much for America's spiritual well-being, circa 1996.

I had dinner the night before the flight with my intermediary, Lt. Gen. Robert Beckel (Ret.), at a restaurant that looks down on a lagoon in which two full-size pirate ships attack each other every hour. In a distinguished career, General Beckel flew 313 combat missions in Vietnam, including close air support during the siege of Khe Sanh. He also flew the U-2 and SR-71 "Blackbird" reconnaissance planes, the latter so fast (Mach 3, 1,800 mph) that, as he put it in terms even a math imbecile like myself could understand, "If you fired a .30-06 rifle from Los Angeles and took off simultaneously in the SR-71, the SR-71 would get to New York five minutes before the bullet." Later, as head of the 15th Air Force, he commanded the B-52 bombers that gave permanent nervous tics to the Iraqi Republican Guard during Desert Storm.

For two years in the mid-1960s, General Beckel flew the solo position with the Thunderbirds. He has the gentle manner that I've found in all but one of the numerous war heroes I've met. "If it's possible for one man to love another man," he tells me of the Thunderbirds, "this would be it." I don't think he's spent much time in New York or San Francisco, but I got his drift. The Thunderbirds, eights pilots and 130-odd enlisted men and women, are a tightly knit group.

He told a story about the time actress Yvette Mimieux—remember her? the girl Rod Taylor rescues from the Eloi in *The Time Machine*— went up for an "orientation ride" with the Thunderbirds in the mid-sixties. Normally, the Thunderbird's narrator is the one who takes visitors up for rides, but in this case the leader asserted droit du seigneur and took her up himself. A few days later the Air Force chief of staff opened the newspaper to an article featuring the very lovely Miss Mimieux in the cockpit of one of his planes, alongside the headline, OPERATION BEDSIDE. The story was full of breathless quotes about how she'd gone three times the speed of sound upside down, five feet above the ground. "Which of course she hadn't," said General Beckel. "And OPERATION BEDSIDE was the name of the program she'd taken part in, and for which this was the reward—visiting servicemen in the hospital. So *that* ended orientation trips for a while."

He talked about G forces, the phenomenon that was going to be a big part of my day tomorrow. G forces are multiples of the force of gravity. Standing, walking or sitting normally, we are under one G. We experience two to three Gs in the seat of a 747 during takeoff. Tomorrow, in the F-16, I would be "pulling" up to nine Gs. My 185 pounds would, if put on a scale during the maneuver, weigh 1,665 pounds. Nine Gs is the normal operating limit of an F-16.

Nine Gs is also the point where your average civilian—such as myself—starts to black out. Astronauts on take-off go through up to twenty-five Gs, but they are lying on their backs. An F-16 pilot is reclining slightly and, if he is pulling nine Gs, is usually in the middle of a dogfight, or trying to shake a heat-seeking missile.

Flying the plane itself, said the general, isn't really all that hard. In the old days, getting the aircraft to do what you wanted it to do was a big part of the whole job. These days, computers do most of that work, leaving the pilot to concentrate on up to 125 possible configurations of guns, missiles and bombs. The stick, which used to be between the legs, is now off to the right, leaving the left hand to operate the weaponry. The stick itself barely moves—a mere eighth of an inch in any direction. Pressure sensors register the slightest touch. In fact, the first modern sticks didn't move at all, until the pilots demanded that a little play be built into them, for feel.

"Now we have what's called 'instantaneous Gs,'" said the general. The slightest pressure on that stick and the pilot can find himself pulling the maximum nine Gs and fighting not only the enemy but also from draining the blood in his brain. Pilots wear a G suit, outer leggings resembling chaps that contain air bladders that inflate automatically under G pressure, squeezing the legs and midsection and forcing blood to stay in the upper body. But G suits can't do all the work, and if you are not prepared for high Gs, you can black out in only three seconds. It takes anywhere from seventeen to forty-five seconds to fully regain consciousness; that's a long time if your nose is pointing to the ground at six hundred miles per hour. It happened recently to an American pilot in the Adriatic.

I remember two other things from that night: General Beckel pointing out that the Thunderbirds were formed in 1953 to convince Americans that jet fighters were really safe, despite the fact that so many of them were crashing in the Korean War; and riding up to my room in the elevator in Caesars Palace with a Roman centurion.

Nellis Air Force Base is a fifteen-minute drive north of Las Vegas. There are no centurions in its elevators, but it is headquarters to the Air Warfare Center, which runs the Red Flag exercises that simulate aerial combat between aggressors and defenders. They keep MiGs and other Soviet planes acquired (one way or another) here. This is where many of the top combat pilots in the Air Force come to train. It's also home to the U.S. Air Force Air Demonstration Squadron, known more generally as the Thunderbirds. It's a crisp desert day punctuated by the sound of screaming turbofan engines.

You do not just show up and immediately go whooshing up into the wild blue yonder in your F-16, white scarf whipping from your neck. First you report to a flight surgeon, in my case, Capt. Jack "Harpo" Shelton, who checks your vitals and looks in your ears to make sure that you can do the Valsalva maneuver (holding your nose and blowing to vent inner-ear pressure). The flight surgeon tells you, from personal experience, that riding in the backseat of an F-16 can be a "nauseogenic experience," but that there are ways to compensate. (1) Don't look down into the cockpit, (2) find the horizon and keep looking at it, (3) increase oxygen flow through the mask to 100 percent. Most people, he said, tend to get sick after the acrobatics because it's then that the adrenaline stops pumping, so—"try to keep excited." He reassures me that "less than half" the people who go up for rides throw up. I ask him if I can take the herbal antimotion-sickness tablet that I've brought with me. (I'd been told not to use patches or traditional drugs as these would only "diminish the experience.") Fine, he says, can't hurt.

Next comes the lecture about compensating for G forces. "It's an interesting sensation the first time you feel it." I'll know, he says, if the blood is draining from my head when I start to lose peripheral vision. "It will eventually narrow down to where it looks like you're staring out through the opening in a straw." I sense that this could be a real disadvantage in a dogfight.

The solution, according to the Air Force handout he hands me, is "straining like you're having a hard bowel movement." Ah, the romance of the wild blue yonder. . . . It occurs to me that a hard bowel movement would probably come very easily to me in the event I saw a surface-to-air missile in my rearview mirror. Anyway, the idea is to tighten every muscle below the waist so as to give blood draining from the upper body nowhere to go. Also, Captain Shelton advises, fill your lungs to three-quarters, hold your breath for three to four seconds, then very quickly inhale and exhale in a sort of bizarre parody of Lamaze birth classes. What this does is to constrict the muscles and heart, thereby forcing the blood to stay in the brain. Keep that brain full of blood, was the message I took away from flight surgery.

I practice all this in the car on the way back to the Thunderbird hangar with my escort, SSgt. Chuck Ramey. Constricting my buns and breathing like a porpoise, in combination with an impending sense of dread, gave me some insight into what it might be like to drive to the delivery room in labor. Leave it to a nineties male to discern similarities between childbirth and flying in a fighter jet.

I was now turned over to a Life Support Specialist. I rejoiced in his title, and soon in SSgt. Jeff Kessler himself, to whom it falls to dress visiting backseaters in flight suit, G suit, explain how to use the parachute and survival harness, helmet, oxygen mask, and generally to condense three days of safety briefings into one hour.

This can have unintentionally comic effect, as it did when, during the "Post Ejection Procedures" portion of Sergeant Kessler's briefing, he described how I must angle myself when falling between high-voltage power lines (feet together, head to one side; and may you never have to use this information) and how I should then "be relaxed" for the landing. "Be relaxed" was item number 42 or thereabouts on my post-ejection agenda, starting with being blasted out of the cockpit while going hundreds of miles an hour, possibly upside down. All the makings of a bad air day. In my youth I once jumped from a plane, and so I know from experience how wretched a prospect it is, even when done for obscure recreational reasons.

I paid more attention to Sergeant Kessler than I did to any college professor, for no college professor ever said to me, "The pilot will say 'Eject, eject, eject,' three times. By the third 'eject,' he's going, so you might want to, too." I felt a warm rush of relief when Sergeant Kessler said that the pilot has the option of ejecting both of us. Confident that my brain—assuming it had any blood left in it—would react hysterically to any syllables remotely sounding like "eject," I rejoiced in this datum. Consolation, however, turned to consternation when he began displaying the one-man life raft that would be dangling from my waist on the descent. "A raft," I asked. "In the desert?" Oh well, don't ask, don't tell.

Now he showed me the survival radio—the same type that pilot Scott O'Grady had with him during his five days on the ground in Bosnia, instructing me that I must turn off my emergency beacon before I could use the radio. Finally there was the laminated 121-page Air Force survival pamphlet. I flipped it open at random and saw that I was to rub my body with dirt to disguise body odor, and how to make good use of animal organs. The last two pages confirmed the adage that there are no atheists in foxholes:

WITH OTHER SURVIVORS:

   A. PRAY FOR EACH OTHER
   B. SHARE SCRIPTURES AND SONGS
   C. APPOINT A CHAPLAIN
   D. TRY TO HAVE SHORT WORSHIP SERVICES
   E. WRITE DOWN SCRIPTURES, SONGS, OR LITURGIES THAT ARE REMEMBERED
   F. ENCOURAGE EACH OTHER WHILE WAITING FOR RESCUE
      1) GOD LOVES YOU
      2) PRAISE THE LORD

In walked the Thunderbirds themselves, back from their morning practice. In one month, they would leave for their two-hundred-day annual tour, during which they give about seventy shows. There are eight pilots, six of whom perform in the show. The other two are the operations officer and the advance pilot/narrator who goes on ahead to make arrangements and then narrates the shows, describing to the crowds what it is exactly that the Thunderbirds are doing, other than apparently trying to commit synchronized suicide in front of tens of thousands of people.

It's an interesting sensation being in a room with eight Thunderbird pilots. When I reported it later to my wife, she swooned, "Be still my heart." The leader, Lt. Col. Ron "Maxi" Mumm makes Tom Cruise, star of the movie *Top Gun,* look like Pee Wee Herman. The others, some of them veterans of Desert Storm who flew F-117s and F-4G Wild Weasels, were not lacking in the stud department.

But then what were you expecting, chopped liver? These men are the cream of the cream, the top gun percentile of the U.S. Air Force, chosen not only for their ability to fly upside down on top of each other at 400 mph, but for the image they collectively present. The Thunderbirds are nothing if not Public Relations. Seventy-five percent of Air Force recruits say that they have signed up because of the Thunderbirds. With a yearly budget of $1.9 million, roughly one-tenth the cost of one F-16, that makes the Thunderbirds a very cost-effective recruitment device; they don't even have to take out ads on late night TV promising that swabbing decks is going to be an adventure, not a job.

I was introduced to my pilot, Thunderbird No. 8, Capt. Daniel R. Torweihe, a thirty-six-year-old handsome, broad-faced, blue-eyed former bricklayer from Wisconsin, looking quite knightly in red show suit, white "fram" ascot, and blue flight cap. I could see why he'd been selected as the team's narrator: he has a Disneyland-upbeat tenor: "O-*kay*, Chris, if you're ready, we'll walk out to the aircraft and *go flying*. It looks like we're going to have a *great* day!" I liked him immediately, but then you bond quickly with someone who is going to fly you upside down at nearly the speed of sound.

Commander "Maxi" Mumm told me that the visibility was "hundred miles—plus" and, as I was leaving, asked if I wanted some of his lunch chili. I considered two possibilities behind his offer of spicy Mexican food moments before subjecting my stomach to nine times the force of gravity: this was either fighter jock sangfroid, or an evil practical trick on his colleague Capt. Torweihe. I politely declined, and instead made one last visit to the head, where I noticed that the autographed photo from the Navy's Blue Angels flying team hangs over the urinal.

Tom Wolfe wrote in *The Right Stuff* that the astronauts, just before blasting off from Cape Canaveral, would utter the silent prayer: "Oh Lord, don't let me f- - - up." I made my own prayer into the bathroom mirror: "Oh Lord, don't let me throw up."

We walked out onto the apron, where nine Thunderbird F-16s sat gleaming in the sunlight, cockpit canopies up like broken shotgun breeches.

Two F-117 stealth fighter-bombers were in the line of planes next to ours, looking like high-tech bats. I asked, "What's it like to fly one of those?" Dan shrugged, "It's really just a *bomber*." There isn't much aesthetic grace to an F-117, only low-hung, black malevolence, whereas the F-16 Fighting Falcon has the sleek, sporty lines of a Ferrari. Paint it military gray and fit it out with AIM-9 Sidewinder missiles and Mk-82 Snakeye 500-pound bombs and you have a Tom Clancy wet dream. In sparkly red, white and blue Thunderbird colors, devoid of the instruments of war, it almost smiles at you.

We walked past nine planes, over a quarter billion dollars worth of aircraft, to Thunderbird No. 8. Two very friendly, upbeat crew chiefs named T-Bone and Mike helped to strap me tightly into the backseat, and connected my oxygen mask and parachute harness. *Whatever else comes of this,* I thought, *I will never again feel scrunched in economy class.* T-Bone pointed out the switch to the cockpit video camera mounted on the dashboard, presumably so that I could turn it off while I threw up, or blubbered with fear. Just before the canopy closed down, sealing me inside my snug metallic cocoon, Mike stuck two small plastic bags with ties into my G suit at either knee. "You won't be needing these," he grinned illogically.

Capt. Dan was now in his front seat, though I could only see the top of his red helmet over the headrest. "How're we doing?" he said over the intercom. I was breathing through my oxygen mask like Darth Vader in *Star Wars: pssshhttt* Great *pssssshhttt.*

He started the engine, a low whine that steadily built, making the cockpit needles quiver and the people on the tarmac cover their ears. A word about this Pratt & Whitney F100-PW-220 turbofan engine: it produces twenty-five thousand pounds of thrust. We would weigh twenty-three thousand pounds on takeoff. Any craft with a thrust-to-weight ratio greater than one-to-one is essentially a rocket. Cut off the wings and it will still fly, if erratically. Craning my head to one side, I could barely make out the wings. The total wingspan is only thirty-two feet.

Over my amplified breathing I could hear Dan request a "straight climb to sixteen thousand" feet from Nellis Control. During the pre-flight briefing he had told me that we would take off and then accelerate to 400 knots and then climb vertically, straight up, to sixteen thousand in about eight seconds. Nellis is at about two thousand feet above sea level, so our rate of climb would be seventeen hundred feet per second. The Empire State Building is 1,472 feet. So clearly this is a rapid way of getting to sixteen thousand feet.

"O-*kay,* Chris, if you're ready, we'll be taking off. Here we go."

I'd be dishonest if I said that I remembered much of it, but reconstructing: we lifted fifty or so feet off the runway at 150 knots. Dan increased speed. "O-*kay,* now I'm going to add the afterburners. . . ." I do remember an amazing sensation of speed and being shoved back into the seat.

We increased speed to 450 miles an hour. (Big commercial jets take off at about 130.) I think I remember another hearty "O-*kay*" from the front, but then my world went weird. I recall that it became suddenly very eerily quiet inside. How they manage that, I don't know, since being near one of these birds on takeoff will leave you saying "Beg pardon?" for the rest of your life. I suppose Mr. Doppler has something to do with it. Either way, I remember no sound, only a vise squeezing everything below my waist. The G suit had automatically inflated to compensate for the four Gs of our vertical ascent.

The video records that I turned my head to the side, but I have no memory of that, only of Dan's reassuring voice saying, with wonder in it, "Seven thousand, ten thousand . . . O-*kay,* leveling off at fifteen thousand, five hundred feet," at which point I found myself looking up through the canopy at Nellis Air Force Base, three miles below. We were upside down. Nice touch.

"How'd you like that?"

I wish I could report that I said something more interesting than, "Wow," but it's all on video. I did have the presence of mind, at least, to ask where was the drinks cart. And the sense to reach back and toggle myself some 100 percent pure oxygen, as my stomach was telling me, "I don't think we're in Kansas anymore, Toto."

"Okay, Chris, we'll fly about forty miles to the northwest, and then I'll turn the aircraft over to you."

I liked the just-flying-straight for forty miles part, though I wasn't at all sure about the taking over the aircraft part. We were now going about 400 mph. There was no sense of speed, other than the airspeed indicator. And, come to think of it, the clouds that were going by sort of briskly.

We did our forty miles in no time and were now over a much-practice-bombed quadrant of the Nevada desert called Indian Springs. It was here, in January 1982, that the Thunderbirds suffered their worst disaster: four T-38s flying the "line abreast" formation did a loop and crashed into the ground. The four scorch marks in the desert floor were eerily symmetrical. The reconstruction revealed that the stabilizer—the part of the tail that keeps an aircraft flying steadily—on the lead pilot's plane had jammed, so that instead of coming out of the loop, the equivalent of a back flip off a diving board, he went into the ground at 478 mph. The other three pilots, eyes trained to stay on the next man, followed him into the ground. A total of eighteen Thunderbirds have been killed since 1953.

"Okay, Chris, I'm going to do an aileron roll now."

We rolled upside down and over. All very smooth and effortless.

"All right, you have the aircraft."

I used to fly a Piper Cherokee, which is to an F-16 what a bumble bee is to a falcon. I remember struggling with the trim tab to get the wheel so that I didn't have to push it or pull it to fly straight-and-level. I took the stick in my right hand and nudged it to the left, imperceptibly, ever so cautiously. Immediately we were upside down.

"Fan-tastic!" said Dan, as if I had performed brilliantly. This is simply Thunderbird politesse. Another nudge and we were right side up again.

"Ready for a loop?"

It would be nice to report that I was indeed avid for a loop, but the truth is I was avid for something else. I turned off the camera, not wanting this moment to became a permanent part of the record. Here I had a fleeting moment of panic wondering if I would be able to remove my oxygen mask in time. This is essential to the operation I was about to undertake, unless you want to fill your lungs with breakfast. (I understand this is medically undesirable.) It came off—Praise the Lord—in one swoop. I hoped the intercom would not be too unpleasant for poor Dan. So much for homeopathic antimotion-sickness remedies.

I felt much better afterward, despite the sweat that was pouring off my face and collecting like a puddle inside the oxygen mask. I was ready, more or less, to do the loop.

"Okay," said Dan, "let's add the smoke. . . ." The smoke trail allows you to see how round a loop you have done. My G suit inflated and I strained and grunted against four Gs. All in all it feels as though an extremely fat person has suddenly plumped down onto your lap. At the apex of the loop there was a confusing moment of upside-down five Gs—if I've got this right—weightlessness, essentially, followed by decidedly positive Gs as we came out of the loop into our own smoke trail. That part of it *was* cool. But now it was time again to avail myself of the baggie at my knee.

"How we doing?" Dan asked. After listening to my imitation of a distressed walrus, he said solicitously, "Remember, we're up here to have fun, so we can do as much or as little as you want. If you want, we can just do some sight-seeing."

If it is possible, as the general would say, for one man to love another man, that was the moment; but merely to sightsee would have been like taking a Ferrari out on the track and driving around it at 65 mph.

We did a vertical roll. I can report that this was the most nauseogenic of our maneuvers. Indeed, watching the videotape of it, on my bed a few minutes ago made me blanch anew and my scalp tingle with sweat. First we dropped down to about a thousand feet off the ground, then it was back on the throttle and vertically up, up, up for many thousands of feet, only this time rotating 360 degrees three times.

"How was that?"

"Great," I gasped. After availing myself of the baggie for the third time, I declined Dan's kind offer of performing another vertical roll myself. Instead we did a zero-G maneuver: a brief parabola at the apex of which you become weightless. Dan instructed me beforehand to remove a glove. The video shows the glove levitating off my lap, bouncing off the canopy. He said that on long, boring flights, pilots sometimes play a little game where the front-seater sips some water and does the parabola, then spits it out and with the stick guides the suspended droplet, quivering in the air like a silverly ball of mercury, backward until it plops down onto the lap of the guy in the back seat. I don't think they do this while bombing Baghdad.

We did something called an eight-point roll, a 360-degree rotation in eight, jerky installments. "One-" jerk "two-" jerk "three-" jerk . . . My own eight-point roll was considerably less fluid than Dan's.

It was now time for the thing I was frankly not looking forward to, the nine-G turn. Dan kept politely insisting that we did not have to do nine Gs, but I had read enough about the Thunderbirds to know that "orientation fliers" such as my sad-ass self are divided into two kinds, those who do nine-G turns, and those who do not.

Dan's tone of voice became slightly more businesslike, instructing me to tense all my muscles and hold my breath, put my hands on my lap, keep my spine straight and head back. I recall thinking that it can't be possible to throw up during a nine-G maneuver, since everything is pressing *down*.

"Okay, I'll put the nose down now so we'll gain some speed . . . add the afterburners." I felt a surge forward as the F-16 accelerated to .85 Mach, or 550 knots.

"Okay, Chris, are you ready?"

"Uh hunf." I was already tensed to the consistency of granite.

"Okay, here we gooooo . . ." We were sideways to the ground now. Dan pulled back hard on the stick and we went into a tight turn.

The G suit inflated to the maximum. My hands pressed down onto my crotch. A crushingly heavy weight pushed down on my body. My helmet was nailed to the headrest. I was aware of a slight shuddering. The video shows the wings shaking. Somewhere a voice I did not recognize said, "Bingo, bingo!" Dan later explained that this was a fuel-warning device he had preset. At cruising speed, the F-16 carries enough fuel to stay aloft for two hours and ten minutes. With the afterburners on, it will use up all its fuel in fifteen minutes, which pretty much limits the number of nine-G turns you can do while dogfighting over enemy territory. In one hour and ten minutes of flying, we used two and a half tons of fuel.

But now I was aware of Dan's voice again . . .

". . . Seven . . . eight . . . there it is, nine!"

"We did it?"

"You sure did!" I appreciated the "you," even if all I had done was to strain through the bowel movement from hell. But there it is on the video of the heads-up display, the pilot's TelePrompTer-like screen that displays all his instruments, a little digital "9.1" at the lower left-hand corner.

The entire turn had lasted five seconds. I had not blacked out, or even lost any peripheral vision, my solitary, pathetic moment of triumph that morning. I don't think I could have lasted another two seconds without blacking out. During their aerial shows, the Thunderbirds execute a seven-G turn lasting *eighteen* seconds, at a hundred and fifty feet above the ground. No margin of error for blacking out there. That is why Thunderbirds tend to be in their early thirties and possessed of great physical strength.

The audio portion of the video records a high-pitched whine as we came out of the turn. I think that was me. The camera shows me looking pale, but giving two wan thumbs-up. Then I turned it off, not wanting my memento of the day to show the gastrointestinal aftereffects of nine Gs.

We did a victory lap over Hoover Dam. Just before landing, Dan did two tight three-G turns to shed airspeed, but by now they hardly amounted to shucks, and then we were on the ground. The canopy was lifting, fresh, desert air filling the cockpit. I came down the ladder slowly, stood wobbly beside Dan for a photo while he pinned a Nine G button on my flight suit. Then I crawled to the Life Support Room where I availed myself of a trash basket in the corner. We did the debriefing, watching the video, Dan sitting beside me hungrily eating an aromatic nitrite-red weiner with chili.

The nine-G turn doesn't look like much on the video. All you see is a shifting of sunlight and a dark-visored figure crushed inert in his seat. The only sound is the loud, three-second exhalations, the strange "Bingo, bingo," and a high-pitched whine that might have been the last of my air being crowbarred out of my lungs. I had to make a conscious effort to stay awake in the debriefing room, even though I was watching a video of myself in the cockpit of a fighter plane. But there was an insight in this fatigue. This is how they will feel, a lifetime of dinner guests glancing frantically at each other: *Oh God, here it comes, his Thunderbirds video. Tell him we have a baby-sitter and have to get home.*

—*Forbes FYI*, 1996

Macho Is
as Macho Does

One night I had the words "fuck off" tattooed on the outside edge of my right hand. Some explanation is, obviously, in order.

I was eighteen and drunk, both on the six-pack of beer I'd been plied with to ease the pain of the far more elaborate (and tasteful) tattoo being applied to my biceps and with the thrill of being a young merchant marine on my first night of shore leave in Hong Kong.

But, you logically ask, why those particular two words? A joke on the ship's officers. The offensive phrase was burned through my epidermis on the part of the hand most visible to the recipient of a salute. Get it? I didn't either, on waking up to discover three regions of acute distress: my head, my biceps, and my hand. In a nice bit of karmic comeuppance, my assigned task that day was to swab clean the cargo winches: twelve hours of 100-degree heat, with my newly embroidered hand immersed the whole time in kerosene. Every letter sizzled memorably.

The second question begged by this act of juvenile idiocy is Why do men do these things? I don't mean, Why do men have four-letter words tattooed on their hands? The only other instance that I know of is the Robert Mitchum character in the 1955 movie *The Night of the Hunter*. (How lovely to share this distinction with a famous psychopathic murderer. I must have a swastika tattooed on my forehead and achieve affinity with Charles Manson.) No, what I mean is, Why must some men play the tough guy?

One of the nice things about not being eighteen anymore is looking back on all those times when you practiced smoking in front of the mirror, impressed your date by revving the engine at the stoplight, tried on twenty pairs of sunglasses until you found the kind Paul Newman wore, talked fuel injectors and .357 Magnums while holding a long-necked beer bottle, and wore blue jeans so tight that you ended up with sore balls and a rash. Yes, one of the nice things about being forty-one and happily married is that you understand how ridiculous all that really was—and how ridiculous it still is.

Sometime between eighteen and forty-one I learned something: that the ones who are really tough never act tough. Unless—as with the saying about never drawing a gun unless you plan to use it—they intend to be tough, in which case it's usually over very fast.

After the merchant marine, I went to Yale, where there was very little macho posturing going on. A lot of intellectual posturing, for sure, but no "Me Tarzan" stuff. This was the early 1970s—Nixon, antiwar demonstrations, women's lib, Alan Alda, *homo sensitivus*—and anyone who even tried to look tough would have been laughed at and told to go enroll in TM (transcendental meditation, for you Generation Xer's).

It wasn't until I started work in New York City as a magazine editor that I met my first genuinely fake tough guy. He was a writer. (Surprise!) He wore mirrored sunglasses—the kind that look exactly like mirrors, that is—and he would come to the office wearing a Porsche racing jacket crammed with stripes and patches. It was made of this silvery material—faux flame-retardant?—so shiny it looked as if it had been made with cast-off astronaut-suit material. At first I was mightily impressed. After four years of Shakespeare, Blake, and Joyce, here was a real-world writer. He smoked Camels; drank "Stoli, up"; made a show of annoying our boss, the editor; and told lurid stories of hanging out with extremely brutal South Bronx street gangs to research the big piece he was doing for us.

But after a time I started to wonder. (The best thing about a good education is it equips you with a good shit detector.) His teeth were unappetizingly brown from nicotine. He coughed a lot and wheezed after climbing a flight of stairs. The editor whom he cast as Walter Burns to his Hildy Johnson confided to me with wry amusement that he had been escorted every inch of the way by New York police during his research on the South Bronx gangs. As for the jacket, it became pellucidly clear that he had never set foot in a Porsche or any other racing car.

The mirrored shades were, I suspect, to cover up the aftereffects of too many Stolis, up, at Elaine's, or, more subtly, perhaps they were just the perfect sunglasses for the Me Decade because they let the beholder see himself in the reflection, invariably improving his opinion of their wearer.

He died ten years later, in his early fifties, of a heart attack, on the tennis court. Not a terribly macho end.

It was partly my memory of that jacket that led me years later to lock horns publicly with one of my heroes, Garry Trudeau. I'd been working at the White House, writing speeches for then vice president Bush. At the time, Trudeau was going after Bush mercilessly for what he perceived as Bush's slavish loyalty to Reagan, raking him over the coals in strip after strip for sacrificing his "manhood." When the next Banana Republic clothing catalog arrived, I saw in it an effusive endorsement by Trudeau for a leather navy pilot's jacket. Bush had gone off at age eighteen to fly torpedo bombers in the South Pacific against the Japanese; Trudeau had not. I pointed out this irony in a repercussive letter to *The Washington Post*.

Ever since, I've been averse to military fashions on civilians. Flight jackets ought to be earned. Imagine standing in an elevator wearing one with a 388th Fighter Wing insignia and the door opening and someone who'd actually *been* with the 388th getting on.

I'm averse, too, to civilians who talk military, saying things like "Lock and load" when they're merely going into a meeting, or shouting, "Incoming!" when the boss sends down a sharp memo. One of my closest friends served with the Special Forces in Vietnam, and I have never, ever, heard him say, "Lock and load" or "Incoming!" because something wasn't going well that day at the office.

The White House, as anyone who's worked there will confirm, is a veritable platform for macho posturing. I was there during the early Reagan years, and while it's true that the place did not lack for cowboy boots, the smell of testosterone roasting around the campfire was by no means peculiar to the Reagan era. Nixon's chief of staff wore a crew cut, and JFK's people liked to one-up one another with the question "Is your wife pregnant? Mine is." White House toys are too tempting for many men (and women): flashing lights, motorcades, *Air Force One*, phone consoles with lots and lots of important-looking buttons, Uzi-toting Secret Service agents, and, most coveted of all, a White House pass on the end of a chain around your neck. I saw people wear those chains around their necks at dinner parties, pretending they'd forgotten they still had them on. *Whoops. So then I said to the president . . .*

The most conspicuous practitioners of macho on any White House staff are the advance men, the ones who arrange presidential movements and events. They wield a kind of plenipotentiary power. Who's going to tell them no? They work for the president of the United States. I've seen twentysomethings reduce governors of consequential states to fuming impotence—and relish every second of it. I watched one tell a government official of a significant foreign power, after viewing the spectacular nineteenth-century palace where the bilateral event would take place, "The facilities will be adequate." The documentary *The War Room,* about the Clinton campaign staff, shows the swagger that develops when young men get a taste of power. The advantage of the American system of government over, say, the Rwandan system is that in ours the tools of power consist of pagers and passes, theirs of guns and machetes. It is harder to laugh off the macho pretensions of a sixteen-year-old Hutu pointing an AK-47 at you.

Guns are certainly more attention-getting than even the coolest sunglasses or the flashiest Porsche jacket. Posturing with guns became literal in the 1980s with *Miami Vice,* when Crockett and Tubbs held their *biiig* pistols with both hands, in the combat stance. Up until then, TV cops had been content to hold their weapons in just one hand. (The cooler combat stance was the result of *Vice* producer Michael Mann's having previously directed and produced the film that is recognized by both security and military types as the only one to portray the world of killers with technical realism—*Thief,* starring James Caan.) Dirty Harry managed to empty his .44 Magnum—"the most powerful handgun in the world"—with only one steady hand, but by the 1980s guns were too serious to handle with just one.

I've noticed, too, that guns have become icons of masculinity. Street gangs today initiate members by having them kill whichever passing motorist signals to them that their headlights are off. The last issue of *Spy* magazine carried a piece in which well-known rap musicians talked with fondness about their guns. Clearly we've arrived at a weirdly evolved stage of gun macho. A few weeks ago I was on a jury that convicted a man of it. He had drunk "about twenty-four" beers one day—this according to his own defense witness—and then, when no girls would dance with him at a party, stuck a loaded .22 revolver in the temple of a man who'd got on the elevator at the wrong moment. The police call this type of posturing "ADW (Gun)," assault with a dangerous weapon. It can get you about ten years, but I have little doubt that he'll be back among us soon, probably in need of an even more urgent expression of his compromised manhood.

He was just a small-time punk loser, seeking to impose his own loser status on the other guy. The tough-guy act I find most repellent is the one affected by some Wall Streeters. Michael Lewis got their number in his book *Liar's Poker* when he wrote about show-off million-dollar bets and swaggering traders with their cigars, scatologies, and crude misogynies. Most of the really sick jokes—of the *Challenger* disaster or the Michael Jackson variety—I'm told, originate on Wall Street.

Tom Wolfe found the perfect name for this breed of puffed-up bantam cock in *The Bonfire of the Vanities:* Masters of the Universe. In the ridiculous movie version, poor Tom Hanks did what he could with Sherman McCoy, given the deplorable script, and managed a few nice moments of swagger, as when he shrugs over losing half a billion dollars of a client's money and grins and says to a fellow MOTU, "We're not going to get upset about $600 million, are we?" Michael Douglas did a fine job of showing the effect of too much money on the prostate with his portrayal of Gordon Gekko in *Wall Street,* shouting "Lock and load!" to his assistant as he launches another hostile takeover.

Give me the posturing of the businessmen of yesteryear any day. At least this one: Sally Bedell Smith, in her biography of William Paley, founder of CBS, recounts a gem of an instance. Paley was visiting his Long Island neighbor John Hay Whitney, owner of the *Herald Tribune.* "To Paley," Smith wrote, "Jock Whitney embodied the ultimate in American masculine style. . . . A gentle rivalry flecked their friendship as a result. Once while watching television with Whitney at Greentree, Paley wanted to change the channel. 'Where's your clicker?' Paley asked, figuring Jock would have a remote-control switch at his fingertips. Jock calmly pressed a buzzer, and his butler walked up to the TV set to make the switch."

Whitney had grown up in the era of Teddy Roosevelt's "Speak softly and carry a big stick." (And clicker.) Lately, U.S. foreign policy seems to be all talk and no dick. Here was Clinton on the campaign trail: "The Serbian aggression against Bosnia-Herzegovina . . . must end. It is time for America, acting in concert with its allies, to exert strong leadership." This is not to suggest that America ought to send in the cavalry in an attempt to eradicate religious and ethnic hatreds that go back half a millennium: only that talking tough without follow-through looks as ridiculous on nations as it does on eighteen-year-olds, but with far worse potential for trouble. Bush's words after Saddam Hussein's invasion of Kuwait, "This will not stand," would now sound pretty hollow if Saddam were still receiving his mail in Kuwait City. General Colin Powell was not putting on the macho when he announced his war plan with a matter-of-factness startling to our government-pronouncement-jaded ears, "First we are going to cut [the Iraqi army] off," he said. "Then we are going to kill it." Powell was the most plainspoken military man since Sherman.

People made fun of Reagan for playing the tough guy, just an old ham actor turned president, but in the end there was somehow something convincing about his toughness. Certainly, the Evil Empire was convinced; after the fall of the Soviet Union, it was learned that in the early 1980s the Kremlin thought Reagan was planning to go to war against them if they pursued their policy of foreign aggression. This said more for their paranoia than it did for Reagan's bellicosity, but they blinked first, and the Iron Curtain came down within a year of Reagan's leaving office, so the historians may decide it was more than just acting. He certainly demonstrated toughness of the personal kind when he took Hinckley's bullet in the chest. It's a test I fervently hope I never have to take, but in the event I do, I hope I'll have the scrappiness, as he did, to ask the doctors as I go under if they're all Republicans.

The tattoo? The one on my biceps is still there, a little faded but clear enough to alarm small children on the beach. The one on my hand is no longer there.

About ten years after that night in Hong Kong, I was in the Zarzuela palace interviewing the king of Spain—a *muy macho* fellow and very admirable—and about halfway through our hour I noticed his eyes being drawn to my hand, which I then assiduously tried to hide, not wanting to have to translate "fuck off" into Castilian for His Majesty Juan Carlos de Borbón y Borbón, king of Spain. When I got back to New York, I went to a dermatologist. It was prelaser back then, so it took an old-fashioned glistening steel scalpel to cut it out—thank God I hadn't asked for "Don't Tread on Me"—and fifteen stitches to close it. It hurt, and this time there was no six-pack to ease the pain. Now, I look at the scar and think, What was I thinking?

—*Allure,* 1994

Hardly
Roughing It

Would You Belíze?

There are drawbacks to group travel, it occurred to me as I sat trapped in the back of the van listening to a woman I had only met an hour before acquaint me in immodest detail with the vicissitudes of her husband's lower colon. I was more interested in Belize, the small, coastal Central American country that I had always wanted, for some reason, to see, and where now I finally was. I nodded as politely as I could throughout her unbrief discourse on the virtues of Manchurian ginseng, as she eye-droppered some onto the tongue of her docile husband. I managed to keep an impassive face as she lectured me urgently that "you can't just dump everything into your liver—you've *got* to clean out the lymphs," but when she said brightly, "That's why Bill and I are into colonics," I averted my eyes in the direction of a jungle-covered Mayan hillock and thought, *It's going to be a long ten days.*

At the end of a disastrous experience traveling with F. Scott Fitzgerald, Hemingway announced to his wife his new rule: never travel anywhere with someone you don't love. That's not always practical, but I had made sure to bring along my good friend Tom. If you are going to spend ten days with a dozen people you've never met, it's prudent to bring some insurance along. As it turned out, our group was a collection of pleasant and varied people, including a bond broker who is a great-great nephew of Warren Harding; a Canadian real estate man with a passion for remote-controlled airplanes; another Canadian couple, he an accountant, she a former navigator in the RAF; a retired chief operating officer of a Big Board company; a couple of spry and engaging older ladies, one a children's portrait painter, the other a botanist; a well-read Connecticut couple, he a college administrator, she a bibliographer; and the colonically inclined California couple, who introduced themselves to everyone we came across as "Vegans." This turned out to be not a reference to a home planet in Alpha Centauri, but the word denoting strict vegetarianism. Watching them describe their draconian dietary requirements to the mystified peasant folks who cooked our meals in remote hamlets was a memorable part of the trip; you have not truly lived until you have witnessed a tank-topped blond from Los Angeles explain the evils of chicken to an emaciated Central American.

But there is this to be said in favor of group travel, especially with a pukka outfit like Butterfield and Robinson: everything is done for you—visas, transport, food, lodging, and if anything goes wrong, you get to yell at them and they're not allowed to yell back. I wish Butterfield and Robinson guided New York cab rides. *Eric, would you please tell Mr. Abouhalima to SLOW THE @#$% DOWN, GODDAMNIT!*

And there's this: you get to see a country like Belize through the eyes of a Jaime Awe. (Pronounced *Ah-weh.*) Jaime is a native Belizean, a professor of Mayan archeology at Trent University in Ontario, smart, funny, street-wise, someone you'd want in your lifeboat.

Not that there were any lifeboats around. We were in the interior. More than half the people who go there, go for reasons having to do with the gin-clear water off Belize's coast, for the fishing, scuba diving, beaching, tanning and general lying about. There would be some of that at the end of our trip, but now we were on our way west, climbing gradually from the mangrove swamps along the Caribbean coast, through grassy savannahs, to the foothills of the Mayan mountains in the interior. Belize doesn't have a whole lot of interior; at no point is it more than about sixty miles wide. The whole country is only slightly larger than Massachusetts, but unlike Massachusetts, it has a functioning economy and a good record on human rights, which is so rare in these parts that the country ought to be stuffed and mounted and hung above the General Assembly at the United Nations. They also speak English in Belize, so you don't have to shout at the natives in English the way you do, say, in Mexico in order to make yourself understood.

Belize used to be British Honduras. By the time we got there, last January, the British were down to about fifty troops, owing to the fact that the United States, in a rare instance of actually accomplishing something hemispheric without making a hash of it, quietly told Guatemala to drop

its idiotic, centuries-old irredentist insistence that Belize really belongs
to Guatemala. That is why, despite the fact that it has been independent
of the Crown since 1981, the British commandos stayed on, and will remain, conducting jungle warfare exercises, helicoptering out tourists
who've stepped on fer-de-lance snakes, and performing various other
vital functions, like giving the Guats the willies.

Earlier on, Belize was passed over by the *conquistadores,* probably because a lot of its coast looks like an advertisement for Off! mosquito repellent. It was finally stumbled upon by wet, disoriented, shipwrecked
British sailors in the early 1600s. There followed a period of the usual
rapine and plunder, with the difference that the economy was based on
fishing and mahogany logging, instead of on banana or sugar or coffee
plantations, so the country didn't end up being a basket case run by a lot
of resentful and voluble descendants of slaves. What slavery there was was
abolished in 1838, and the British magistrates, while strict, were fair, so
people saw that democracy, though flawed, was better than shooting up
the National Assembly every other Wednesday.

All of this was irrelevant to our purposes, since we'd come to check
out the birds, who really don't care who's in charge as long as they don't
govern by DDT, and to see Mayan ruins and caves. I like birds, and wish
them well generally, and only shoot them about once a year; but I
wouldn't say to my wife, *C'mon hon, let's go spend two weeks in Belize looking at birds.* However, if you are a bird person, then Belize is for you.
Forty percent of the people who go to Chan Chich Lodge are birders,
the other forty percent are naturalists. Put the two together, and you've
got the makings of some of the dullest conversation in any hemisphere.
The remaining twenty percent, such as ourselves, come to chill out
thirty-five miles from the nearest phone at a place where you can spend
all day reading in a hammock listening to the plummy warbling of
Orapendulas, get drunk on rum punches and then go stumble down to
the nature trail and moon the electric-eye camera set up by the Wildlife
and Conservation Society that snaps flash pictures of jaguars, pumas and
coatimundi with alarmed expressions on their faces. That's *really* getting
to know a country.

It dawned on Tom and me that we were on something perilously close
to an "eco-tour" when at the end of the first day, after a stop at the justly
famed Belize zoo and after checking into our first wilderness lodge,

Chaa Creek, we were taken for a short walk on the Pantı trail and shown in mind-numbing detail, a bunch of trees and vines. Chocolate trees, Cohuna palm trees, hog plum trees, bayal trees, trees with black orchids (the Belizean national flower), mahogany trees, cedar trees, red gumbolino trees, fiddlewood trees, sapodilla trees. There were trees that could cure dysentery, impotence, ringworm, purge amoebae, ward off evil spirits, make antibiotics, termite-proof Chippendale furniture and mask filters for World War II pilots. When, two hours later, I heard the words, "Now this is another kind of gourd . . . ," I began to feel pangs of sympathy for those Brazilian cattle ranchers who are supposed to be ruining the planet. At the herbal remedy shop at the end of the Panti trail tour, one of the women bought a bottle of something that was supposed to help her husband with his marital duties. She mentioned it a couple times over dinner, which, to judge from the expression on her husband's face, may have been a couple of times too many. This is a drawback to group travel: having twelve people know that your wife thinks you need a bottle of Belizean erection tonic.

That night at Chaa Creek, a pretty collection of hibiscus-, bougainvillaea- and poinsettia-covered thatched-roof bungalows set in a verdant valley—actually, pretty much everything is verdant in the jungle; if you sit down for more than five minutes, *you'll* be verdant—Jaime gave an interesting lecture on the Maya, specifically on their obsession with caves. I'll condense it for you: the Maya were *really* into caves. A good thing, too, since the whole region is filled with them, owing to the heavy rainfall eroding the porous limestone underneath. The Maya thought caves were the entrance to hell. Having grown up using the New York City subways, I immediately understood why they would think this. They left food in caves, sacrificed animals and humans in caves, buried their honored dead in caves, and ate hallucinogenic mushrooms in caves while ritually mutilating themselves, generally by piercing their tongues and penises with long, obsidian needles. I got all this from Jaime, and he has a Ph.D. in it, so you know it's true. Jaime speculated that the Maya had disappeared due to problems resulting from population stress. My own theory was that people who eat psychotropic mushrooms and crawl into caves to perforate their tongues and penises are not going to make it to the Super Bowl.

The next day, we went into a cave. This was unquestionably the high point of the trip. Jaime told us that only about 2 percent of people who come to Belize do this, which was encouraging to hear, since, as a group trudging up the steep hill with our expensive cameras, expensive hiking boots, our fanny packs and our multicolored clothes and cute hats, we collectively looked like a bunch of dorks. That's another problem with group touring, trying not to feel like a dork.

At any rate, we went in about three-quarters of a kilometer, however much that is, and about three hundred feet down (a hundred meters). I discovered that I am not a cave person. Despite the amazingly preserved Mayan pots we saw along the way, dating to 500–600 B.C., I kept saying to Tom, "I've seen enough. Let's go back." But Tom, being a lawyer, wanted to press on, probably sensing a massive class-action suit against Butterfield and Robinson. I was left to conclude that I was the only real dork in the group. On we went, until we came to a small opening in the damp limestone. We lowered ourselves by rope down into a chamber about one hundred and twenty feet high by seventy feet long. In the center of the packed-earth ground was a stele about the size and shape of a tombstone, surrounded by a circle of smaller ceremonial stones. This was the spot, Jaime explained, where they cut out the hearts. This produced in me intense stirrings of numinousness and wonder, as well as a keen appreciation for not having been born in Belize in 500–600 B.C.

We had lunch nearby at Checem Ha. We ate chicken with rice and red beans, coleslaw and fried plantains, liberally covered with Marie Sharp's Hot Pepper Sauce, the catsup of Belize, and washed it down with ice-cold Belikin beers. It was about the best meal any of us had ever had. Except for the Vegans. They complained to the lovely, toothless woman who cooked our meal about the horrors of animal fat; then they ate some rice and beans. The She-Vegan, as Tom was now privately calling her, produced a bottle of Beano, from which she made the He-Vegan take an ample spoonful. This is another downside to group travel: being made to swallow antiflatulence medicine by your wife in front of twelve people who by now have concluded that you really are a dork.

Back at Chaa Creek we talked with its owner, Mick Fleming, a hearty, burly, outgoing British expatriate. He told funny stories about a roguish jaguar hunter and Mayan tomb-looter. He said that we wouldn't have to worry about banditos tomorrow. Banditos had been preying on his customers on the road to the Mayan ruins at Tikal, across the border in Guatemala. They would jump out of the bushes and stick 16-gauge shotguns in your face. They were doing it quite regularly, up to three times a week, until Mick got the Belizean Defense Forces to persuade the Guatemalan armed forces to do something about it. They'd caught them six weeks ago. I had mixed feelings, hearing this. It would be nice to say back home that we'd been robbed by banditos, but being mugged is being mugged in any language, and a 16-gauge shotgun makes a big hole whether you measure it in inches or centimeters.

The next day we drove to Tikal. Guatemala is to Belize what Ireland is to England: the butt of the jokes. The standard of living and the quality of the roads drop the moment you cross the border. Also, you see lots of soldiers, not a good sign; in ten days in Belize we saw one policeman, and I don't think he had a gun. Even the traffic cops in Guatemala seemed to have the latest submachine gun. In the last thirty-odd years, Guatemala has had an on-again, off-again civil war going that has killed a hundred thousand, about half the population of Belize, another reason Belize is not eager to be annexed by Guatemala.

Tikal was one of the great Mayan cities. It covers nine square miles, has eighteen huge temple structures and 2,080 stone roof structures. Between 1956 and 1969, one hundred scholars from the University of Pennsylvania excavated it, with some help from one thousand local laborers. They uncovered eighty of those 2,080 buildings. Jaime said that there may be as many as ten thousand other buildings underneath all that jungle. Just keeping what's been excavated from turning back into jungle is work; for instance, they have to scrape the Temple of the Lost World once a year with spatulas to ward off the green crud. They pile rocks outside the entrance to temples to protect the frescoes inside. Rocks attract snakes; snakes deter looters.

The temples are steep. A guide had recently fallen down one of them to his death. In six hours of climbing we did a year's worth of Stairmaster. Our local guide droned on in an amusing, Victorian English monotone under the hot sun—"We are now in de central acropolis, built on top of de previous structure, obeying de needs of time . . ."—as he told us what had happened here between 600 B.C. and A.D. 1000. As usual with Mayan temples, sacrifices were the main event. The victims, Luis the guide told us, "were narcotized, then degraded, de arms and leg joints dislocated, then dey were tied over the stone, decapitated, the blood collected and offered and burned with herbs." One unhappy prisoner was kept for seventeen years of bloodletting rituals before having his head cut off. They played a version of basketball, with a human skull coated with hard rubber; the losing team ended up on the sacrificial slabs. To date, archeologists have found no evidence of any baseball strikes in Tikal.

It was a society in which you were really better off being a noble. That's true of 99 percent of civilizations, but given what went on here, being a noble at least kept the scalpel-wielding priests at arm's length. The Maya had a keen grasp of the advantages of class. If they'd had an airline, it would have been all first-class; coach passengers would have been tied to the wing, with the flight attendants coming by to poke holes in their tongues. The better neighborhoods at Tikal were strictly off-limits to the common folk. The only way you got to the top of one of those temples was if you were building it or depositing your heart on it. The nobles wore lots of jade—Lord Ah Cacao's robes contained sixteen pounds of jade—and got to eat a special diet containing more protein than the working-class schmoes, as a result of which their skeletons are on average ten centimeters longer than the others. Luis mentioned that they were given to "ritual enemas, with powdered [hallucinogenic] mushrooms." On hearing this, the Vegans began to murmur among themselves. The nobles wore beautiful headdresses of quetzal feathers and hummingbird wings. According to Luis, "They made themselves cross-eyed as a sign of beauty." I don't know how they managed that, but you can see it in the frescoes. They all do look cross.

I remember two things of Tikal. The first was a scratch of Mayan graffiti, perfectly preserved, showing a skull beside two vertical bars and two dots. Each dot represents five, each bar, one; the skull represents death. It means "twelve dead." Whether from disease, or losing at basketball, or in battle, no one knows, but there it was on the wall, twelve hundred years later.

The second was watching the sunset from the top of Temple IV. Lord Ah Cacao finished Temple IV in A.D. 741, a year before Charlemagne was born. We were almost two hundred feet up, above the jungle canopy, looking down over all of Tikal, watching the lengthening shadows and listening to a cacophony of macaws, red-lored parrots, black falcons and howler monkeys. Hurrying back to the Jungle Lodge through the gloaming, Tom and I got briefly lost, which was not a comforting sensation in this vast, tangly agora of bats and ghosts; but soon we were swigging white cane rum with Jaime as two British women swam topless in the dirty pool.

By 1:00 P.M. the next day we were back in Belize, "civilization," as our driver smiled once we'd made it across the border. A de Havilland Twin Otter STOL (Short Takeoff and Landing) flew us to Gallon Jug, where a bus took us to a miracle of exotic hospitality built on the plaza of a Mayan ruin. Chan Chich Lodge consists of twelve thatched-roof bungalows, very good dining room, very good bar, nature trails, birds, jungle cats, monkeys, unexcavated ruins, a forbidding river, and that's about it. It was the brainchild of Barry Bowen, who owns the beer and Coca-Cola concession in Belize. When you control the flow of beer and Coke in a hot country, you're doing very well. He hired two ex–U.S. Special Forces officers, and the wife of one of them, to build and run this sequestered Xanadu. It's run extremely well. The only complaint I heard in our three days there was from the Vegans, who, apparently, were simply not getting enough protein.

Jimmy Carter had been there recently, with seventeen of his children and grandchildren, and the usual battalion of Secret Service agents. It's not quite the same as hearing that George Washington had slept there, but in the jungle you take the cachet as it comes.

By now Tom and I had had enough tree lore to last us the nineties, so we mostly lay in our hammocks reading, secure in the knowledge that no phones would ring, the ultimate luxury. There can't be many places on earth as lovely as the porches at Chan Chich, entangled with hibiscus, bougainvillaea, wisteria, golden shower, wandering Jew, avocado, poinsettia, flame of the woods, ginger and oyster plants. Toward sunset, the birds start to go bonkers. Ornithologists probably have a more precise term for it, but whatever it is, it's loud, starting out as a crepuscular Vivaldi string quartet, with the *poip-poip* of the tree frogs, and gradually building, with a little help from the ubiquitous oscellated turkeys, to an 1812 Overture. But it is nothing compared with what wakes you up in the middle of the night. The first morning, Tom said to me, somewhat shaken, "Did you *hear* that?" Yes, I shuddered. What *was* that? It sounded like the Primeval Id, being denied antacid tablets. The answer—Jaime had all the answers—was several hundred very agitated howler monkeys. "It was probably," he said, "some male dominance issue." Whatever it was, you would not want to get in the middle of it. No wonder the Maya went into caves and perforated their penises.

In the midmorning heat you could walk to where the real birdwatching action was—at the dump. The smell was a bit high, but the mounds of ordure were covered with enough feathered delights to keep any birder scribbling happily in his logbook. At night, after dinner, we hung by the bar, listening to Tom and Norman, the two Vietnam-era Green Berets who built Chan Chich, with twenty or so laborers in just twenty months, for $400,000. One story they told was an object lesson on why the omens are not good for the human species.

Some Mennonites and Belizeans and Guatemalans had been illegally logging Guatemalan mahogany and hauling it over the border into Belize, on Barry Bowen's land. Tom and Norman found a pile of it worth about one million dollars. They told Bowen about it and offered to burn it. No, Bowen said, we need to let the government know about this. Thus did the Belizean government and the Guatemalan government enter in and start a game of diplomatic Ping-Pong. The Guatemalans said, We'll come and get the lumber. The Belizean government, well aware of Guatemala's smouldering lust for annexation, said, No, we'll bring it to you. Oh no, said Guatemala, no Belizean trucks on Guatemala's sovereign soil. Stand-off. So, said Tom, we now have Guatemalan troops in Belize guarding the lumber while Guatemala builds a road through a nature preserve in order to get to it. He shook his head. "The lumber will have rotted by the time they get to it, and squatters will come in on the new road and settle in the biosphere." Tom and Norman had some perspective on it, anyway, having survived a previous jungle conundrum.

The next day we STOL-ed to Ambergris Cay, on the coast. It rained and was buggy, and the beaches were full of waste. It would be stretching it to call Ambergris Cay "paradise." Some went scuba diving, and reported great success, some of us hung around San Pedro, shooting pool and eating stone crab claws at Elvi's. Every time we heard a plane take off, Tom and I would look up longingly, like the people in Rick's Cafe in *Casablanca* at the flight to Lisbon. It was time to go home. We had half an hour between planes in Miami to call up the Vegans' airline and cancel their special meals.

—*Forbes FYI,* 1994

One Way to Do
the Amazon

◻

Day One

On way from Newark (freezing) to Manaus (steambath) aboard Forbes's Boeing 727, *The Capitalist Tool,* I read aloud to company from Alex Shoumatoff's remarkable book *The Rivers Amazon.* Contains graphic medical descriptions of various ways Amazon can ruin your entire day—including nose dropping off, blindness from insects crapping in eyeball—and memorable section on toothpick-size catfish with fondess for "mammalian orifices," which must be surgically removed.

"Unh," says someone.

About to move on to snakes and furry arachnids, am told to shut up.

We land. *The Highlander* and *The Virginian* are waiting at the dock in Manaus, guarded by men with shotguns. Glenn Ellison, *Highlander's* second steward, pipes us aboard with bagpipes.

Forbes—hereinafter, Malcolm—gives us the Cook's tour: The topmost deck is a solarium, as if a *bateau-mouche* had been grafted on top. There are four guest suites in addition to Malcolm's master suite, with its whirlpool and steambath and Spanish-galleon rear picture window. I draw Burgundy. Others are Blue, White, and Gray. The king of Bulgaria says, "It's clever. This way no one is offended by being given 'Cabin Number Four.' "

After dinner our omnicompetent guide, Silvio Barros, gives us a brief sketch of what's ahead. Tomorrow we'll see the famous Manaus opera house, built by the rubber barons at the turn of the century, when Manaus was booming. Contrary to popular legend, Enrico Caruso did not sing there. Silvio apologizes that no operas are being currently put on.

"It's the perfect opera house," observes Kip Forbes. "You can see it but you can't hear it."

Day Two

We bus around Manaus. The public market, built by Eiffel, reeks of putrescent catfish. Vultures swarm over shantytowns. At the opera house we learn that after a military coup in the seventies, the military government decreed that the beautiful rose-colored building be painted—gray, to conform with all official buildings. The kings of Greece and Bulgaria, having extensive experience of the military mind, shake their heads.

A buffet is spread at the Hotel Tropical. We're given drinks made of *cachaça*—napalm-strength sugarcane rum—and passion fruit. Eyeballs poached, we eat grilled local fish, *tucunaré*. For dessert, a manioc pudding with cloves. "Let's hope the prussic acid has been leached out," says the king of Bulgaria, diving in.

We cross the Rio Negro, a major Amazonian tributary, and hike a short distance into the jungle to Salvador Lake.

Lucky Roosevelt to Malcolm: "You know, Archie's grandfather died of his trip to Brazil. He caught a fever and he was never right after that."

The appearance of a three-foot-long crocodilian inhibits immediate gleeful scampering into the lake, though everyone's faint with heat and soaked through with sweat. Lucky, Esteban, and Kip gamely jump in.

Archie: "They say alligators only take small pieces out of you."

Guide: "Yes, but sometimes the wrong pieces."

Later, during cocktails on the *Highlander,* Pat Kluge appears, stunning in crinkly white cotton shirt, with boa constrictor, Gus, coiled around her arms. Gus belongs to our sous-chef, David, and eats day-old chicks and mice. Mice hard to come by in Manaus. Rats plentiful, but generally too large for Gus to swallow.

Dinner of cold pear soup, tiny lamb chops, rosettes of baked mashed potato. Dessert is piped in by the steward to the tune of "The Green Hills of Tyrol": three sherbets garnished with mint leaves and candied violets, all inside brass incense pots from Thailand.

Kip explains his father was served petits fours inside these at a hotel in Thailand, with dry ice smoke pluming out of the holes. He expresses disappointment because the Manaus dry ice factory was closed until tomorrow afternoon. "We'll just have to make do." Guests feel insulted and complain bitterly. After dinner, Cuban cigars courtesy of Hassan, king of Morocco, via diplomatic pouch, hence not illegal, Malcolm emphasizes.

The *Virginians* are piped ashore to "Auld Lang Syne." The passengers and crew of the Greek cruiser docked across from us are leaning over the rails to get a glimpse of the Greek king and queen. As Constantine returns their waves, the ship issues three deafening blasts from its stack— "Go with God" in marine signal language. The crowd roars, the scene suddenly charged and cinematic.

The big ship pulls out, eventually becoming a blazing wedding cake of strung lights in the distance. We watch it recede in the darkness.

"It's interesting," says Simeon. "Tino (the king) went aboard before dinner to have an ouzo with the crew. But the captain never showed up. So he thinks he must have views."

Day Three

Up early for canoe trip into jungle. Malcolm advises us to oil up against mosquito bites—the local variety is chloroquine-resistant—with something made by Avon (Ding-Dong) called Skin-So-Soft. It's a body lotion made for soft-skinned ladies, but apparently the malarial anopheles mosquitoes detest it.

"Who told you about this?" I ask, skeptical but nonetheless smearing myself all over.

"Nancy Pierpont."

"Who?"

Kip interjects, as Kip often does: "You know Nancy. She has a *great* sense of humor."

Above us we see a half-dozen monkeys of the "smelly" macaque variety, but our nostrils are filled with the sweetness of *damas de noche* blossoms.

Back to the ship for Malcolm's press conference. He enters with Gus wrapped around his arm and assures twenty reporters that Brazil's $100 billion foreign debt will just have to be "restructured." (He does not add, "because your government is inept." We are guests here.) The press greatly relieved. Front-page headline next day: "Forbes: No Crisis in Brazil."

Day Four

We (finally) shove off. Ten miles downriver we pass from the cola-red of the Rio Negro into the café-au-lait of the Solimões, the river that will carry us the twelve hundred miles to Iquitos, with some help from the twin GM 900-horsepower diesel engines. The meeting of the two waters is dramatic. They don't mix for a long stretch, owing to differing density, speed, and coloration.

Glenn the bagpiper appears in full regalia at the bow to pipe us through to the tune, naturally, of "The Meeting of the Waters."

"Know why the waters don't mix?" asks Dr. Nunez. He is a young and friendly Brazilian specialist in tropical diseases who Malcolm thought it prudent to have along.

"Speed, density—"

"Racism," he smiles.

After lunch Kip and I inflate the wading pool we bought in the market at Manaus and splash about. The only thing the designer left out was a pool. We are three degrees under the equator, and the sun blazes hot—about 105 degrees at midday. After no more than fifteen minutes, skin turns pink. After thirty minutes, precancerous.

Later that afternoon, sitting in the fantail salon with the wonderful dioramas of whaling scenes and shipbuilding, I hear a bang-bang-BANG underneath. Should I tell the captain? Minutes later the crew are pulling up the floorboards and frowning. Half an hour later they're donning wet suits. Dr. Nunez, who has a bit of the perverse about him, watches them while calling out the names of various things they are apt to run into down there.

"Pirarucu!" he trills. These get up to ten feet, two hundred fifty pounds.

"Piraiba!" Six feet, three hundred pounds.

"Piranha!" Small, but massively inconvenient.

We tender over for dinner with the *Virginian*s, Lucky not altogether happy about bats diving in and out of flashlight beams. Kip clutches a catalog on the Forbes collection of Victoriana. "I thought King Constantine might be interested, since he's Victoria's great-great-grandson." Simeon is related as well. My eyes fasten on a photograph of a huge pair of bloomers. Item number 44: "Personally Hers." I suppress the temptation to ask Kip what a pair of imperial bloomers goes for.

John Kluge shows us around. The *Virginian* used to be the *Highlander IV*, so Kip is familiar. John, like Malcolm, collects. An entire wall of beautiful and rare seashells. Also, various early U.S. Navy dirks and cutlasses; an arrow from the *Mary Rose*, Henry VIII's flagship; a letter from Nelson; a hammock hook from the USS *Constitution*. His other interests, past and present: *Cats* (22 percent); Ice Capades; Harlem Globetrotters; a collection of seventy-two carriages; serious quantities of art, including a personally financed ten-year project of "narrative art" entitled "Seven Lagoons"; Democratic party politics. John is the only Democrat I know worth $4 billion. Come to think of it, he is the only *person* I know worth $4 billion.

Kip talks about Trinchera Ranch, his father's place in Colorado. Originally 170,000 acres. "It was nice, because everything you could see from the house was ours. Then Pa bought an additional eighty-seven thousand acres and it was even nicer, because everything you saw from the plane was ours." I like Kip.

It dawns on me uneasily that I am the only one calling the king of Bulgaria Simeon.

Day Five

Malcolm helicopters in from meeting with President Sarney.

"How was he?"

"In better shape than he should be." I take this as a reference to Brazil's foreign debt, now over $100 billion.

He showers and changes into a pair of extremely loud WASP-psychedelic-pink slacks with smiling lions heads and plays bridge with the Roosevelts and Kip.

I read Jacques Cousteau's enthralling book on his Amazon expedition. The river we are on has ten tributaries longer than the Mississippi, produces twelve times its outflow, and could fill Lake Ontario in three hours.

The current here is swift, five knots, bringing huge trees that crash against the hull at night, starting you awake. At first I wondered why the ship swerved so sharply at night; now I know why. The current also carries floating islands of *canarana* grass, which King Constantine and Lord Romsey shoot at with deer rifles.

Silvio arrives as we dive into butterscotch sundaes and says the *Virginian* has radioed. Some of them are planning to spend the night in the jungle.

"Why?" asks Malcolm. A *wise* question.

"They want to hear the sounds of the jungle," says Silvio.

Malcolm ponders this. "We'll supply them with a tape."

Kip and I volunteer to go along. Rather, Kip volunteers and I go along. Comfortable trips make the worst stories. Best to have something to complain about.

Tonight is Archie's sixty-ninth birthday. Some of us learn for the first time that he was in the CIA from 1947 to 1974 and that he will publish his memoirs this year. Lucky reveals he speaks "about twenty" languages.

After dinner we watch rest of Cousteau documentary, in which Amazonians tell him about pink dolphins seducing women and getting them pregnant.

Day Six

We go ashore and hack our way several hundred yards into the jungle to get flavor of it. After three minutes Malcolm, dripping in sweat, tells Silvio, "I think we've got the point." Hearty agreement all around, but we are urged on by the guides and press on, providing a banquet for ants and mosquitoes.

At lunch Simeon recounts the story of being driven out of Bulgaria by the Communists at age ten, after the Soviets murdered his father, King Boris, and his uncle, the regent. His mother was convinced they were never going to be allowed to leave. When the train carrying him and his mother mysteriously stopped just short of the Turkish border, his mother thought their "Varennes" was at hand: a summary firing squad against the siding. But it was the engineer who had stopped the train, refusing to go any farther. "I will not be the one to drive the king out of Bulgaria!" It was probably his death warrant. A Turkish engineer was sent for, and Simeon and his mother made it safely out of their country.

Halfway through this much more detailed and spellbinding story, he stops and says, "I think I must be boring you."

"My God," sputters Malcolm. "Most of us have to read history. We don't get the chance every day to talk to it."

Simeon is a remarkable man: scholarly, pious, a natural raconteur. That night I start calling him "Your Majesty." He is amused by this and starts calling me "Your Excellency."

Day Seven

We're about half the way to Iquitos, six hundred miles from Manaus.

Breakfast conversation fixes on the enormous black beetle that has affixed itself to our upper deck during the night. I do not join in the excitement over the errant coleoptera because Kip and I are preparing to helicopter forty-five miles upriver to join up with the *Virginian*s for our night in the jungle.

We land in a soccer field in the town of Fonte Boa, and are swarmed by small children—one of whom I see is wearing a Banana Republic T-shirt—and the king of Greece. Furious preparations are underway aboard the *Virginian* for our expedition. Lord Romsey is packing a Walther PPK, the king has a .38 tucked into his waistband.

Two very hot and unpleasant hours later we are paddling in dugout canoes through the *varzea,* the flooded forest. Piranhas dimple the surface and larger things splash behind half-submerged rubber trees. Vines droop like snakes. The Cutter mosquito repellent—God bless you, Mr. Cutter—burns like acid on our sweat-drenched faces.

The king and Lord Romsey go off to shoot deer—or anything furry or feathery that moves. We sit miserably in the dugouts, provender for ectoparasites, chiggers, mosquitoes, and protozoans. (As I write this two weeks later, I scratch at a bubbly rash that has turned my body from head to toe into a Rand McNally relief map.)

After a series of loud shotgun explosions, the king of Greece hoves up in a dugout, looking content and smoking a cigarette. "We had a very nice wander through the forest," he says. "Shot a few trees. One of these fellows," he grins, thumbing back toward the native guides, "was told who I am. He'd never heard of the term. He said to me, 'How do you get to be one of those?' " He laughs. "He said, 'Is it like the ones in the Bible? Why don't you have your crown?' I told him, 'Well, it's a bit hot.' Then he asked me if I knew any pharaohs."

Kip and I end up in a native hut politely but firmly declining the gracious offer of a shared meal of catfish—with head and guts—boiled in Amazon water and poured on manioc.

Hundreds of thousands of fireflies. The guides paddle silently through the forest making a *"Whoaan! Whoaan!"* sound to attract jacares—the Amazonian crocodilians. Enormous insects flit in and out of flashlight beams. Something the size of a bird—but not a bird—lands on my face.

Hours later, back at camp, the king, Pat, and Norton arrive with two small crocs, speared but still alive and looking distinctly pissed off.

We eat a dinner of tomato soup, fruit, and chocolate. Dripping with sweat, reeking, and eyes and cuts stinging with Cutter's, we spend a fitful night in hammocks covered in mosquito netting, listening to the sounds of the guides in the distance hunting jaguar.

Day Eight

A hard rain falls as we paddle back to the *Highlander,* which to these itchy eyes looks like Paris. Breakfast of eggs, bacon, muffins, juice, coffee. It turns out the others went crocodile hunting last night as well. My sense is everyone greatly relieved not to have seen any. While sitting in the back of a dugout, our helicopter pilot, Chuck Dixson, was backed into a termite nest. Chuck is reportedly not in a good mood this morning.

John Kluge arrives to play a few rubbers of bridge. I turn the thermostat to forty below and go to bed between clean sheets.

Kluge is an interesting guy: He made $7,000 playing poker while a scholarship student at Columbia—he was a classmate of Thomas Merton's, whom he remembers as a "playboy." To judge from lunch conversation, he has creamed the *Highlander* crowd at bridge, though he *says* he hasn't played it in fifteen years. Malcolm abdicates his seat to Kip. One must consider before sitting down to cards with the second-wealthiest man in America—the man started with zilch.

That night I start out of my sleep at 3:00 A.M. when a huge log *thunnngs* into our hull. I walk forward in the hailstorm of insects and stand awhile as the *Highlander's* searchlight sweeps back and forth across the water. No lights on either shore. The *Virginian* is behind us, slaloming through the logs.

Day Nine

Nearing Peru now, the river getting narrower, more interesting. Instead of a solid wall of green at river's edge, the jungle opens here and there, revealing emerald pastures and cavernous hollows with liana vines for stalactites. Another new sight: Natives paddle out in their dugouts, waving, to surf in our wake. A strange, but not unwelcome, absence of vultures.

Malcolm announces that the *Virginians* will be coming over and there will be skeet off the aft deck before lunch. We practice with the 12-gauge pump guns we have aboard to repel terrorists. Simeon and Margarita, veterans of many Spanish shoots, knock the clay birds down one after another.

Unfortunately, their king and their lord beat our king and our queen. Checkmate.

"The last thing I shot was Germans," grins Malcolm, declining a turn.

Dinner aboard *Virginian*. The Kluges lay on another fine spread: slices of beef rolled around horseradish cream on fried toast, caviar atop blue cheese, a dripping Brie *en croute,* fresh cakes, and a beautiful split of icy-cold German dessert wine.

Lots of congratulations on having made it through our night in the jungle. "Hold on," I demur, "and see if two months from now we're all covered with scarlet blotches and our noses fall off." (Prescient, that.)

Day Ten

Glenn the steward/bagpiper says he gets up every morning before dawn to practice his bagpiping on the top deck. He says the villagers come down to the water's edge and clap and dance. "It's really something." The crew is, without exception, exceptional.

We visit an Indian village a mile up an estuary, guided by Chuck above in the helo. I crouch in the high-speed Donzi as we make our approach to the village, figuring: Here are two high-speed boats and a helicopter in an area way off the beaten path. If I were the local coke baron, I'd guess I was under attack by a bunch of gringo drug agents disguised as rich WASPs.

But the villagers are welcoming. We exchange gifts and poke around. Everyone wears a little wooden cross around the neck, even the babies.

Later this afternoon we arrive at the junction of Brazil, Colombia, and Peru. As various officials of all three countries amuse themselves with the ship's copier, we go ashore.

Leticia is, you might say, a freebase-port. They assemble untaxed elec-
tronics components here, but the city's economy essentially runs on cocaine, brought down from the nearby mountains in paste form, called
pasta básica. It's sent on from here for further processing into cocaine hy-
drochloride, the alkaloid that has done so much to improve the quality
of life in the United States and elsewhere.

We motor past a flotilla of boats and seaplanes confiscated from drug
runners. Carlos, the guide aboard *Virginian*, keeps up a running mono-
logue as we walk through the streets.

"Over there I watch a man shot. Pow! He have a suitcase with one
million dollars. Cash. You see this hotel? The owner killed a few months
ago. He wouldn't sell. There on the corner—with the mustache. He was
in Manaus three years prison for cocaine. Every day in Leticia—pow!"
He shakes his head and frowns.

Day Eleven

Getting close, now. The river continuing to narrow; the ship at times
steering so close to the bank we can peer deep into the jungle. A curi-
ous and not unpleasant sensation, doing that while sitting amidst a
Gainsborough and a Toulouse-Lautrec, air-conditioned and sipping
Bloody Marys. A Conradian experience this is not.

Sad that tonight is our last—the Captain's Dinner, as the occasion is
formally called. We have covered nearly twelve hundred miles. Malcolm
is an antidote to the horror stories about extreme wealth. He's generous
as hell and he likes to have fun.

This afternoon I run into him. He has the run of the most luxurious
yacht afloat, yet there he is—oddly—alone, sitting on the top deck reading a book. We chat as the equatorial sun melts gloriously in an El Greco
of blues and oranges. I ask him, well, why the trip? Malcolm looks off
into the jungle, probably out of politeness. *What a stupid question.*

"I don't know," he shrugs and smiles.

Despite our magnificent insulation, it has been possible to absorb one
or two impressions of Amazonia. What will be memorable ten years
from now? Probably that night in the jungle, squatting in the native hut,
trying, politely, to fend off a dinner of stewed catfish *dans son jus*. How
freely it was given! That and the hard maize was all there was for this

large family. If we'd eaten, someone else would not have. I like to think that the spirit of the Amazonians is reducible to that one single act of generosity. An absurd proposition, of course. Shoumatoff writes of watching two Indian boys stoning a dog to death one afternoon out of sheer boredom and wickedness. But we will have our illusions, and the meal in the jungle will remain mine.

As for the river and land, what has surprised me is not the remoteness and the sparseness of the inhabitation, but just the opposite. Given what dire extremes nature has provided—heat, floods, disease, dangers from predators great and microbial—you wonder that man has survived here at all. Even the soil is not the rich land it is popularly supposed—a "counterfeit paradise," in the words of one biologist. That's why, in part, so many Big Thinkers like Daniel Ludwig and Henry Ford have gone bust trying to cultivate it. And why jungle can be turned into permanent desert with the aid of a few bulldozers. Once the web of interlocking fungi beneath the topsoil is disturbed, the verdure turns to moonscape, and remains so.

My own pathetic fallacy would be to say that it has great wit, the Amazon. It outfoxes everyone, from billionaires to bleeding hearts. A few years ago everyone was screaming because it was supposed to be the major source of our oxygen, and the deforestation was said to be tampering with our most basic need, the air we breathe. Now science has determined that our oxygen comes principally from marine algae. The current environmentalist worry is that the extensive deforestation may be playing havoc with the planet's budget of nitrous oxide. The proposition is as wonderful as the river itself: that by plundering the Amazon we are endangering our chief source of laughing gas. I am sanguine. For I know that most laughing gas is manufactured by politicians, not plants.

Malcolm breaks out a Margaux '78 for our last night on the Amazon. After the chocolate sundaes have been piped in, Malcolm is lavishly toasted. Archie reads a poem composed for the occasion. Malcolm toasts his pair of kings—a good hand—and says how ironic it is that the restoration of democracy in their two countries should depend on a restoration of the monarchy. Simeon rises, tears welling, and thanks him. We are on the verge of sentimentality, so Malcolm stands up, signaling coffee and cigars. "You see," he turns with a wink to the king of Greece, "the advantages of *owning* the boat?"

Day Twelve

We arrive at the dock in Iquitos. The current runs at five or six knots, so fast you think you're still moving. Braided and holstered officials swarm over us, wanting to check our milk. Our Ultra High Temperature *milk!*

We thank, inadequately, the crew for having got us here and pile into cars. The humidity is suffocating; shirts that were crisp five minutes ago are sopping. Only Simeon, dapper in gray suit, seems unwilted. As we pull away I have a last glimpse of King Constantine leaning over the rail of the *Virginian,* a dozen microphones thrust at him, the beautiful Lady Romsey at his side, translating.

Right after takeoff in *The Capitalist Tool,* Malcolm says, "Shall we buzz the ship?" He disappears forward and soon we are on a low run over the harbor. There below is *Highlander,* looking, for the first time, miniature, like one of the toy boats her owner used to float down the creek by the house he grew up in, dreaming of adventures.

—*Condé Nast Traveler,* 1987

Christmas at Sea

I grew up in Connecticut, and always felt sorry for people who didn't get to have their Christmases there. My mother was brilliant at them, and some of my happiest memories are of those long-ago, frosted times: shopping with her for wreaths and pine roping, decorating the house, making the crèche (using real moss for grass), buying the tree, delighting in the smell of it in the station wagon on the way home, writing my wish list to Santa Claus, a long one because I was an only child. She stuffed my *two* stockings, made of infinitely expandable wool knitting, until they were gorgeously misshapen and lumpy. (I learned the utility of doing this years later as a parent myself: it buys you an extra hour or two of sleep.) Then the great moment would come and there were the wonders beneath the tree, assembled late at night by my dad as I slept. After I spent hours of flying my new helicopter or manning the new battleship, my mother would announce that lunch was *finally* ready and in we would all go to immensities of roasted turkey and pheasant, browned stuffing, mashed potatoes, sweet potatoes, pureed chestnuts, creamed onions, cranberry jelly, buttermilk biscuits, barges of gravy; followed by flaming plum puddings with crunchy hard sauce, mince pies, sugar cookies and candies. To fight off the post-festivity blues, we'd pile into the car in the darkness of late afternoon and go see a movie. My father would fall asleep, as he always did at movies, and awake with a snore every fifteen minutes to demand a plot summary from my increasingly out-of-patience mother. Such were my child's Christmases in Connecticut.

My first Christmas away from home found me working on a Norwegian tramp freighter crossing the Pacific Ocean. I had been aboard for nearly a month, and so far no one had spoken to me, beyond to tell me what my duties were: sweeping, painting, chipping, standing watch, moving heavy things, moving other heavy things, and basically swabbing everything that didn't move. I was a deckboy, lowest of the low, and the only American on board, which was why no one had talked to me. They couldn't figure out what I was doing aboard, so they ignored me. After a month of hard physical labor and not being spoken to by anyone, and many thousands of miles of often rough ocean, I was gloomy that Christmas Eve, thinking back on all those happy times at home.

I was reading—*Siddhartha,* I think—in my cabin, with the sound of loud partying going on in the mess hall, forward. I had to go to the bathroom. I went, and tripped over the prostrate body of one of the oilers, a tall, young man of twenty or so. He was lying face down by the toilet. When he gave no response to my inquiries after his general health, I turned him over and saw some blood clotting at the corner of his mouth. I checked his pulse. There was one, I could tell that much. I remembered from the movies that you were supposed to check their pupils, though I had no idea what for, specifically, but I checked anyway. They seemed more or less normal, for someone passed out bloody on a bathroom floor.

I rushed forward to the mess hall, where the party was going on and stuck my head in diffidently and told them that the oiler appeared to be in some distress and shouldn't we alert the chief mate, who was the ship's medical officer? This brought grunts of laughter. The carpenter, a large, round-faced man named Fitter, got up and tottered, bracing himself against the bulkhead and told me to lead him to the stricken oiler. He gave him a cursory look-over and pronounced, "Is drunk." I volunteered that we should carry him back to his cabin. "No," said Fitter, "Better he stay there so ven he"—he mimed copious vomiting—"is near toilet." I agreed that this made good sense and was about to return to Govinda and the great brown river god when Fitter put a meaty hand on my shoulder and beckoned, "Come, is Christmas. Have a drink."

I was thrilled to be included in the festivities. I don't remember a lot of what followed. I do remember being handed a beer—Ringnes. And another. And another, and another. I remember smoking, offering and accepting dozens of cigarettes. We all smoked cigarettes, of course. They were plentiful and cheap from the tax-free ship's stores: one dollar a carton. (The Ringnes was three dollars a case.) The conversation, shouted

above the raucous din, consisted mainly of: "HOW MANY BROTH-
ERS AND SISTERS DO YOU HAVE?" I remember the singing of
songs, the telling of jokes, all of which had as their punch lines some
graphic detail of syphilis, clap, crabs, or some exotic, penicillin-resistant
chancre the size of a golf ball. I remember learning a toast in Norwegian
that translates, "Shall we go to the attic and f- - -?" The last thing I remember was that we started to drink aquavit sometime after midnight.

I reentered consciousness on Christmas morning with a pounding on
my cabin door by Loo, the Chinese messman, shouting, "Eggah!" This
was his standard morning wake-up call, indicating "Eggs," that is, breakfast.

At eighteen years of age, I had experienced a hangover or two before,
but no youthful excess with vodka and Fresca had prepared me for this.
Many years later I saw a wonderful movie called *Withnail and I*, starring
my favorite actor, Richard E. Grant, and heard him use a phrase that
aptly describes my predicament that day: "I feel like wild pigs have shat
in my skull."

I crawled to the toilet. The oiler was still there. I knelt on his chest and
threw up several times. Took aspirin, which my stomach rejected a few
minutes later. There was nothing to do but crawl back into my bunk and
yearn for premature death. But then there was a hand shaking my shoulder. I looked up into the unforgiving face of the bosun, a grizzled seadog
in his seventies with an IQ to match and a fondness for extremely young
girls . . . at any rate, he was here to tell me to turn to. Ship-speak for "go
to work."

We were a day and a half from Manila, and the captain had decreed
that he wanted the ship spruce for our arrival. Most of the men were delighted at the prospect of having to work on Christmas day because it
paid triple-time. My own pay was twenty dollars a week; my overtime
rate was sixty cents an hour. As much of a windfall as a buck-eighty was,
it was far from enough to propel me from my death shroud of nausea and
headache. What was enough was the prospect of wimping out in front of
people who had just decided to accept me the night before. Slowly, very
slowly, I made it to the deck.

The temperature that day was 105 degrees. A swell rocked the ship
from side to side. I located the bosun and by means of a croaking sound
alerted him to my existence. He gave me my assignment: spray painting
the outside of the bridge.

Spray painting is a messy job of mixing paint with compressed air and then applying it with a large nozzle that looks like an assault weapon. A mist envelops everything within a three-foot radius of the nozzle. So you wear a suit that entirely covers you, even your head. You see out through built-in goggles. You smear petroleum jelly all over your hands, so the paint won't stick to them. You are, in other words, completely enveloped.

I got into the suit and began woozily to spray. I couldn't see very much because the steam coming off my body collected on the inside of the goggles. I'd taken off my shoes; soon my feet were squishing inside the suit, so much sweat had puddled around them. I don't know how hot it was in there. I've been in saunas heated to about 150 degrees. It probably wasn't that hot, but before long a condition the seamen called "heatsick" had taken over. The first sign is loss of rationality. I was now painting the windows of the bridge, to the violent consternation of the second mate. Painting the windows of a ship's bridge is equivalent to painting over the windshield of a car: it makes it hard to see where you are going.

At some point I was no longer vertical. I was on the deck, and they were trying to get the suit off me. Someone emptied a bucket of water onto my head. Just like in the movies. I was between two of the men, who were trying to get me to stand and walk, but my legs were rubber and kept going out. They got me down to my cabin and Loo was assigned the job of trying to get me to ingest fluids, a complicated task as my hangover had left standing instructions with my stomach to repel all boarders. I dismally recall an exfusion of Coca-Cola through my nostrils.

Fitter came with a bottle of Ringnes. The sight of it brought forth a shudder like a death rattle. I told him wanly, please, go away, but a tough Norwegian ship's carpenter is a fair match for an enfeebled teenager from Connecticut and he poured the reviving, ice-cold golden liquid into me, and for the first time that Christmas, 1970, I thought that I might not end the day inside a stitched sack tossed off the poopdeck and committed to the deep; though to this day I still cannot drink Ringnes.

Life Is a
Hotel

"I knew it. I knew it. Born in a hotel room
and, God damn it—died in one."
—Playwright Eugene O'Neill, just before
dying in the Hotel Shelton, Boston, 1953

It was pneumonia that finished him off, not the room service hamburger
or distress that the Late Night Adult Movie that he wanted to watch was
"UNAVAILABLE AT THIS TIME." But O'Neill's last recorded lament will
probably send a little shiver of recognition up the spine of the business
traveler. J. Alfred Prufrock, T. S. Eliot's Common Man, measured out his
life in coffee spoons. We measure ours out in check-ins and check-outs.
Nearly a third of those who travel regularly spend a month a year in hotels. My uncle died in a hotel room. My father was once rushed to the
hospital from his hotel room with an apparent heart attack that, thank
heavens, turned out to be an "acute gastric episode," the term hospitals
use for five thousand dollars' worth of heartburn. I spend maybe two
months a year in hotel rooms. My only hope is if the Grim Reaper
comes to me there, that he won't empty out the minibar on his way out,
driving my heirs and assigns into bankruptcy.

One rite of passage I had in a hotel: my first tryst. I was barely seventeen. It was the first time I had approached a check-in counter other
than with my parents, and I was at pains to impersonate an adult. While
my inamorata, an escapee from the Convent of the Sacred Heart, hov-
ered tremulously behind a potted palm, I managed to secure a room for
the night.

"Your luggage, sir?" the clerk enquired.

I gave him a deer-caught-in-the-headlights stare and mumbled pathetically that the airline had lost it.

"I *see*," he said. Our night of dolce vita was interrupted by bangings on the door by phantom hobnail-booted, truncheon-wielding vice squad police shouting, "We know you're in there, Buckley! Your parents and headmaster have been notified, along with all the colleges you've applied to."

Many years later, while staying at a splendid, multistarred Caribbean resort that caters to the well-heeled, I fell to talking with one of its employees in a bar off premises. After a couple of rum tonics he loosened up sufficiently to tell some delicious out-of-school stories. Quite a few people, he said, bring their mistresses there. In some cases, they like it so much they return with their wives. To avoid embarrassment, the hotel discreetly puts in the computer record of such clients the letters DNR, standing for "Do Not Recognize."

"Last month," the employee chuckled, "one of the staff really messed up really good. At check-in, he said to the guest, standing there with his wife, 'Good to see you again, Mr. Jones!' "

His warm and hearty Caribbean welcome turned Mr. Jones's week in paradise into twenty-four hours of inferno. Mrs. Jones demanded a separate suite, at a cost of thousands per day. And this was only the beginning of Mr. Jones's pecuniary woes. The next day she chartered the most expensive plane she could to come and pick her up, and flew back into the arms of New York's most expensive divorce lawyer, resulting in the eventual reduction of Mr. Jones's net worth by half. I wondered if upon check-out the cashier chirruped pleasantly to Mr. Jones, "We hope you enjoyed your stay with us!"

What is it about hotels that invites people to indulge the lesser angels of our nature? John Belushi ate and snorted himself to death in L.A.'s tony Chateau Marmont. Margaret Sullavan committed suicide at the Hotel Taft in New Haven, where my own mother stayed during the senior prom. Every day it seems you pick up the paper to read that some rock star or tormented Hollywood bohunk has trashed, torched, or in some cases, utterly demolished his hotel room. Is it the rootless loneliness of finding themselves, yet again, in a hotel room? Is *this* reason enough to set fire to the carpet and hurl the television out the window?

Yet even quite respectable, stable types do strange things in hotels. Some years ago I was on a swing through Europe with then–Vice Presıdent Bush. There were eighty or so of us in the entourage, staffers and Secret Service, and we were installed in the Hotel Crillon, one of the great hotels of the world, right there in the center of Paris on the Place de la Concorde. What a jewel it was. I was a lowly speechwriter, but my room seemed grand enough to have been used by a minister negotiating the charter for the League of Nations, which happened right there.

I took a long hot shower in the marmoreal immensity of the bathroom; turned off the water and reached for a towel. No towel. Odd. I looked about. Nothing, nowhere. Not so much as a hanky. Grumbling and rehearsing my outrage in rusty French, I dripped my way to the phone and gave the housekeeping staff to understand that this was an affront not merely to me, but to the dignity of the United States of America.

A few minutes later I was brought a towel by a distinctly unapologetic maid. A single towel, not even a big towel, barely enough to dry my delicates, and this in a hotel known—esteemed throughout the *monde*—for its huge, fluffy, monogrammed terrycloth bathrobes.

I sat down moistly to see if I could work in a caustic aside about the Crillon's lack of towels in the vice president's speech about deploying Pershing missiles. But as a procession of damp and disgruntled White House personnel came through the staff room it transpired that every single member of the VP's entourage had met with the same, towelless fate. This was no casual negligence.

Eventually we learned that a month earlier, Secretary of State George Shultz had been through the Crillon with his staff. In the best tradition of maintaining good relations with the allies, they had looted the Crillon of monogrammed terrycloth robes, towels and other absorbent mementoes. Indeed, said one of my colleagues, who had dried himself with toilet paper, patches of which still clung wetly to his neck, it was a wonder they had not made off with the drapes.

Other than that the Crillon was the kind of hotel that makes la vie en roads tolerable, even worth it. Perhaps if he'd checked out for the last time there, O'Neill wouldn't have been so bitter, though his last words would probably have been less piquant. "Where are the Goddamn towels?" doesn't quite have the same éclat.

—*Forbes FYI*, 1996

Babes

Mom,
Fashion Icon

□

I wasn't aware that my mother was much different from other mothers until one day at boarding school, when I was fourteen. It was the Monday after Parents' Weekend. One of the older boys said to me, in front of some other older boys, "Hey, Buckley, your mother's a piece of ass."

I stood there with my face burning, trying to figure out what, exactly, the correct response was. I wasn't even sure that what he had said was an insult. There was no higher accolade at Portsmouth Abbey School, Hormone High, circa 1967, than "piece of ass." But when it was applied to one's mother it had the whiff of fightin' words. The ensuing scuffle was over in five seconds, with me on my back on the floor and the older boy kneeling on my chest, explaining that what he'd been referring to was "her clothes."

Further evidence that my mother was different came from the school switchboard operator—a fat, gossipy woman who regularly pored over the "Suzy Says" society column in the *News*. "Your mutha went to a big party last night for Walter Cronkite!" she would yell out into the crowded mailbox room as I tried to disappear. "She wore an Eves Saint Lawrent dress! Musta cost a *fortune!*"

It was around then that the phrase "the chic and stunning Mrs. William F. Buckley" entered my family's life. Typically, my mother would use it when she was coming in from the garden—dirty, in jeans and a black T-shirt, her hair pulled back, no makeup. "So much for the chic and stunning Mrs. Buckley," she would say to the house guests.

"Where did that phrase originate?" I asked her a few weeks ago. We were having lunch at an expensive Italian restaurant on the Upper East Side. She was wearing a knockout Oscar de la Renta beige suit, pale stockings, bone-colored pumps, huge costume-gold bracelets and ear-rings. Her hair was freshly coiffed. She had on makeup.

She didn't remember, except to say that she was pretty sure it hadn't come from *Women's Wear Daily,* the trade journal that, along with its glossy cousin, *W,* has been covering her intensively for the last quarter century or so. (Headline, 1977: "AN ORIGINAL: PAT BUCKLEY"; 1985: "THE POWER OF PAT.") In 1975, two years after she first made the best-dressed list, the *Times* headline read, "BEST-DRESSED PATRICIA BUCKLEY: PROUDER OF ROLE AS HOUSEWIFE."

"This linguine," she pronounced, "is inedible." I had to keep coaxing her back onto the topic of fashion throughout the lunch. She kept get-ting off it, giving me new recipes. "Oh," she interrupted herself at one point in the midst of a discussion of French versus American designers. "I have made the most extraordinary discovery. Knorr fish stock. It comes in cubes, like bouillon. It has *changed* my life."

Chic and stunning, I pressed.

"I don't know," she said. "Probably in 'Suzy.' Call Aileen. She'll know. Your father has invited sixty-two people to this concert Friday. Where am I supposed to seat them all—on my lap?"

Eventually we decided that it was Suzy. There was another phrase much in Suzy's repertoire then: "*belle poitrine.*" As in, "Mrs. Buckley, of the *belle poitrine.*" For years, I laughed along with it; then, one day in French class, we got to body parts, and I discovered it meant "great tits."

Over the *linguine alle vongole* (which I found quite good), we did a sort of *Recherché du Hemlines Perdu,* going back over all the different fashion phases she has gone through. For the last twenty years or so, it's been mostly Bill Blass and Oscar de la Renta, with a little Donna Karan, Isaac Mizrahi, and Calvin Klein thrown in. Before the era of Blass and de la Renta, there was the era of caftans (the mid-seventies), and, before that, maxis. (Never midis: "that ugly creation," she told the press at the time.) Before that—the sixties now—there was her "Native American period. Beaded headbands, long buckskin skirts, high boots. There is no broth in this pasta at all. Big silver jewelry. If I was feeling particularly frivolous, a feather. I loved Mary Quant. When was she? I fell for her clothes in a big way. I think I started wearing short skirts before almost anybody, mainly because of my beauteous legs. Who wants to read this kind of crap? Does yours have any broth? The mid-sixties, Pucci. All my bathing suits, pants, tops were Pucci." And back in the fifties, before her New York life began—before she had friends named Nan, Mica, Jerome, Chessy, Estée, Slim, Rocky, and Pano—she was a suburban Connecticut car-pooling housewife and mom. "Classy country clothes, probably from Lord & Taylor. But I always had my sort of hooker side at night."

Who taught her about fashion?

"Me. I think I've always had an eye. For my own kind of style. Mind you," she added heavily, "there have been *many* mistakes made."

This part took no coaxing. She relishes stories in which she is the figure of fun. "About four years ago. It was a Blass, made like an Austrian shade, all wired and pleated. When I was having my fitting, no one said, 'Sit down.' The minute I went out in it, I sat down, and the whole thing came up over my head. People were in total hysteria. I had to stand up to eat."

She went on, "Bill Blass was the first designer I took very seriously. I adored him. It was because I became enamored of—how would you call it?—the classic American look with a tweak to it. Maybe 'tweak' isn't the right word. There's a certain casualness, but there ain't no grunge there. Have you seen the latest Chanel outfits? Please. Bill is a classic American designer. He never loses sight of taste. I didn't mean 'tweak,' I meant 'twist.' A little added . . . If he's dressing you somberly, there's always something to take the somber out of it. And his evening clothes are very romantic."

My mother's parents were Canadian. Her mother was born in Win-nipeg, Manitoba; her father was from Toronto. They lived in Vancouver, British Columbia, where my mother was born and reared. Her father was a mountainous, gruff self-made man who at various times made his money in timber, cattle, gold mines, oil, gas, and racehorses. His name was Austin Taylor; his wife's name was Kathleen. She had soft Irish skin, beautiful red hair, a great, matronly bosom. She was called Babe. They were always well turned out, in a classic sort of way, but they never would have thought of themselves as fashionable.

"One time," she said, "the *Province* or the *Sun* ran a picture of Daddy on the front page and the caption underneath said, 'Sartorial Gem.' He was in such a rage that he went out to the farm and stayed there for three days."

I think this is where her profound ambivalence about the big-city part of her life comes from. Many times, I've heard her describe herself as "a simple country girl from a frontier town in British Columbia, whom my father named after his favorite hunting dog." To put it politely, this is total bullshit. There is nothing simple about my mother, and it's been a long time since she left Vancouver. The part about being named for a springer spaniel may be true. But something in her upbringing—I can hear my grandmother's voice admonishing her (*"Pat!"*), and even when she was in her late thirties I noticed that she wouldn't smoke in front of her father— has kept her grounded throughout many a New York vanity bonfire.

In 1975, Enid Nemy wrote in *The New York Times*:

> Sometimes she describes herself as a jolly green giant. Other times, she thinks she looks like a pregnant stork. She hates shopping, and her closets wouldn't give anyone an inferiority complex. . . . She likes fashion, but it isn't a passion. It's more in the nature of an evanescent flirtation, fun when there is nothing else to do. In Mrs. Buckley's case, there's something else to do most of the time.

From her mother, she inherited civic-mindedness. In Stamford, when she wasn't carpooling, it was the Junior League. In New York she got involved with the Institute for Reconstructive Plastic Surgery, Memorial Sloan-Kettering and, more recently, St. Vincent's Hospital, the Metropolitan Museum's Costume Institute, and many other institutions. The "most of the time" referred to above is spent taking care of my father—a job that would keep all of Brigham Young's twenty-seven wives busy. "I guess the only thing I really do well is run a house," she once told a reporter. That is complete bullshit, but she has the gift of self-deprecation.

My father has the fashion sense of a Romanian country-parish priest, but he appreciates beauty on a woman, and has always done his best to be encouraging. When she made the Best Dressed Hall of Fame, the Valhalla of Seventh Avenue, he called me up to tell me, "Be sure to make a fuss. This is apparently a *very* big deal." I called her and made a big fuss. She changed the subject, if memory serves, to the dog's bladder infection.

Does my father still make a fuss?

"Yes. I don't understand why the food is this way. I had exactly the same thing here last week, and it was delicious. Whenever I come out in a new dress, he always makes a point of saying, 'A new dress. I think it's absolutely divine.' The other day, I came out in a fifteen-year-old Madame Grès, and he said, 'Ducky, that's absolutely divine. Who is it— Bill or Oscar?' He'd seen it twenty times."

At last, she is slightly warming to the subject. She likes fashion more than she will admit. Bill Blass and Oscar de la Renta are two of her best friends. At some point in the late seventies, their photographs, framed in silver, turned up on her crowded bibelot tables. For more than thirty years, she has been very close to Nan Kempner, whom she calls "probably the best-dressed woman I know."

Yes, thank you, she's finished with the *linguine alle vongole*. "Fashion is fun. As long as you don't embarrass your husband. I remember last year coming down the staircase at the apartment in an outfit that I thought was absolutely, startlingly gorgeous, and your father said, 'You look absolutely gorgeous. Where's the rest of the dress?' It was up to the kazoo. Don't use the word 'kazoo.' "

Another time: "I remember it was a Victorian show, and Blaine"— Blaine Trump—"got herself rigged out in some fancy-dandy outfit, and I was standing with Robert"—Blaine's husband—"and some other man. Blaine was wandering around in bustles and furbelows and God knows what, and this man said, 'My God, did you get a load of that?' And Robert said, 'I not only got a load of it, I'm *married* to it.' "

"Espresso, please. I won't tell you what designer it was, but I went about a year ago to order my fall outfits down on Seventh Avenue, and out comes this dress with cutouts here." She points to just below her still–*belle poitrine*. "Black velvet, with net. And I said, 'My God, I think I'm too old for this.' And the designer said, 'But Brooke Astor's just ordered it in four different colors.' Do you want dessert? I really shouldn't. I can't fit into any of my clothes."

I have been hearing her say this since the mid-nineteen-fifties, when my memory began.

"The Italians are not good at pastries. Do you want more cappuccino? I don't know what else to tell you about fashion. Except what I'd really like to do. My wildest fantasy would be to dress like Cher."

Pat!

"Just dreams one has. Although, much as I'd like to go around looking like Cher, I can't. Why? Well, Cher and I, shall we say, *share* different ages. No no no, this is my treat. Where are my glasses? I can no longer see anything. You'll have to calculate the tip. I'm sorry it was so dreadful. It must not be their regular chef. I'm sure all this will be riveting. Just remember that I never take myself seriously about fashion. In fact, I never take myself seriously at all. Given my taste in clothes, I'll probably come back as RuPaul."

—The New Yorker, 1994

Really
Something

If the end of George Bush's presidency marks a generational shift in American politics—the last time the office will be held by someone who fought in the Second World War—his mother's death could be said to mark the passing of an American era, all the more poignantly for her having died so close to the precise moment when the baton was passed. Dorothy Walker Bush died at her home in Greenwich, Connecticut, just after five o'clock on the afternoon of Thursday, November 19th. She was ninety-one years old. Since Mr. Bush had lost the election little more than two weeks earlier, it was not surprising that he should say, when he spoke to us by telephone from Camp David the day before the funeral, "Well, it's been a kind of emotional time for all of us."

Much has been said and written about the way young George Bush strove to live up to his father, the late Senator Prescott Bush. Yet, by all accounts, Dorothy Bush was a much more dominant force in his life. Barbara Bush once told an interviewer that her mother-in-law had "ten times" the influence on her son that his father had.

Dorothy Bush was the daughter of Loulie Wear Walker and of George Herbert Walker, a well-to-do Midwestern investment banker named for the seventeenth-century metaphysical poet and Anglican priest George Herbert. She grew up in St. Louis and attended finishing school at the Farmington School Academy, in Connecticut. At Kennebunkport, Maine, in 1921, she married Prescott Bush, a handsome young Yale man, who went on to become a partner in Wall Street's extension of Skull and Bones—Brown Brothers, Harriman & Company—and, in 1952, United States senator from Connecticut. She reared four sons and a daughter, was active in civic and volunteer work, excelled at sports and games, and divided her time—as they say of those who have more than one house—between Greenwich, Kennebunkport, and Jupiter Island, in Florida. She was a matriarchal American aristocrat.

The impulse toward what her president son once referred to as "noblesse noblige" came, perhaps, from her faith. Her father was an Episcopalian, her mother a Presbyterian. She herself was an Episcopalian—indeed, so much of one that the designation "Anglican" seems almost more appropriate. Dorothy Bush was a deeply religious woman, and she read from the Bible to her children every morning of their young lives. Two days before the funeral, Jonathan Bush, the president's younger brother, recalled, "She went through life with Dad and Christ. Those were her two great companions, and she believed that all things were possible with prayer."

On the phone, the president said, "She led a life of faith. She was totally convinced—not just in her further-along, advanced years—of the life hereafter, and of God's love: all those principles that for us her life really epitomized. She was something. She was really something. She became after Dad's death the leader of our family. All the cousins and aunts, you know, I'm sure loved their mothers, but would cite Mother as the perfect example of the giving, caring person."

The president has often told a story about one morning at Christ Church in Greenwich, where the Bush family attended services ("*every* Sunday," her daughter, Nancy Ellis, groans, "*never* missing a Sunday"). The minister, descanting on Song of Solomon 2:5, got carried away and kept shouting out the line "Comfort me with apples." "He said it about three times," the president recalls. " 'Comfort me with apples! Comfort me!' Pressie"—the eldest brother, Prescott Bush, Jr.—"and I burst out laughing. Mum was giggling, and the old man threw us out. He pointed—*out*. We couldn't contain ourselves. There were a lot of incidents like that with her." "The pew shook," Nancy Ellis says. "She got the giggles. She was a person who got the giggles. She was fun."

Mrs. Ellis also says, "An *enormous* athlete, Mother. A beautiful shot and a good horsewoman and a fabulous swimmer—and tennis, and golf, and paddle tennis. And a fantastic game player. Bridge, Scrabble, anagrams, backgammon, Peggoty, gin rummy, Sir Hinkam Funny-Duster— marvelous card game, Mother was a champ at it. Russian bank, tiddledy-winks. No wonder George runs from horseshoes to the golf course."

For such a competitive woman, Mrs. Bush was remarkably—indeed, legendarily—adamant that her children not boast of their prowess on the playing fields. Vic Gold, the cowriter of the president's 1987 campaign biography, *Looking Forward,* has come up with a scene that his editor cut from the book: "He"—the president—"was eleven years old, and just coming off the tennis court, and he said, 'My game was off.' And his mother said, 'Young man, you don't have a game.' And he told me, 'Right then and there is where I learned the idea of humility.' She had this basic code of American sportsmanship." Mrs. Ellis echoes the thought: "She hated that expression 'my game.' "

The president recalled, "She was always right in there. 'I got three goals in soccer!' 'But how did the *team* do?' She was . . ."

"Tough?"

"Oh, yeah, and a great competitor. In all the athletic events and stuff, she was unbelievable. But there was always this message: good sportsmanship, caring, don't ever humiliate the other guy. She just lived all of that."

Mrs. Bush's other pet peeve was self-obsession, or anything even faintly resembling it. During her son's first run for the presidency, in 1979, she called him after hearing him on television and said, "George, you're talking about yourself too much." Alixe Glen, a longtime family friend and aide to the president, thinks that the mother's lessons may ultimately have cost her son the presidency. "Mrs. Bush hammering that into him—'I don't care how many home runs you made, it's how the team did'—for *so* many years, even as an adult, is what made him unable to brag about himself as president, which many people, myself very much included, feel was part of his demise."

Despite her intervention in 1979, Mrs. Bush made few calls to the White House. "But," the president said, "she did have the marvelous one when she called me early on when I was vice president. She said, 'George, I just noticed how wonderful it is that Ronald Reagan *waits* for Nancy coming off the helicopter and holds her by the arm and is *unfailingly* polite.' I said, 'Mom, is there a message in this here? Are you trying to—' She said, 'No, I just mean that he *never* walks ahead of her and he *never* is anything other than totally considerate.' And so"—he laughed— "I got the message loud and clear."

He also recalled another matter she once phoned him about. While watching Ronald Reagan give his State of the Union address, she noticed that her son, sitting behind the president, seemed not to be paying attention. "I've seen it in print, but it's true," the president said, wryly. "She told me I shouldn't be looking at the papers, you know, sitting, Tip O'Neill and I. That was really funny. I said, 'Mom, I'm just following the text.' 'I know, but you just listen to what he's saying and then you won't need to follow it.' She was great."

Dorothy Bush's health began to fail at about the time her son became president. The photographs of her at the swearing-in, on the West Front of the Capitol, show a frail but sprightly woman—deep in prayer, it appears—holding the hand of Marilyn Quayle as the oath of office is administered to her son. Afterward, she watched the inaugural parade as she sat in her wheelchair, pushed up to a window in the Queen's Bedroom, looking down on Pennsylvania Avenue. Mrs. Ellis recalls, "Things got confusing for her in the last years. The last time she went to the White House, I said to her afterward, 'Oh, Mother, wasn't it lovely, the Queen's Bedroom?' And she couldn't remember that she'd been there."

The family is not sure whether she understood that her son had lost the '92 election. "I don't know," the president said. "I talked to her after, but I couldn't really tell. I think she probably did. My brothers, they think she did, but I would call her, and 'Oh, how sweet of you to call, this is the *nicest* thing in my life, *oh,* I'm so pleased,' you know, and I'm sure she did the same thing to the next cousin who checked in." He laughed. "But she was awful close to us, to Barbara and to me. She made all of us feel that way."

Two weeks after the election, Mrs. Bush had a stroke, at her home in Greenwich. The morning of the day she died, Mrs. Ellis called the president, and he left Washington for Greenwich at 8:35 A.M. on a small Air Force C-20, accompanied by his daughter Dorothy Koch (Doro), who was named for her grandmother. The three of them were "the Bawl Brigade," Mrs. Ellis says. "We'd sit there holding her hand, then we'd get all weepy and leave the room. She was so adorable, and she was so frail at the end, like a little bird in your hand."

"Doro had joined the Brigade in Houston," on Election Night, the president said. "Then her brothers also became members, all of them. So on this little trip to Greenwich, I have to admit, I could well have been elected president of the Bawl Brigade. 'Cause we were awful close. She was struggling. Boy, she was struggling. I couldn't tell how much she knew that it was me and Doro there. I like to feel she knew we were there, and who we were, but Nancy has that very generous interpretation on it"—that Mrs. Bush was holding on until he arrived to say goodbye—"but I couldn't tell that, to be candid. She just opened her eyes and looked over at us, and Press said, 'It's George, Mom, it's George and Doro,' and she kind of looked over and there was some glimmer of recognition, but not her typically warm smile. She'd had a stroke, you see."

The president and his daughter stayed with her for about an hour and then flew back to Washington. Dorothy Walker Bush died at 5:05 P.M. Mrs. Ellis called the president, and got his secretary, who told her he was in another part of the White House, accepting ambassadorial credentials. "He called back about suppertime," Mrs. Ellis says.

Was he devastated?

"I'm sure he was. It's always that fresh sense of loss you have with death, even though you're expecting it and the person is ninety-one. But I talked to him that night, and, you know, he's strong. He said, *'Oh, gee whizz.'*"

On the morning before the funeral, the president said that he had no plans to give a eulogy the next day: "God, no, I couldn't do it. I would choke up. I would be permanently ensconced as a member of the Bawl Brigade. I can't. I'm *terrible* at those things. I've had trouble paying my respects to the fallen soldiers on the *Iowa,* or the dead out of Desert Storm, without getting emotional. I'd love to, but I know my limitations. I even got choked up here at Camp David last night. We had our choir singing. We had a little vespers program with Amy Grant. It was so beautiful, and I found myself choking up. We had a bunch of friends up here, and 'Oh God,' I said, 'please hold back the floods.'"

—*The New Yorker,* 1992

You Got
a Problem?

□

Eppie Lederer, all hair, cheekbones, and dimples, stands in the doorway of her Chicago apartment. "Hello," she says, with a bit of a Mae West purr. It feels a little odd saying this about a seventy-seven-year-old great-grandmother, but there is something ineffably sexy about her. Maybe it's the voice, or the perfume, or the rustle of silk, or the knowing, Listen-honey-I've-heard-it-all eyes. Maybe it's the aura of unshockability she projects. You feel you could tell her something truly dire about your secret life and she'd just nod understandingly and tell you not to worry, she hears from people like you all the time, and she'd give you the phone number of some specialist at Johns Hopkins with a Hungarian-sounding surname who deals with this particular weirdness. At any rate, the woman the world knows as Ann Landers looks younger than seventy-seven, by quite a lot, and she *has* heard it all before.

"The changes I have seen," she once wrote, "would twirl your turban." In mid-October she quietly marked her fortieth anniversary of working seven days a week dispensing advice to the lorn, the afflicted, the battered, the diseased, the lonely, and the confused. According to the syndicate that distributes her column, it currently runs in over twelve hundred newspapers, with a total circulation of ninety million.

Ann Landers has brought Eppie Lederer fame, fortune, authority, and power. She uses honorary degrees for wallpaper. Presidents fawn over her, institutes put her on their boards. A plug from her can send a book onto the best-seller list. All this has brought her enemies, too—chiefly gun owners, pro-lifers, and laboratory-rat huggers. On occasion, she has faltered: she has been caught recycling old letters, fiddling with the wording of others, and, in one instance, causing an organ-donation controversy that resulted in the unfortunate headline "ADVICE COLUMN MAY HAVE LIFE-THREATENING CONSEQUENCES." In each case, she has quickly come clean, and self-administered her trademark "forty lashes with the wet noodle." If readers disagree with advice she has given, she prints the letters. She has never caused a sex scandal, got drunk (she has never touched alcohol or smoked a cigarette), endorsed products, or done infomercials. "People know I'm on the level," she says.

A *World Almanac* poll once named Ann Landers the most influential woman in the United States. A few years ago, a Cornell professor spent four years computerizing, summarizing, and analyzing every column she had written, and came to the same conclusion. Her willingness to grapple with social taboos just as they are about to burst out of the national closet has given her a credibility, even a certain aura of progressiveness, when in fact her values are generally straight-down-the-middle American. Through four decades of change, she has remained tolerant, traditional, cautious, and concerned more with the consequences of behavior than with its inherent morality. She was against the Vietnam War but visited the troops. She is an ardent feminist, but believes that a mother's place is with her children during their early years.

Her apartment overlooks Lake Michigan. She gives me a short tour, high heels clicking on parquet. In the library, there's a Dali bust of J.F.K. and the framed front page of the *Des Moines Register* of July 4, 1918 ("HUNS FAIL IN COUNTER BLOW"), the day she was born. Beneath this, also framed, is an odd tchotchke: one of Mary Todd Lincoln's handkerchiefs. She does not think it is from that night at Ford's Theater. I'm tempted to linger and contemplate the significance of having on your wall the *mouchoir* of the fruitiest First Lady in American history, but we're off to the living room, which has a nearly photographic Picasso self-portrait, and then we move on to the Tudor dining room, all dark paneling and mullioned windows and escutcheons. Somehow, we find ourselves in the master bathroom, an arresting chocolate-and-red eighteenth-century Italian-mosaic-tile fantasy installed by the apartment's original owner. "A nut," she pronounces.

Time to leave for dinner. Bobby, Eppie's chauffeur, is waiting downstairs with the Cadillac limousine to take us around the block to her usual dinner haunt, the International Club, on the mezzanine of the Drake Hotel. Ignoring my protests, she had insisted before I left home on sending Bobby to fetch me at O'Hare. Bobby had further been instructed, despite vehement objections from me, to wait outside the Drake while I showered, and then to convey me the five hundred feet to the entrance to her apartment. It was like visiting an attentive, rich grandmother; and I might as well confess, at the risk of impaired journalistic integrity, that I enjoyed every minute of it.

At the restaurant, the maître d' fusses over her and leads the way to her usual table, designated by a brasslike plaque inscribed "MRS. EPPIE LEDERER." She orders escargots and crab cakes and water, and I ask how she came to grow up in Sioux City, Iowa. Her parents, fleeing czarist pogroms, had emigrated from Vladivostok, by way of Manchuria, in 1908, indigent and speaking no English. Her father, Abe Friedman, started out peddling chickens in the Midwest and ended up owning, as she puts it, with affecting lack of boastfulness, "every theater in Sioux City except the Orpheum." His twin daughters, Esther (Eppie) and Pauline (Popo), born in Sioux City on July 4th, 1918, eventually became, as Ann Landers and Abigail Van Buren ("Dear Abby"), the most widely circulated advice columnists in his adopted land. In the words of Yogi Berra when he was informed that a Jew had been elected Lord Mayor of Dublin, "Only in America."

In 1939, Eppie married Jules Lederer, a salesman who later started a company called Budget Rent A Car. (Money has never been a worry, and therefore never a motivating factor, in Eppie's life.) They had a daughter, Margo (she is now a freelance writer, has three grown children and three grandchildren, and lives in Cambridge, Massachusetts). They moved to Wisconsin, where Eppie's volunteer work soon got her elected chairman—even now she does not use "chairwoman"—of the Eau Claire County Democratic Party; and in 1955 they moved to Chicago. That year, she became famous.

The original Ann Landers was a nurse whose column ran in the *Chicago Sun-Times* and was syndicated in about two dozen newspapers. When she died unexpectedly, Eppie applied for the job, along with about thirty other aspiring advice columnists. They were all asked to answer an identical set of hypothetical letters from readers. The first set out the dilemma of a woman whose walnut tree was dropping nuts onto her neighbor's property. They had exchanged words about it. Who owned the walnuts? Eppie had been an assiduous networker during her years as a Democratic Party official. She called up her friend Supreme Court Justice William O. Douglas and put the question to him. The answer was that the neighbor could do anything she wanted with the walnuts except sell them. The next question was from a worried Catholic who wanted to marry a Protestant. Eppie turned to her friend Father Theodore Hesburgh, the president of Notre Dame University. Hesburgh advised that the marriage could proceed, but only if the Protestant agreed to raise the children as Catholics. And so on.

She submitted her extravagantly sourced answers. The editor in charge of the column called her up and sputtered, "You can't use these people's names! They'll sue us!" Marshall Field, the publisher of the *Sun-Times,* telephoned her a few days later and said, "Good morning, Ann Landers." The column was an immediate success. She stayed with the *Sun-Times* until 1987, the year she bolted across the street to the *Tribune.*

Her sister Popo, recognizing a good thing when she saw it, followed her into the advice-column biz a scant three months later. This did not do wonders for sibling relations. Indeed, Eppie and Popo did not speak for years. Creators Syndicate says that "Ann Landers" appears in about twelve hundred papers. The Universal Press Syndicate, which distributes "Dear Abby," claims a suspiciously similar number of papers. Both companies adamantly refuse to provide a list of their client papers. As for the principals, they wisely refuse to discuss the rivalry, preferring to rise above. By way of calming the tempest in this particular teapot, suffice it to say that the two nice Jewish sisters from Sioux City, Iowa, eventually kissed and made up.

What a kinder, gentler time the fifties seems! The letters that flooded in to Ann Landers then were, for the most part, about acne, or not having a date for the senior prom, or having an inattentive husband. But there were others, too.

In her first year, Eppie published a letter from a young man who wondered how to get Mom and Dad to accept his romantic partner. Homosexuality, of course, was still locked away deep in the closet, behind the winter overcoats. She suggested family counseling. The publisher of the

St. Joseph, Michigan, paper refused to print the column, and told the syndicator that he would run a front-page notice explaining that "Ann Landers" would not appear that day because it dealt with a subject not fit for family reading.

Recalling the episode forty years later, she is still indignant. "I called the publisher up and said, 'This is a human problem, and that is what I do.' He said, 'I'm not going to print it.' I said, 'Fine. Then everyone in St. Joe is going to buy the *Detroit Free Press* to see what you won't print.' I called the *Free Press* and told them to get ready for a lot of extra sales"—throaty laugh—"because I know human nature. They're going to buy the other paper to find out what it is, this 'isn't fit for family reading,' I said. Well, that was the last time I had to do something like that. From then on, boy, that St. Joe paper printed every damn word I wrote."

That was then. Earlier this year, she got into trouble with gay readers for recommending that the longtime boyfriend of a bridegroom's father not attend the impending nuptials if his presence would be an embarrassment. "Well, my God," she says, launching into a riff based on sackfuls of fulminant mail that that bit of advice had brought. " 'What do you mean, "embarrassment"? This is his partner for seventeen years and you want him to leave him home? Are you crazy?' It was amazing to me how much flak I got for that." She agrees with her critics. "Unfortunately, I did not show the gutsiness I should have shown," she concedes, administering herself a lash with the wet noodle.

Despite the changes that have sent her turban twirling over the past forty years—she's gone from bad breath to AIDS, from spoiled brats to machine-pistol-wielding ten-year-olds, from a puff of pot to crack babies (about 15 percent of the letters she gets now are drug-related)—she still sounds somewhat reassuring. "The problems basically have not changed in forty years," she told me. "The basic problems are family problems. This is No. 1. It's always been that way, and I suspect it's always going to be that way."

DEAR ANN LANDERS:

Last May my husband asked me if he could wear one of my housedresses while painting the kitchen. He said it would be more comfortable. I said OK. He did look awfully cute, and I told him so. Ever since that time he has been wearing my dresses and wigs and makeup when we

are alone. He has asked me to call him Linda when we "play girl friends"
as he calls it. . . . I can truthfully say I don't mind. . . . Is there anything
wrong with it?

> Happy Woman Who
> Loves Her Husband

DEAR WOMAN:

My opinion is of no consequence. The only thing that matters is what
you think, and apparently you think it is just fine. . . . Just make sure the
doors are locked and the shades down. And say hello to Linda.

"Now," she says after the waiter assures her that the crab cakes are on
their way. "What about you?"

This is a legacy from her father, Abe, who once told her, "You never
learn anything while you're talking." But there is nothing to learn from
me, other than my yearning to wear a housedress and Manolo Blahniks
and have my wife call me Lulu, so we talk some more about her, about
a few issues of the day, and about people who have figured in her very
public life.

How much money the column earns her: "Oh, I wouldn't answer
that. You know that. But when I started to do this I was not interested
in the money. I was married to a man whose wealth supported me very
well."

Her sister's column: "I just don't discuss her in any piece on me. And
there have been a lot of good pieces on her, and my name doesn't come
up, and I think that's the way it should be."

Politics: "I make a concerted effort to keep politics out of my column.
You can't tell from my column whether I'm a Democrat or a Republican."

David Brinkley: "A master at letting other people talk."

George Will: "He can't resist the temptation to tell you how smart he
is."

Ted Koppel: "I've always thought that he would make a terrific
lawyer."

Geraldo Rivera: "Oh, he's so trashy."

Guns: "The proliferation of guns in this country is unreal."

The National Rifle Association: "I have nothing more to say to these people."

Interracial marriages: "One subject I have not dealt with in a column, because the roof would fall in, and I don't need that."

Marijuana laws: "Ridiculous. I don't want it legalized, but I don't think you should have to go to jail for ten years if you get caught smoking a joint."

Eleanor Roosevelt: "A great woman. A great woman. Big woman. I was amazed when I met her. I mean, she's *huge*. She asked a lot of questions, which I found interesting."

Senator Joseph McCarthy: "Living in Wisconsin, I would run into him and he would grab me and hug me. And I couldn't bear it. Because I disliked him intensely."

Nixon: "Same thing with Nixon. He would always greet me very warmly, and I couldn't bear it. He never got it."

Joseph Kennedy, Sr.: "A monster. Duplicitous, mean-spirited, anti-Semitic."

Meeting President Kennedy in the Oval Office when she went there as the national chairman of the Christmas Seals campaign against TB: "He was so attractive. A knockout. Sex appeal oozed from his every pore. He was the womanizer from Hell. I mean, this guy had women all over the place. In the swimming pool, the locker room. Of course, he had a bum back, for one thing, and the women had to do all the work."

Teddy Kennedy: "A superb senator. Superb. Standing up for all the right things. . . . I know, Chappaquiddick—and being drunk is no excuse, and he was plenty drunk that night, plenty drunk. But he certainly— If you can redeem yourself from a thing like that, he has done it."

Ronald Reagan: "A sweet guy. You know, he's totally gone. I had a letter from Nancy just a few weeks ago, and she said, 'I feel like half a person.' "

Nancy Reagan: "People used to make fun of the Nancy gaze, but she really meant it. They really were so in love with each other that they had no room in their hearts for their children. This is one of the sad things."

Hillary Clinton: "I like her enormously. She's badly mistreated by the press, badly mistreated. . . . She doesn't deserve this."

Bill Clinton: "I don't think he's fooling around anymore. Nor do I think he will. I read that Hillary threw a lamp at him. I read that. Did you read that? You know something? I think she did."

Bill and Hillary Clinton: "They make their own fun, those two. They make their own fun."

Vince Foster's suicide, Whitewater, etc.: "Not much fun there."

Her friendship with Father Hesburgh: "The greatest unfertilized romance in the history of the world."

The Catholic Church's problem with priests who can't keep their hands off the altar boys: "Terrible. They just move them around. They don't throw them out. Now they're getting a little smarter, because they're getting sued. I think, with these problems, eventually the Church is going to have to let the clergy marry."

Bishop Fulton J. Sheen: "Do you remember him? He was a friend of mine. He was charismatic beyond belief. I first heard him speak when I was living in Eau Claire, Wisconsin. I went backstage to meet him. He looked at me and said, 'The metaphysics of a dimple is more profound than simple.' I said, What is going on here with this guy?"

Her visit with him in Washington: "He opened the door at this gorgeous home, great big St. Bernard, like a country gentleman. Living in this estate with this wonderful dog and a Lincoln and driver. I said, 'Not bad for a fellow who took the oath of poverty.' And he said, 'Well, Esther'—he called me Esther, which I thought was interesting—'I'm not an order priest, I'm a diocesan priest, and I didn't take the oath of poverty.' I said, 'Good for you. You did it right.' He had converted Clare Boothe Luce, and people thought maybe this was going to happen to me, and when I told them I was going to visit him they said, 'Uh-oh, be careful.' I said, 'This is not going to happen. I'm Jewish for life.' "

On meeting Pope John Paul II: "Looks like an angel. He has the face of an angel. His eyes are sky blue, and his cheeks are pink and adorable-looking, and he has a sweet sense of humor. Of course, he's a Polack." Laughter. "They're very antiwomen."

Why she hangs out with so many Catholics: "I don't remember my father having any Jewish friends. They were all goyim. He seemed to gravitate to the Gentiles, especially the Catholics."

The North Carolina judge who announced that raped women could not get pregnant because "the juices don't flow": "Did you ever hear of anything so crazy?"

The British Royal Family situation: "It's so sad."

Roseanne: "A psychopath."

The dessert tray: "Forget about that. I've got a divine lemon-meringue pie at home."

She leads the way to the study in her apartment, through corridors hung with drawings by her grandchildren and editorial cartoons in which she is mentioned. Her study is crammed with four decades of trophies: keys to what seem to be most American cities and some foreign ones as well; a huge collage of more than a thousand logos of papers that carry the column, including the *Oneonta Star*, the *Calgary Herald*, and the *Lubbock Avalanche-Journal*; and a host of photographs of her standing next to famous people. The shot with President Jimmy Carter shows him clasping her in a rather intimate clinch. ("He wasn't just lusting in his heart," she wisecracks.) Here she is with Walter Annenberg ("wonderful dancer"), with Hubert Humphrey, with Reagan. A framed triptych of Ted Hesburgh shows him on the day he began at Notre Dame, during the middle of his reign, and on his last day, cleaning out his desk. It is signed, "To Eppie, L but no K, Devotedly, Ted." The "L" stands for "love," the "K" for "kisses"—a long-standing joke between them. Among the dozens of honorary degrees hung on the wall, she points out a photograph of Hesburgh and her, both in cap and gown, after receiving honorary degrees from St. Leo College, in Florida. The priest is planting a big wet K on her cheek.

She has lived alone in the apartment since 1975, which is when she split up with Jules, her husband of thirty-six years. When the reporters found out that Ann Landers, who for twenty years had been advising couples to stick it out for the sake of the children, was getting divorced, the result was—surprise!—a full-court press stakeout downstairs.

She wrote about the divorce in the column, telling her readers that she wanted them to hear it from her and not from the *National Enquirer;* and that she and Jules had had a wonderful relationship but had now decided to go their separate ways. The column was shorter than usual. She asked editors to leave the rest of the space blank, in honor, as she put it, of a great marriage that never made it to the finish line. She received thirty thousand tear-drenched letters of support from her readers.

"What happened was," she says in her sharp Midwestern voice, "he had another dame." An eyebrow arches, the right dimple deepens like a

Florida sinkhole. "He told my daughter about it, but he didn't tell me. And this went on and on. Finally, my daughter told him, 'This is a pretty lousy thing you're doing here'—he was keeping this woman in our apartment in London. 'I'm going to give you thirty days, and if you don't tell her I'm going to tell her.' On the thirtieth day, she called him up and said, 'Well, thirty days is up.' But he couldn't quite bring himself to do it. So she called me and said, 'When Daddy comes home for dinner, ask him if he's got anything he wants to tell you.' And I said, 'Oh, boy.' So I did. And he said he's had this other woman for three years. 'That's the way it is,' he said. And I said, 'I'm glad you told me. The marriage is over.' 'Oh,' he said, quite surprised. 'Maybe we can work something out.' I said, 'No. No way.' He asked me to give him a few months to move out. I said, 'I'm not going to give you a lot of time, but I'll give you some time.' Finally, it occurred to me that he wasn't going to move out. He was just hanging around hoping I'd change my mind. Five weeks went by, and he's still there. I said, 'Look, Jules, I don't think you've got the message. I'm going to Athens in two weeks to get an honorary degree. When I come back, I want you out of here.' I went out and bought two dozen pairs of black socks, two dozen pairs of brown socks, two dozen handkerchiefs, a dozen shirts, and a dozen pairs of shorts; wrote down the number of the doctor, the drugstore, and the cleaning establishment, and a suggestion for a laundress. They know *nothing* about this. And I said good-bye and good luck. And that was it."

She is single but not unattached. Her companion—she calls him "my gentleman friend"—is a prosperous, well-connected lawyer. They dote on each other, travel together, and synergistically network in the Democratic stables. A month before I went to Chicago, there was this message on my answering machine: "It's Eppie! I'm in the Lincoln bedroom at the White House. I'm having a very good time with the Clintons. I'm calling everyone I know to show off."

On the bookshelves in her study are copies of *Miss Lonelyhearts, Balm in Gilead, The Joy of Sex, Portnoy's Complaint,* and *The Bonfire of the Vanities.* A bust of Lincoln looks down on a desk strewn with photographs, clippings, and correspondence, including a thank-you letter from the Hereditary Disease Foundation in Santa Monica. Eppie explains, "A reader in Michigan wrote and said, 'I have money but I don't like my family, what should I do?' And I said, 'Give it to the Hereditary Disease Foundation.' " He did. The thank-you letter is, as you might guess, effusive. According to the *Chicago Tribune,* a single column she wrote on another occasion resulted in $100 million for cancer research.

Amid the desk clutter are five bottles of Liquid Paper correction fluid. She writes at home on an IBM Selectric III. She has eight secretaries and two clerks at her *Tribune* office, ten blocks away.

About a thousand people write to her each day. The assistants winnow the letters down to about two hundred, and sort those into categories. She shows me her bundles, piled on a chair near the desk, and asks, "What have we got today?"

Today we have "Bad Doctors," "Singles," "Chivalry," "North Carolina Judge," and "Jewish."

I ask to see what they're talking about in "Jewish."

She reads, " 'Dear Ann, We are Jewish parents whose thirty-three-year-old daughter says that she is a Jewish Christian. Jesus is the messiah and Jews and Christians worship the same god. How do you react to such a daughter? We are both shocked and distraught.' "

What's happening in "Chivalry"?

A recent column featured a letter from a woman in her ninth month of pregnancy who complained that no one on the bus would give up a seat. The men, Eppie says, are writing in. "This one says, 'They want equal rights? We'll give them equal rights. These macho women have brought this on themselves.' " She pulls out another: " 'Dear Ann, I have come up with a simple solution. Why not let the women sit on the men's laps? This will completely eliminate the seating problem and no doubt bring joy and frivolity all along.' Signed, 'Bus Rider in Florida.' "

The copy of *Miss Lonelyhearts* on the shelf prompts my next question. Her answer is, "You have to insulate yourself against what is coming at you. Otherwise, you go right to pieces. I've had some letters that are very, very sad. And hopeless. 'I'm a twenty-seven-year-old and I've never had a date, and I probably never will, because I've been in a wheelchair for ten years. I just wish that some nice man could see beyond the wheelchair.' What do you tell them? What do you *say* to these people?"

She talks about a trip she made to Vietnam in 1967. She had been getting a lot of letters from the boys. "They were not happy warriors, and I decided to go and visit them in the hospital, and that was a tremendous experience. I would sit on the bed, which you're not supposed to do, and they loved the closeness. They said, 'Boy, I haven't smelled perfume in two years.' And I said, 'You could be dangerous.' You know—just to have a lot of fun with them." She brought back three hundred phone numbers. "Calling them took me three days. I had notes—'Leg gone,' 'Eye out,' 'Gerald Swanson, he lives in Akron, call mother.' I called up these people. 'This is Ann Landers and I'm calling from Chicago and I just got back from Vietnam and I saw George. He's in the hospital. He has a cold, and they didn't want it to get any worse.' " She adds, "A lot of colds. I just was not going to get into any kind of injuries. The telephone conversations I had with these people! I made friends for life."

It's getting late—the time of night when you can hear the clocks ticking. She talks about her father's coming over from Vladivostok. We speculate. What if Abe Friedman had stayed in Russia? Assuming he escaped the pogroms, would she still be there, a babushka, shoveling snow and taking in washing for extra cash? She says she regrets never asking her parents about their parents and grandparents—the only regret she has expressed all evening. Suddenly, she blurts, "Who *cares*? It's what you are today that counts, not where you came from."

She says she's been lucky, adding, "I knew what to do with the luck, that's the difference. Some people don't know what to do with it. I recognize an opportunity. But I never envisioned anything as huge as this."

She has no plans to retire. "I plan to die at the typewriter. Just keel over at the machine."

Ann Landers will die with her. "I own the name. There will never be another Ann Landers. When I go, the name goes with me. I've had offers, and I mean in the millions, for that name, and I've absolutely— No way am I going to sell the name. The name is mine and that is me, and when I go the column goes with me."

It's after midnight. I'm tired; she isn't. When I leave, she will deal with "Chivalry" and "North Carolina Judge" and "Jewish" for a couple of hours. She asks the elevator man if the night doorman got the cookies she brought back from dinner for him.

"Yes, Mrs. Lederer."

Riding down, I miss the quiet and the closeness and the smell of perfume. A few days later, there is a message on my machine: "It's Eppie. All I did was talk about me. We didn't get to talk about you."

—The New Yorker, 1995

Formative Years

Stoned in New Haven

It was the eve of the 1975 Harvard game, and two days after Generalis-simo Franco had finally, after one of the most protracted deathbed vigils in history, given up the ghost. Three Yale students climbed a three-story fire escape and made it up onto the catwalk of the billboard that still looks down on Broadway, urging new generations of Yalies to smoke, drink, eat and bank. They had brought with them a gallon of black paint and two rollers with which they wrote across the billboard in enormous letters:

NOV 19——FRANCO

NOV 22——HARVARD

The cops arrived just as they reached the bottom of the fire escape and arrested them. After frisking them, they lined them up against the wall, just as in the good old days. At this point, a burly sort of sergeant stepped forward and said, "Okay, which one of you guys is Franco?"

I don't want to ruin the story—a habit I picked up as an English major—but as an objective correlative of my era at Yale, it's pretty good. It works (I can hear Mr. Thorburn saying) on *all* levels: the perpetual misunderstanding between gown and town; the jubilation of my class-mates at the death of fascism in the face of a far greater ethic: Beat Har-vard. By 1975 Yale was much less uptight than it had been when I arrived, and they became heroes for a while, these three.

September 6, 1971, was gray, humid and horrible. Apart from the dis-orientation brought about by Orientation Day, I remember an extraordinary fear of the place and of the people, professors and classmates. Many of my peers must have felt the same fear, to judge from the number of visits I made to see them at the Yale Psychiatric Institute. By the time I graduated, I was familiar with the Thirty-Day ward, as well as the Ninety-Day ward, and knew some of the doctors by their first names.

I will not be using *we* or *us* here. The dangers of the first person plural were made unwittingly and excruciatingly clear by Joyce Maynard, who matriculated with the class of 1975, but who left before graduating and eventually turned up in Vermont with J. D. Salinger.

Miss Maynard wrote an article for *The New York Times Magazine* in the spring of freshman year entitled "Looking Back at Eighteen." It was a well-written, sensitive piece about Growing Up with the JFK assassination, Vietnam, Nixon, the killings of RFK and Martin Luther King; all the rest. A subsequent piece in the "My Turn" section of *Newsweek* argued that *we* were all looking for heroes; and a third piece, which appeared in a fashion magazine under the title, "The Embarrassment of Virginity" was about how her freshman year roommates—while she chose herself to remain chaste—used to stay up all night swapping abortion stories, birth control pills and tales of Lucullan sexual repasts that seemed a letter from *Penthouse* than Vanderbilt Hall.

This was only the third year of coeducation. There weren't nearly enough women at Yale and the really sharp-looking ones had been made paranoid by the hormonal effrontery of the more than "one thousand male leaders" that President Brewster had alluded to in a recent speech. The King was crucified for that statement, and so was poor Joyce Maynard, for her defense of virginity and for her observations on behalf of her generation. She had said nothing especially controversial or offensive in any of her articles. It was the *we*'s that did her in.

A generation likes to be spoken about—but not spoken for. *Co-opt* was one of the buzz words then (as in "The Movement has been co-opted by registered Democrats"), and I guess everyone felt as though his *Weltanschauung* had been co-opted by Joyce Maynard, because they (we) all came down on her pretty hard. Before a year had gone by, an article ran in the *Yale Daily News Magazine* entitled "The Embarrassment of Joyce Maynard," a clever but nasty little bit of invective in which the author likened her to one Consuela de la Profunda Oscuridad, publisher of an insolvent Madrid periodical of the early 1800s known chiefly for her theory that the military power of the Iberian people depended on the traditional chastity of Spanish women. A few months later she left Yale and did not return. And that was the last time anyone in my generation ever used that goddam pronoun; unless it referred to a specific group of less than six people.

Another casualty of the period was Erich Segal. *Love Story* had opened recently at the theaters, and the nation had its hankies out. His best seller had made him terribly famous, but at Yale his name invited ridicule. I give you the following, from the same issue of the *YDNM*. It ran beneath a wonderful caricature by Joel Ackerman, after David's "Death of Marat": "By dispelling the notion that to be a success in such diverse fields as track, popular writing and scholarship one has to be discerning and tasteful, Segal has given the student hope for a life after Yale." He was denied tenure and left for Princeton, where I'm sure he does not miss Yale. He gave a very good course, The Satires of Juvenal, Latin 49b.

At any rate, there was the Course Catalogue to contend with those first few days—the Blue Book: 412 pages of rules, descriptions of majors, and listings of courses. Concerning the first there didn't seem to be much problem: only troglodytes flunked out, and since Yale did not admit troglodytes, no one flunked out. QED. Actually, two F's meant you were encouraged to spend a semester away from New Haven reordering your priorities, or however the dean put it; but two F's were hard to come by, unless you really asked for them. Dope was okay. No one was kicked out for smoking pot or dropping acid (coke was still more or less unheard of). The rumor was that New Haven cops had to notify the campus cops if they were going to bust any students, and that the campus cops always notified the student in time for him to clean out his room. I suspect this was nonsense. During the balmy evenings of that Indian summer of '71 the smoke was so thick, in my entryway at least, that it once set off the fire alarm, causing an amok evacuation of McClellan. Soon people learned to ignore the fire alarms on the Old Campus, and they would go off all the time, unheeded. The campus cops got even by taking longer and longer to turn them off, until one of Yale's first lessons had been learned: accommodation. But I don't think anyone was ever busted. There was a sense of immunity and impunity behind the walls of the Gothic fortress.

The Blue Book was carried everywhere in clammy palms the first two weeks. The number of courses led to a lot of impulse shopping, naturally. Six weeks into Anthropology 43b, Maroon Societies seemed less intriguing than they had at the outset.

Some courses sounded irresistibly exotic: French 91b, *Le roman Africain de langue Française de 1950–1965:* "A critical approach to the novels of Mongo Beti. . . ." English 29 offered readings in Homer, Aeschylus, Sophocles, Euripides, Aristophanes, Shakespeare, Racine, Molière, Goethe, Ibsen, Chekhov, Beckett, Brecht, Vergil, Dante, Cervantes, Joyce: from the *Odyssey* to *Ulysses.* What a long journey that was. I remember my feet propped up on the windowsill in Linonia and Brothers on a wet spring afternoon, magnolia and wisteria blossoms outside in the courtyard, reading Molly Bloom's last lines, ". . . he could feel my breasts all perfume yes and his heart was going like mad and yes I said yes I will Yes"—the feeling of triumph that brought; and the feeling of doom sitting down afterward to begin a ten-pager on "Agenbite of Inwit."

Skill was needed in choosing a curriculum, and it was only after a few years of practice that one became adept at writing obsequious applications to the vastly oversubscribed Residential College seminars (Dear Mr. Cosell: My fascination with sports broadcasting goes back to the first time I saw you on television. . . .), or at spotting a good gut.

Guts . . . no curriculum was well-rounded without a gut or two. It wasn't until sophomore year that you became really good at spotting one by its description in the Blue Book. There were clues. For instance, the "(o)" next to the course title that meant no exam; the tip-off description, ". . . intended for students whose interests are not primarily technical . . ." or, "Enrollment limited to 100 students." Word of a new gut was passed around as carefully as *samizdat* lest too many find out about it. Some departments offered guts as a way of inflating their budget allocations. For instance, I think there were less than two dozen classics majors each year, but Classical Civilization 32b, Greek and Roman Mythology and the European Tradition, otherwise known as "Gods for Bods," drew over three hundred, mostly from the ranks of the football team, the hockey team and the *Yale Daily News.* The total enrollment of the Classics Department thus rose greatly, giving the department chairman a reason to petition the administration for more money with which to hire teaching assistants and, presumably, a new professor for The Satires of Juvenal. Thus Yale's second lesson was learned: Pyrrhonism.*

---

* *Arch* · excessive or pervasive skepticism.

There were pitfalls in choosing a gut. One professor of a course all too famous for being a gut found himself on the first day of classes staring out at hundreds of eager faces. So he announced a twenty-five-book reading list (not counting the *optional* reading), weekly five-page papers, random quizzes, a midterm, final, *and* twenty-page paper. There was a stunned silence, and at the class's second meeting the number of students attending had dropped to less than ten. The professor kept up the subterfuge for two weeks, until the deadline for course enrollment had passed, and then announced a change in course requirements from the above chamber of horrors to one five-page paper. The true-blue guts of my era were Rocks for Jocks (An Introduction to Geology); Monkeys to Junkies (Darwin and Evolution); TV 101 (Popular Culture); Pots and Pans (American Visual Arts, 1812–1870); Nuts and Sluts (Abnormal Psychology); and Moonlight and Magnolias (The Antebellum South and the Civil War, 1815–1865), this last one taught by the late, great Rolly Osterweiss. The ne plus ultra gut, which set the standard by which all others were judged, was George Schrader's The Self and Others, Philosophy 49b, described in the Blue Book as an "Exploration of the structure and dynamics of interpersonal relatedness . . . with particular attention to the writings of R. D. Laing." One three-page paper on your roommate.

Guts mattered because the Yale of the early seventies was an academic pressure cooker. It may have been hard to flunk out, but it was a lot harder to get to the top, and the job market was at a record low in those days. The first campus-wide controversy I remember, one month into freshman year, wasn't about Vietnam but rather a plan to cut back on the hours of Sterling Library. There followed such an uproar that it was withdrawn. May Day and the Panther Trial and the strike and the days of Abbie Hoffman were over (thank God), and it was once again important to get into law school, med school or Harvard Biz. A full-page ad taken out by Kodak in the *Yale Daily* read: *Maybe the way to change the world is to join a large corporation.*

All this led to something called *Weenie*-ism, as it was dubbed by a *Yale Daily* columnist. A weenie was identifiable by a bluish skin pallor, a result of overexposure to the fluorescent lighting in the underground Cross Campus Library, thick glasses, pimples, a plastic shirt-pocket guard, a calculator worn on the belt, a shrill, whining lamentation brought on by the loudspeaker announcement that the library would close in fifteen minutes, and a right arm that automatically jerked upward during classes whenever a question was asked of anyone but him. It was not a pleasant thing to watch them come midterms trekking en masse up Science Hill, reciting aloud their ketone syntheses on the way to Orgo, the Homeric nickname for Organic Chemistry, the premed prerequisite that only the dedicated passed, and that meant the difference between a Park Avenue practice and . . . oblivion!

This is not to say there were no weenies in the Humanities; quite the contrary. Horror stories abounded concerning the likelihood of English and philosophy majors obtaining gainful employment in what was always referred to numinously as Life After Yale. A history teaching assistant mused woefully over coffee once that there were exactly *two* openings for history Ph.D.'s in the country that spring. There were academic skirmishes in the Cross Campus Library: staking out a study carrel before thy neighbor did; hiding Closed Reserve books where no one else could find them. President Brewster, looking more and more like his Doonesbury counterpart, took note and made a speech decrying "Grim Professionalism." The term quickly entered the Yale consciousness and became a buzz phrase for all that was lowly, bourgeois and mean in human nature. "Grim professional!" replaced "Eat my shorts" as the epithet of choice. The deteriorating situation was not helped when the administration, discovering that something like half of the senior classes were graduating with some kind of honors, decided to toughen up the requirements for cum laude, magna and summa, as well as for departmental honors. The keening of weenies, an unearthly, mournful sound, was heard echoing through the stone courtyards long into the sleepless nights.

There was a girl who studied even while walking between classes; when it rained, she covered her books in large plastic baggies so she could continue despite. When at graduation she was awarded the Warren Prize for the highest scholastic standing and it was announced she had gotten *thirty-six* A's over the years, she was booed.

At the same commencement, one of the Class Historians said in his address how much things had changed. He told the story of Gertrude Stein at Harvard turning in her exam booklet unused after five minutes to philosophy Professor William James, saying, "It's too nice a day for taking an exam," to which James replied, "Ah, I see you understand perfectly the nature of philosophy, Miss Stein."

"Well," the Historian continued, "at Yale, during a recent exam, a proctor watched as a student bald-facedly copied off both people sitting next to him and consulted a crib sheet. When it was time to hand in the blue exam booklets, the fellow walked down to the front of the room where the table was already piled high with blue booklets. The proctor confronted him, saying she had seen everything. The fellow looked at her and said, 'Do you know me?' 'No,' she said, upon which he thrust his blue booklet into the middle of the tall pile of booklets and walked out scot-free." The Historian concluded his remarks saying that the true spirit of the Yale class of 1976 had been caught by the anonymous scribbler who had written on a stall of the CCL men's room, "God didn't create the world in seven days. He fucked off the first six and pulled an all-nighter."

> The picketeer and the patrons exchanged insults as the day progressed. Name-calling was fairly mild, however, with only such words as "pig" and "slob" being used.
>
> *Yale Daily News*
> January 24, 1973

Mory's had fired a waiter for trying to organize a union, and Local 217 had thrown up a picket line outside. Mory's meanwhile had lost its liquor license temporarily over its refusal to admit women. The draft had just ended, the peace in Vietnam that had been at hand finally was—for the time being, and Yale had officially contributed twenty-one dead to the war. The Reverend William Sloane Coffin, looking more and more like his counterpart in Doonesbury, was taking a year off "to assimilate experiences." Sophomore John Bobusack did seven thousand sit-ups at Payne Whitney to Kostelanetz's "Light Music of Shostakovich." Jimmy Carter, Governor of Georgia, spoke at the Political Union, and, according to the *News*, "predicted confidently that the Democrats will capture the White House in '76." General William Westmoreland had been prevented from speaking at the Political Union, as had Secretary of State William Rogers, who pulled out when the Yale administration announced it could not guarantee his safety. Drama student Meryl Streep was appearing in *Major Barbara;* undergraduate Sigourney Weaver in *Woman Beware Woman*. The Department of University Health had issued a warning on the effects of nitrous oxide; Ken Kesey had brought along a tank with him on his visit to Yale, and thanks to a complaisant night watchman at National Compressed Gas in North Haven, who would turn the other way for fifty dollars, laughing gas was very in, despite DUH's warnings about hypoxia or blowing a hole through the back of your throat. A copy of Thomas More's *Utopia* was stolen from the vault of the Elizabethan Club. The bursar's office announced that tuition, room and board for '73–'74 would probably go to the unheard-of five thousand dollars a year; and it was calculated that every class cut or slept through cost nineteen dollars, a ratiocination that nevertheless did not increase the number of classes attended. Timothy Dwight College announced it would hold an honest-to-God prom that spring. Ann Landers told an audience in SSH 114, apropos of admitting women to Mory's, "If they don't want you there, forget it." Robert Penn Warren retired. Francis Donahue resigned from the *News* after fifty years. George and Harry's closed after forty-five years. Wes Lockwood, a sophomore member of the Yale Christian Fellowship, a.k.a. the Jesus Freaks, was kidnapped by his parents and subsequently deprogrammed by Ted Patrick, which brought the phenomenon into the pages of *Time* magazine. Several Yale women were raped, ushering in the era of locked gates. The faculty voted to hold exams before Christmas, and an associate professor of theology was charged with having "deviate sexual relations" with a sixteen-year-old boy in a Long Island motel room.

I suppose every generation of undergraduates should have at least one Divinity School scandal. Maybe it's significant that this one went by virtually unnoticed. Deviate undertakings were scarcely confined to the Div School; they were in fact de rigueur. During spring of sophomore year I participated in my first and only Black Mass—for credit, in a psychology course. We (there were five of us) arranged to hold it in the beautiful little chapel at the base of Harkness Tower. We wrote up a liturgy, complete with a backward Lord's Prayer, got the right kind of candles, arranged for a female sacrificial victim—she was awfully obliging about it—dry ice, Moog synthesizer, the works. It almost didn't come off, though, because one of us spilled the dry ice and water all over the chapel carpet and had to borrow a mop from the Branford common room, which at the moment was being used by the Party of the Right for one of their Homage to Franco or Edmund Burke soirées. They asked what the mop was needed for, and being in a hurry I just explained we were having a Black Mass over at the chapel and had spilled dry ice. They grew quite alarmed at this and were preparing to storm over in their pinstripes on behalf of Organized Religion, but the professor arrived and explained it was all for credit, which seemed to impress them and they went away.

The Tang Cup Competition, for which Timothy Dwight's best and brightest trained all year long and which involved swallowing eight ounces of beer in less than one second (I think the record was .8 sec.)— I will not go into. But I should mention the Yale Invisible Precision Marching Band, whose halftime shows Woodbridge Hall began censoring after its Salute to Birth Control one game. The alums were apparently unamused when the band assumed the shape of a coathanger and marched from end zone to end zone playing "You Must Have Been a Beautiful Baby."

Acid use went up precipitously during winters, with some dealers barely able to meet demand, especially when *Fantasia* had its annual showing at the RKO on College Street. The first five rows were usually filled with drug-crazed youth, the rest of the theater with children and their mothers, who were trying to instill in them a love of classical music. Such were the winters of discontent in New Haven.

But the film societies made midwinter bearable. You could go to a movie every night for seventy-five cents and see anything from *Nosferatu* to *A Hundred and One Dalmations*. *Casablanca* was so much a part of life that the posters didn't bother to include the name, only the showing time superimposed on a grainy blowup of Rick and Ilsa on the foggy tarmac. *We'll always have Paris*. A festival of films made by Yalies featured *A Child's Alphabet with Carnal References to DNA Replication in the Garden of Eden*.

Practically every college had its own film society. Berkeley used to put on all-night festivals showing Marx Brothers and Sherlock Holmes until dawn. Every Wednesday at midnight in Linsly-Chit 101 there was a horror movie, part of the Things That Go Bump in the Night series, presented by Gary Lucas and Bill Moseley. They were very *noires bêtes,* these two. Before the showing of *The Texas Chainsaw Massacre* they presented a skit strongly reminiscent of the *mort par cent coupées,* the method of public execution that disappeared in the twilight of the Ch'ing dynasty, with

V–8 juice splashing all over the same stage where that morning Professor Hartman had lectured on "The Rime of the Ancient Mariner." Those contrasts were everywhere: *L'Incoronazione de Poppea* in the JE dining hall, Daniel Ellsberg next door in the common room. Lucas's and Moseley's guerrilla theater of the absurd (they would think me so for putting such a name on it) went on gleefully until they told a reporter for the *Yale Daily News Magazine* that the Bump series audiences were mostly made up of "groyds [Negroes] and fags," thereby enraging both of those undergraduate groups and making Lucas's and Moseley's physical well-being questionable for some time. Moseley called me up at *Esquire* several years later with an idea for an article on cattle mutilations in Colorado. "I've become something of an authority on the subject," he said. I was glad to hear from Bill, even if the article idea didn't go over so well at the next article idea meeting.

Yale was not immune from national viruses, and so for a while people could be seen running naked through the snow outside Yankee Doodle and J. Press. The night that Elliot Richardson, late of the Saturday Night Massacre, came to speak, several hundred Yale men and women streaked through the Old Campus, watched mutely by President Brewster and Mr. Richardson from the steps of Battell Chapel, holding onto their brandy snifters for dear life. The phenomenon was otherwise short-lived. I don't know if all of this made more or less sense than swallowing goldfish or whatever. I guess it presaged some kind of return to post-Revolution normalcy, though there were still some unspent political energies left.

I remember being in the Cross Campus Library one night, holed up, trying desperately to understand Heidegger's *On the Origin of the Work of Art*—I never did—and hearing shouts of "Ho, Ho. . . ." At first I assumed it had something to do with Dean Howard Taft, whose nickname was Ho Ho. But as I poked my head out of the cubicle, the shouting became more distinct: "Ho, Ho, Ho Chi Minh, the NLF is gonna win." The protestors numbered about twenty. They made a quick march through the CCL, drawing venomous stares from weenies and grim professionals, chanting their support for the architect of what has become a nation where concentration camps, genocide and odes to Stalin are commonplace; and left. John Kerry, looking more and more like his Doonesbury counterpart, spoke at the PU.

Yale was a place where generals, Marine Corps recruiters, the Secretary of State, and William Shockley were not allowed to speak, but where Fidel Castro's representatives, Jane Fonda, Ralph Nader, Frank Mankiewicz and, for that matter, anyone who called himself a Marxist, were received with the kind of enthusiasm accorded Neil Armstrong on his return from Tranquillity Base. Every time eggs were thrown and a guest speaker was shouted down, the administration promised a thorough investigation of this flagrant disregard for freedom of speech and appointed a special committee made up of history professors, which did—nothing. During the aborted Shockley debate, black and white students surrounded his opponent, William Rusher of *National Review,* the man who came to *refute* Shockley's thesis that blacks are genetically inferior to whites, shouted "Racist!" at him, spat repeatedly in his face— while campus cops looked on—and stomped up and down on the roof of his car. Nothing was done to the people who did this. Yale once again announced serious action, which by now everyone knew better than to take seriously. This was not an endearing part of Yale, and I cannot phrase my bitterness better than the Reverend Julian Hart once did. He was one of my professors in Religious Studies, and his Religious Themes in Contemporary Fiction was the kind of course—as Richard Sewall's Tragedy was—that made Yale so exciting. He announced one day in class that he would not be returning next semester for what would have been his thirtieth year of teaching. He was asked why, to which he replied, "Anyone who has been around Yale as long as I have has seen the lowest absurdities perpetuated with the highest degree of solemnity."

I have to say—I was warned, early on: February 20 of freshman year. There it was, above the fold in that day's *Yale Daily,* a little story reporting the findings of Professor Jonathan Spence, Yale's distinguished Sinologist, to wit that Mao Tse-tung never would have become Chairman without the help of Yale. You see, after being introduced to Communist theory in Li Ta-chao's Marxist study group in Changsha, the young Mao, aged twenty-six, needed some kind of forum through which to promulgate his political philosophy. The student union of Yale-in-China invited him to be the editor of its journal. Years later in Shanghai, out of money and wanting to form an area branch of the party, Mao once again turned to Yale-in-China, which obliged him by renting him three rooms for his "bookshop." Because of the success of the "bookshop," Mao was chosen as a delegate to the First Party Congress of the Chinese Communist Party, at Shanghai, in 1921. The rest you know about.*

As for my own youthful passion for terrorism, I was lucky, since I could indulge it through the *Yale Daily News Magazine,* where I spent most of sophomore year and the whole of junior year, to the everlasting detriment of my liberal arts education. It was in the Briton Hadden building on York Street that I learned Yale's third lesson—greasing by: perfecting the arts of obtaining dean's excuses, the power cram, killing off imaginary aunts and uncles so as to postpone hourly tests. Most important of all was getting on well with the dean's secretary. They were the *real* power of Yale. All this was necessary in order to write and edit endless copy on the usual lapidary topics: Mrs. William Sloane Coffin, Freshmen Counselors, the legend of Brian Dowling, Politics in the English department, the steam tunnels, Grove Street Cemetery. Our formula was succinctly and accurately described by a subsequent editor as turning major stories into filler items and filler items into major stories. Still, it seemed to work, and on occasion we were able to inflict inaccurate and misleading journalism on our public. One time, when the big question was who would succeed Kingman Brewster as president, we concocted a poll, awarding insignificant percentages to Dean Taft and the three other likely successors and a whopping 40 percent to Professor Kai Erikson—for no better reason than that we were awfully fond of Kai and wanted to give his career a nudge. The faculty took the poll quite seriously and for days Kai's hitherto-unknown-but-immense popularity among the students was a topic of conversation. Actually, Kai got along quite well without our help, because he really is terrific.

Another time we devoted an entire issue to a pet subject, drugs, complete with a poll—this time a real, though not statistically valid one— which showed that 14 percent of Yale students had at some time sold drugs. Anyone who sold so much as a joint to a roommate could answer the question affirmatively, and did. Local television picked it up, as did AP and UPI, and America was informed the next day that ALMOST 20 PERCENT OF YALE STUDENTS SUPPORT THEMSELVES BY SELLING NARCOTICS. Yale was in the midst of the $370 million capital fund-raising drive at the time, so the news was not well received

---

* I have one consolation, though, in a *Yale Daily* headline of the same year

HARRINGTON SEES U S. GOING
TO COLLECTIVE SOCIALIST STATE

at Woodbridge Hall. Dean Martin Griffin spent most of the following week on the phone explaining to choleric alums that Elm and High Streets had not really become the new Haight-Ashbury, while the editors made themselves discreetly scarce. Yale had by then hired a full-time public relations man, Mr. Stanley Flink; and it gave us pride and satisfaction to know we kept Stanley busy. His face got longer and longer until eventually one day it fell off.

Our last issue we were proud of. It contained stories by Tom Wolfe, Anthony Burgess, Ayn Rand, Ray Bradbury, John Cheever, William Styron, William Saroyan, Joyce Carol Oates, Erich Fromm and Art Buchwald, not an undistinguished bunch of contributors to an undergraduate rag. It was John Tierney's brainstorm: send out letters to great authors asking them to contribute to the Mag—at the top scale rate of one dollar per word. (What *Playboy* then paid.) Our budget was one hundred dollars, so we could only afford ten-word articles by ten great authors. Fortunately no more than ten replied, so we were spared the awkwardness of sending Norman Mailer a rejection letter. Contributors were asked to write on the End of the World, a popular theme as finals and graduation approached. Anthony Burgess sent an exquisite poem, all the way from Rome, gratis; Tom Wolfe wrote a sixteen-word piece and asked that the remaining four dollars of his fee be sent to "the Connecticut novelist, William Styron, to help cheer him up"; Ayn Rand said she was all written out on the subject.

I remember those production nights: standing over the light boards for sixteen hours at a stretch; the smell of developing fluid; fingertips stinging from razor blade cuts; the hum and click of the Compugraphic and Morisawa; running up to the Board Room at five in the morning and through a bluish nicotine fog pleading with Lloyd Grove *please* to finish his goddamn lead article; the glazed look on his face as he said he had only three pages to go. *THREE PAGES!?* But Lloyd's copy was always worth the wait. Now they wait for it at *The Washington Post*. In that last issue we ran the story on why there are daffodils in the moats around the colleges each spring. They were planted in memory of a little girl named Barbara Vietor, who died of asthma at the age of nine. I cannot explain why the memory of the daffodils and a child I never knew should mean so much to me still, but it does, and I will always be grateful to Yale for that, as for so much else.

—My Harvard, My Yale, 1981

What Did You Do in
the War, Daddy?
Well, It's Like This. . . .

The day I turned nineteen, I went down for my physical and had my first and only experience of Army life. I took with me a letter from Dr. Murphy, my childhood doctor, describing in uncompromising detail the asthma that had been a major part of my life, occasionally severe enough to put me in the hospital for a week. As I shuffled along the line from urinalysis to the hemorrhoid inspection I tried to look wan and generally tubercular, ready to faint if any voice were raised in my direction. One Army doctor looked at my letter with an unimpressed scowl. My hands got clammy and I wiped them on my forehead, hoping the perspiration would give my brow a nicely febrile sheen. At last I came to the end of the line, to a table at which three doctors reviewed the other doctors' evaluations and ruled on them.

"Asthma?" said one of them, looking up.

I nodded feebly and made an emphysematous sound resembling a yes, intended to make him understand the asthma had left me with a dearth of pleura, which I was conserving in order to participate in the sacrament of last rites, which in my case was obviously more or less imminent.

After the longest pause I have ever waited through, he said, "Rejected."

I waited until I was a few blocks from the examination center before breaking into a full run. (They might have been watching.) I have never since run so fast. When a mile later I hit the campus and saw my roommate and some friends across the quadrangle, I broke into a sprint. A few yards from them I jumped and in midair shouted, "I FLUNKED!" loudly enough to cause nearby heads to turn and wonder, probably, what inversion of academic values had caused this deranged jubilation.

Twelve years later, on a November day in Washington, D.C., I watched as the Vietnam Veterans Memorial was dedicated. At the edge of the crowd where I stood there was a Marine, about forty years old, ramrod-stiff and impeccable in ceremonial dress. He turned suddenly from the proceedings and, walking a few paces away, took off his glasses, put two fingers of a white-gloved hand to the bridge of his nose, and began to weep.

Watching his grief made me feel like an intruder. I felt I had no business there, so I left the grounds.

There was a lot of talk that weekend about healing. It was true the veterans finally did get the welcome home and a measure of the appreciation and recognition that they had always deserved. A group of college students in a Georgetown bar stood up and applauded when a group of vets walked in. That alone seemed a remarkable enough event for President Reagan to make prominent mention of it in a speech shortly afterward.

In a city once known for its spectacular antiwar demonstrations, there were no sour notes, only the ads on television for a movie that had just opened: Sylvester Stallone working out his post-traumatic stress disorders on a small American town—with an M-16 and everything short of close air support. Good timing, Hollywood! But when it was over—the parade, the speeches, reunions, workshops, the fifty-six-hour vigil at the National Cathedral during which the names of the 57,939 dead and missing were read aloud—there was no doubt it really had been a homecoming. Myra MacPherson wrote in *The Washington Post,* "Now there is some meager measure of reconciliation; some who used to taunt them [the homecoming soldiers] at army camps and airports—the student deferred taunting those less privileged draftees or those who felt compelled to serve their country—admit guilt and shame."

It's been ten years now since the troops came home, but until recently I had never once heard anyone admit to guilt or shame over not having gone to Vietnam—not in hundreds of conversations about the war. I find this strange; *meager,* I think, is the operative word.

The gap between those who went to war and those who stayed behind was larger in the Vietnam War than in any other war in our history. Fifty-three million Americans came of age between the signing of the Gulf of Tonkin Resolution on August 7, 1964, and April 30, 1975, the day Saigon fell to the Communists. Of those fifty-three, eleven million served in the military; and of those eleven, fewer than three went to Indochina. That leaves forty-two million Americans who did not serve. Twenty-six million of these were women, who weren't called (though the sixty-five hundred women who did serve were essential to the war effort). About sixteen million were men who were deferred, exempted, or disqualified or who evaded the draft. About 80 percent of the Vietnam generation did not participate in the dominant event of their time. About 6 percent of military-age males saw actual combat.

If the millions tend to blur, consider: How many of your friends went to Vietnam?

It wasn't until the memorial opening that I stood face-to-face with my own guilt and shame. These feelings are, I acknowledge, somewhat illogical. My medical disability is genuine—even as I write this I take periodic hits off my asthma inhaler. Into the bargain I suffer from a rather unpleasant vascular malady called Horton's cluster headache. I did not dodge the draft, starve myself, shoot off a toe, act psycho, or go to Sweden. So whence this permanent malaise? Go figure. Guilt is a pretty personal affair, and it's not my business to tell people how they should feel about not having gone to Vietnam. But now that the vets have finally come home and the healing has begun, it may be time for those of us who do have misgivings about not having fought to think, out loud, about the consequences of what we did—and didn't do.

For those who never left, there is no ceremony and no coming home; if the healing is to be complete, then all the wounds from that war will need healing.

Those of my parents' generation who missed World War II were devastated by not being part of it. When an uncle of mine talks about being just too young for that war, he uses the word *traumatic*. He once told me that for him and many of his peers Korea came "almost as a relief."

But it's hard to compare World War II and Vietnam. A lot of people I know say there's no good reason to feel guilty about having missed Vietnam. There's an echo in their arguments from *Henry IV, Part I*:

> . . . but for these vile guns,
> He would himself have been a soldier.

They say it was a lousy war on every score. They talk about My Lai, body counts, fraggings, Agent Orange, the Phoenix Program, the inability to distinguish enemies from friendlies; about the long list of horrors that seem peculiar to Vietnam. They feel vindicated, and some of them are startled at the question of whether they feel any guilt or shame at having sat out the war. Okay, some say, the "Baby killer!" business did get out of hand. Any movement has its excesses. But it was our movement, our resistance to the war, our not going that convinced the White House and the Pentagon and the Congress to end the war.

True, but six months after the fall of Saigon in 1975 James Fallows examined an entrenched fallacy of the antiwar movement in an article for *The Washington Monthly* called "What Did You Do in the Class War, Daddy?" The article had, in the words of the *Monthly*'s editor, Charles Peters, "tremendous impact. It was a turning point in a generation, being willing to open itself up to other than cliché-left truths about Vietnam."

Fallows described how as a Harvard student he had starved himself down to 120 pounds and affected a suicidal disposition at his Army physical. As the doctor wrote "unqualified" on his form, "I was overcome by a wave of relief, which for the first time revealed to me how great my terror had been, and by the beginning of the sense of shame which remains with me to this day."

His article was a brilliant and scathing indictment of a system that sent the sons of the working class off to fight its war while allowing the overwhelming majority of the sons of the middle and upper classes to avoid it. One of Fallows's most penetrating self-criticisms was that while those in the antiwar movement (of which he was a part) convinced themselves they were the "sand in the gears of the great war machine" by burning their draft cards and marching, the real way—the courageous way—to have ended the war would have been to *go* to war.

"As long as the little gold stars," he wrote, "kept going to homes in Chelsea and the backwoods of West Virginia, the mothers of Beverly Hills and Chevy Chase and Great Neck and Belmont were not on the telephones to their congressmen, screaming *you killed my boy*, they were not writing to the President that his crazy, wrong, evil war had put their boys in prison and ruined their careers. It is clear by now that if the men of Harvard had wanted to do the very most they could to help shorten the war, they should have been drafted or imprisoned en masse."

Fallows's argument seems to me airtight; but there are a lot of people who persist in the fallacy, and this has contributed to the anger that many vets understandably feel. Who made the real sacrifice, anyway? Some who never went to Vietnam or into the military did suffer because of it, though the numbers are relatively minuscule: of 209,517 accused draft offenders, 3,250 were imprisoned and 3,000 became fugitives. But, as Paul Starr, author of *The Discarded Army: Vietnam Veterans After Vietnam,* wrote, "the conflict was waged without any privation at home, and the result has been an enormous disproportion of sacrifice. A few have been asked to die; virtually nothing has been asked of everyone else."

Whatever sacrifices were made at home, the ones made on the field of battle cost more, and it is hard—for me, anyway—to disagree with something James Webb, the twice-wounded, highly decorated Marine and author of *Fields of Fire,* told *Time* magazine apropos the gap between vets and nonvets: "We're going to have to lead this country side by side. We're going to have to resolve this. The easiest way is for people who didn't serve in those years to come off this pretentiousness of moral commitment and realize that the guys who went to combat are the ones who suffered the most. They are also the ones who gave the most."

The hard, psychological evidence is that what most people who didn't go to Vietnam feel is neither guilt nor regret but relief. Two years ago the Center for Policy Research submitted an exhaustive nine-hundred-page study to the Veterans Administration and Congress called *Legacies of Vietnam.* Its results, if not surprising, were interesting. It found that only a bare minority of nonveterans, 3.5 percent, feel that staying out of the military had a negative impact on their lives. Thirty-six percent feel it had a positive effect. When asked how staying out of the service had benefited them, the majority said it was by enabling them to pursue their education and career. The next-highest majority said that staying out gave them a competitive advantage over their veteran peers. A veteran, I think, would find this last datum depressing and disheartening.

The question, though, of whether nonvets ought to feel vindicated by the conduct and results of the Vietnam War is, in a sense, beside the point. War is war and combat is combat, and ever since the first jawbone was raised in anger men have felt a terrible need to prove themselves on the field of glory.

"I have heard the bullets whistle," wrote George Washington about his adventures in the French and Indian War, "and believe me, there is something charming in the sound." A century later, watching a Federal charge be repulsed at Fredericksburg, Robert E. Lee mused, "It is well that war is so terrible, or we should grow too fond of it." Vietnam may have performed a great national service by demonstrating for my generation the truth of the general's remark.

The lore is full of stories of those who got out of the war. But for some, not getting into the Army and not getting to Vietnam had nearly as traumatic or profound an impact as being left out of the Normandy landing had on those of another generation. Their stories are far rarer than the other category, but also worth the telling.

One fellow I know is convinced his entire family has been historically cheated. His grandfather was fourteen when World War I ended; his father was fourteen when World War II ended; he was fourteen when the Vietnam War ended.

Robert Owen was thirteen when his brother Dwight was killed in a Vietcong ambush in 1967. (Dwight's name is inscribed in the lobby of the State Department in Washington, along with those of other recipients of the Secretary's Award, the State Department's highest honor.) Robert worshiped Dwight, and the death hit him very hard.

Six years later Owen was a freshman at Stanford, watching television in his dormitory, when the news showed the first batch of POWs setting foot on the tarmac at Subic Bay. When Jeremiah Denton, who'd been a prisoner of the North Vietnamese for seven years, stepped to the microphone and said, "God bless America," Owen suddenly found tears running down his cheeks.

Not long afterward the Marines happened to be on campus recruiting. Owen had not awakened with the idea of signing up, but when he read an ad in that morning's student newspaper saying, DON'T BE GOOD LITTLE NAZIS: STOP THE MARINE RECRUITING, he went down for an interview. The protesters outside were trying physically to prevent anyone from getting in. Owen, who has the build of a pentathlon competitor, shoved his way through. He signed up for the Platoon Leader program. Then came the physical. He flunked it because of a lacrosse injury to his knee. Then began a long, consuming quest.

During the four years following graduation, he tried to get into a half dozen California police departments. Each time, the knee kept him out.

In desperation, he offered to sign insurance waivers. No one would accept such an arrangement.

Nineteen-eighty found him in the same part of the world where Dwight had gone in answer to his own call, on the Cambodia-Thailand border, processing refugees from Pol Pot's reign of terror for the International Rescue Committee. Then the word came that his father was dying, and he returned home to take care of him. During that ordeal he tried twice to enlist, in the Marines and in the Navy's SEAL (commando) program, but the Achilles' knee kept showing up on the X rays. As he was going out the door the Navy doctor suggested he try some other branch of the government. Now he works on Capitol Hill.

After telling the long story one night recently at a Chinese restaurant in Georgetown, he said he'd finally come to a realization that allowed him peace of mind. After all the attempts to put himself in positions where he'd have to prove himself, he'd finally decided that "if and when the test ever comes, I'm going to get my red badge of courage, or die trying."

In the silence that followed, the fortune cookies came and we cracked them open. His read: YOUR WISDOM HAS KEPT YOU FAR AWAY FROM MANY DANGERS.

My friend Barnaby writes from Paris a fourteen-page letter imbued with something like regret, about what not going has meant to him. (Unlike me, he was never called. If he had been, he would have gone.) He mentions a well-known novelist he knows who, when drunk, tells people he was a fighter pilot in Vietnam. (He wasn't.) But Barnaby understands the novelist's dilemma and alludes to something Hemingway once said: that if a writer goes to war for a year, he will have enough to write about for the rest of his lifetime.

He remembers a man he met once in a bar in Vermont, a construction worker who'd been stalking deer in the woods for a week with a bow. He invited the man back to his cabin for a drink, and the man told Barnaby about his year in Vietnam as a gunner on river patrol boats. This was, incidentally, three years before *The Deer Hunter* opened.

"It had started to rain heavily as we finished the beer. It was a chilly November. I offered him the couch next to the fire, but he declined, saying he had a tent, and that there was an eight-point buck he'd been closing in on for three days. He thought he could get him at dawn. We shook hands at the door and he stepped out into the cold wet night.

There wasn't an ounce of fear in him, and I knew that he thought I was soft—I hadn't been to Vietnam—but he didn't hold it against me, perhaps because of the way I listened to him talk."

Barnaby dwells on the word *pledge*. "I knew [at the time] that we had pledged to support that country. While I never liked the phrase, 'My country do or die,' I get a lump in my throat when I hear the pledge of allegiance. I think the word pledge is one of the most beautiful in the world. . . . To stand by a pledge can be an ordeal, and the pledge is only as good as the man who makes it. I will never know how good my pledge is."

Both Owen and Barnaby were looking for something, obviously: for a test of manhood, a chance to prove themselves under circumstances far more grueling than the challenges civilian, peacetime life throws our way: college exams, job deadlines, love affairs, wind surfing. I think some of the stories we've all heard about getting out of the draft or about antiwar demonstrations have a kind of wistful quality to them, as if those telling them are trying to relate ersatz war experiences.

One friend who was in a lot of demonstrations confessed how disappointed he was that he'd never been gassed, "because then it would have been my war too." Another tells a story of taking multiple doses of LSD before being inducted, which, after an understandably complicated series of events, resulted in his getting off. It's a funny, and in some ways harrowing, story. It's his war story.

There's an undercurrent of envy here. I certainly feel it, at least. I have a number of friends who served in Vietnam. One was with Special Forces, another was in Army intelligence, another with the CIA. They all saw death up close every day, and many days dealt it themselves. They're married, happy, secure, good at what they do; they don't have nightmares and they don't shoot up gas stations with M-16s. Each has a gentleness I find rare in most others, and beneath it a spiritual sinew that I ascribe to their experience in the war, an aura of *I have been weighed on the scales and have not been found wanting.*

The word *veteran* comes from the Latin for *experienced*. But it's not the same experience we gain by passing through the gradual, attenuated rites of passage of lives measured out with coffee spoons. In his extraordinary book about his experiences in Vietnam, *A Rumor of War,* Philip Caputo wrote, "We learned the old lessons about fear, cowardice, courage, suffering, cruelty, and comradeship. Most of all, we learned about death at an age when it is common to think of oneself as immortal. Everyone loses that illusion eventually, but in civilian life it is lost in installments over the years. We [in Vietnam] lost it all at once, and, in the span of months, passed from boyhood through manhood to a premature middle age."

In that passage, they learned something very hard to obtain outside the battlefield: the "communion between men [in infantry battalions] is as profound as any between lovers. Actually, it is more so. It does not demand for its sustenance the reciprocity, the pledges of affection, the endless reassurances required by the love of men and women. It is, unlike marriage, a bond that cannot be broken by a word, by boredom or divorce, or by anything other than death. Sometimes even that is not strong enough. Two friends of mine died trying to save the corpses of their men from the battlefield. Such devotion, simple and selfless, the sentiment of belonging to each other, was the one decent thing we found in a conflict otherwise notable for its monstrosities."

At the heart of Dr. Johnson's saying that "every man thinks meanly of himself for not having been a soldier" are a great many childish, mud- and blood-splattered romantic notions and dreams of glory. In the context of what Caputo is saying, maybe the best reason for agreeing with the doctor is that by not putting on uniforms, we forfeited what might have been the ultimate opportunity, in increasingly self-obsessed times, of making the ultimate commitment to something greater than ourselves: the survival of comrades.

The fragging stories blurred an important realization: if anything is clear about the ethos of the American soldiers in Vietnam, it is that they weren't fighting for democracy, or against communism, but for each other.

Dr. Arthur Egendorf, a clinical psychologist now in private practice who served with Army intelligence in Vietnam and who was a principal author of the congressional study *Legacies of Vietnam,* says that for non-veterans of Vietnam, the effects of not going are "mostly negligible, not the sort of thing to talk about as mental illness. Maybe some feel actual guilt, but mostly what we see is a kind of vague malaise." Guilt—severe guilt—is still having nightmares thirteen years later because, as in the case of one of Egendorf's friends, your unit was wiped out while you were on a reconnaissance patrol. The man in question blocked from conscious recollection the names of his friends who were killed in the attack: "We went to the Vietnam memorial together, and he literally could not mobilize himself to touch the wall because he was so ashamed of not being able to remember the names of those who died. Now," says Egendorf, putting all this in sobering perspective, "*that's* guilt."

But he does have "an impression" about the impact not going had on the generation that in the main didn't.

"If there is one major strand," he says, "that is played out among the nonveterans, it's this whole thing about nonengagement, noncommitment. Service got a bad name in the last war. People who didn't serve felt vindicated for keeping clean. And the main cost of all that is much more social than in any obvious sense individual. You see a declining trust in public institutions of all sorts. It's a suspicion that *I got away with something.* There's no neurotic guilt, but there is a lingering need to cover up and justify a posture of nonengagement. It means that there are a lot of lives that are less vital because of it."

Egendorf is not at all critical of those who, as he says, took a stand against the war on political or moral grounds; in fact, he admires the courage of those who undertook nonviolent protest.

On the other hand, he says that in the course of undertaking the *Legacies* survey, he began to find that a majority of Vietnam-generation males evinced attitudes he describes as "turned-off, who cares, don't count on me."

"*That's* where the main cost lies. The form of the war experience becomes 'I got off scot-free, ha ha ha.' And that is *not* a posture on which you can build a creative, constructive, determined, self-respecting life. Those kinds of virtues come out of a sense of having given oneself, having served, standing for something. Caring enough, putting your neck out.

"So when you have deliberately not done those things—and the zeitgeist was to justify pulling out, cover your duff—then you have people fooling themselves about how to make it in the world. They bullshit themselves into thinking the great virtue is staying aloof, being noncommittal. But that's precisely what *doesn't* work. What works is to commit yourself to what you care about."

Egendorf has two last observations on all this. The first is that this guilt—or malaise—is a waste of time. It doesn't do anyone any good. "At first," he says, "it seems like a badge of worthiness. *At least I'm suffering.* It can lead to a kind of belated hero worship [of vets]. But that's useless, really, and ultimately self-destructive. What we need to muster for vets is dignity and respect. We're all partners in a prearranged marriage. There's no illusion of romance, but we do need to have respect for each other. And if we're going to have that, we're going to need forgiveness—for ourselves."

The other is that "people called the shots as best they could at the time. It's not an excuse, but a question of recognizing that the dumb thing we all do is blame ourselves for not having known what it took some crucial experience to teach us. Guilt becomes a kind of booby prize. What we need much more than that is a fresh look at what now calls for commitment."

Whether it's guilt or malaise, what I do know for certain is that if someday I have a son and he asks me what I did in the Vietnam War, I'll have to tell him that my war experience, unlike that of his grandfather, consisted of a hemorrhoid check.

Most people I know who avoided the war by one means or another do not feel the way I do, and I'm in no position to fault their reasons or their justifications.

But I do know some others who are still trying to come to terms with all this. And sometimes it comes to the surface, a sense of incompleteness . . .

"I didn't suffer with them. I didn't watch my buddies getting wiped out next to me. And though I'm relieved, at the same time I feel as though part of my reflex action is not complete."

. . . of an unpaid debt . . .

"I haven't served my country. I've never faced life or death. I'm an incomplete person. I walk by the memorial and look at the names and think, 'There but for the grace of God . . .' "

. . . of how easy it was . . .

"The dean once told me, 'You know, the one thing your generation has done is made martyrdom painless.' "

. . . of having missed history's bus . . .

"It's guilt at not having participated. At not having done anything. I blew up neither physics labs in Ann Arbor nor Vietcong installations. I just vacillated in the middle. It's still confusing to me. Only in the last few years have I tried to straighten it out in terms of my country. And now I know I should have gone, if only to bear witness."

—Esquire, 1983

Incoming

□

In August, *Esquire* published an article in which I made the apparently startling admission of having regrets about not having served in the Vietnam War. I say "apparently" because in ten years of journalism, I have never experienced the kind of reaction that one article elicited. It twanged some national chord. I was glad, having researched and written the piece in order to find out if anyone else felt this way. But I was genuinely surprised at the volume of the response. A brief consideration of that response might interest those who have thoughts on the matter, pro or con.

What I wrote was this: I was classified 4F, legitimately. At the time I was delighted and relieved. Now I tend to feel that, whatever the circumstances, I got off a little too clean. It was an ill-advised war, but it was a war. Some went and some didn't.

I distinguished between "childish, mud- and blood-splattered romantic notions and dreams of glory," and something else. I wondered if it wasn't possible that by not going "we forfeited what might have been the ultimate opportunity, in increasingly self-obsessed times, of making the ultimate commitment to something greater than ourselves: the survival of comrades."

None of this struck me as especially novel or insightful. I did not have to look under rocks or call up *Soldier of Fortune* magazine for sources. Among those I quoted were Philip Caputo, James Webb, Robert E. Lee and George Washington. James Fallows had broken the ground in *The Washington Monthly* eight years ago.

My piece was a kind of footnote, something I had been mulling over, and which had coalesced as I watched the dedication of the Vietnam

Veterans Memorial in November '82. It was neither an endorsement of the Vietnam War nor an endorsement of war. It appeared before the Beirut bombings and the invasion of Grenada and the article in the Style section about the Airborne Rangers who got their jollies by "stomping to death" a homosexual.

I should have known something was wrong when the *Phil Donahue Show* called. (I declined.) Then the *Today* show called, followed by PBS, a number of radio stations. People writing books on the aftermath of Vietnam called.

Bob Greene wrote a syndicated column, slightly missing the point, which said he felt the same way, too, i.e., that those who didn't go were cowards. I still cannot find where I said that, but never mind. Mike Royko, who doesn't like Bob Greene, read Greene's column and weighed in with a puzzlingly titled column, DRAFT DODGERS BORINGLY BLUBBER THEIR GUILT—puzzling because neither Greene nor I had in fact dodged the draft. Royko was royally peeved and ended his column with a suggestion: "Oh, shove it."

Vermont Royster of *The Wall Street Journal* found it a reasonable thesis, and wrote a thoughtful piece placing it in historical perspective. Jules Feiffer did a very funny strip in which a "shallow $50,000 a year journalist" and a "glib $65,000 a year attorney" effetely fret at the tennis net over not going to Vietnam. "Of course, I wouldn't want to get hurt," says one in the last frame. "No," concludes his partner, "I'd prefer to see others shot and learn from it." My laughter over that last line has a nervous quality.

Then Richard Cohen of the *Post* wrote an ideologically guided epistle, describing my article as "something out of Kipling, or maybe Tennyson." That is not such bad company, but it wasn't meant as a compliment, for he viewed my article and the invasion of Grenada and the bombing of Beirut as all of a piece. "Once again, we are in love with war," he wrote. "This is a dangerous infatuation." I felt a bit misunderstood at first, but calmed down on reflecting that Cohen reminds us conservative warmongers at least once a week that war is bad. I am sorry to disappoint him, but I agree with him.

All this, however, has not been half as interesting as the letters that four months later are still coming in. For the most part they are extraordinarily well-expressed, moving, provocative—and not necessarily sympathetic.

A twenty-seven-year-old counselor of Vietnam vets writes with the world-weary maturity of one who might have served in that war: "Don't envy the soldier's experience. . . . I admire them all for trying to hold up considering what they went through. But it is dangerous business to start looking even remotely fondly, for whatever reasons, at Vietnam. This is the first step towards forgetting all the many lessons we can learn from the war, and this is the first step towards getting ourselves in such a travesty again."

A vet who returned in 1967 and who has had a hard time of it writes that he found in the article "a rare empathy, brimming with the recognition of sacrifice made by those like me, from those like you. This was all I ever really wanted. A recognition I never got from the junior personnel executives, the multitudes of them I have had appointments with. The ones who went straight from high school to the college campus to the business world, uninterrupted."

Then two letters from the same person. The first is dated September 10 and explains that after years of malaise over having been in the Special Forces in the late '60s but not having gone to Vietnam, he is volunteering, at age thirty-six, for the Airborne Rangers.

The second letter is dated November 15. It begins, "Whatever guilt I might have felt by my not participating in the Vietnam War has all been erased by recent adventures in Grenada. . . . Unfortunately, we lost three killed and six seriously wounded in three helicopter crashes on our last raid before pulling out." It ends, "Please continue doing whatever you can to further the cause of Vietnam vets."

I now understand that any rumination on any redemptive aspect of Vietnam, especially with American soldiers' dying in another what-are-we-doing-here conflict, is bound to strike some as utter folly. If I glorified war, then I was the fool. It is such a delicate matter that praise for those who went should be prefixed and suffixed with ritual denunciations of war in general. I do not say that cynically; that is what the emotionalism of the public dialogue appears to require.

Among my article's faults was that it wholly neglected the effect of the war on women. Some of the most compelling letters I am getting are from women. One writes to say she feels something like guilt over her inability to have a child. It has left her with a sense of unfulfilled womanhood. Another correspondent reports the very good news that Joe McDonald, late of Country Joe and the Fish, minstrels of the antiwar movement, now holds benefit concerts for San Francisco–area Vietnam vets. What troubles her still is that she never asked her boyfriend about his war experiences. "You were correct," she ends, "when you said that most people are comfortable with the course of action they took during the war years. I, however, am not one of them."

That this article should have provoked so many disparate interpretations may mean that there are still a lot of people out there like her.

—*The Washington Post,* 1983

A Few More
for the Road

A.C.
in D.C.

I read somewhere that air-conditioning was invented in order to provide a measure of relief for poor President Garfield as he lay dying during a Washington summer from Guiteau's bullet. I feel bad for the man. Bad enough to be shot by a maniac with a French surname, but to linger on to spend your last July and August in Washington. . . . It was so hot on the top floor of the President's House, as it was then called, that a crew of navy technicians was tasked with devising some means of cooling him down. They came up with a system of forcing air through pipes chilled by ice and salt. Valiant as this effort was, I can't imagine it helped much. I'm convinced of this because I used to spend summers in the top floor of a house in Washington. I wasn't able to call in the navy, but I called in just about everyone else, and it's still hot enough up there to finish off a *healthy* president.

Air-conditioning did not become the most important thing in my life until I moved to Washington in July 1981, almost a hundred years to the day after President Garfield was shot. I soon developed the habit of opening the freezer of any refrigerator I passed and inserting my head in it.

To make matters worse, I lived for the first five years in Foggy Bottom, a part of the city named for the swampland it once inhabited. (The State Department is nicknamed Foggy Bottom, an often appropriate bit of metonymy.) In President Garfield's day the army kept its stables there. There was also a slaughterhouse nearby, as well as a canal running along what is now Constitution Avenue, from the Lincoln Memorial to the Ellipse, just south of the White House. Apparently a lot of carcasses from the slaughterhouse ended up in this canal. The miasma would then waft on up to the President's House. A few years later President Cleveland decided, Enough already, and moved his summer residence to higher ground three miles to the northwest, where the air did not smell like cholera soup. A hundred years later, my wife and I followed him to what is now called Cleveland Park.

The first thing I asked the realtor was, Does it have central air-conditioning? Yes, she said. Sold, I said.

I set up my office in the small, third-floor attic room that gives out onto a rooftop deck from which you can see the towers of the National Cathedral and pluck apples from the branches of the old apple tree in our backyard, assuming you enjoy severe stomachache. I thought I had found Writer's Heaven, an aerie it might please a passing muse to light upon.

It was early June, already well into the Washington summer. On my second day in my new office I noticed that by 9:00 A.M. it was already a bit stuffy up there. By ten I was downright clammy, and by eleven I was starting the old summer striptease. Then I thought, *Hold on, you have central air-conditioning, schmuck. Turn it on!*

I approached the control panel with some trepidation. I'd never had central air-conditioning, only the window "units" that shake, rattle and drip and cause the lights to dim. I turned the switch to On. The whole house shook for about five seconds. I took this for a good sign. I imagined a great polar bear stirring after a long winter's hibernation. I went back up to my office and put my hand under the register and there, by gum, was a cool stream of air. Soon the house would be a veritable igloo. I sat down contentedly and went back to work.

I spent the next few days trying to convince myself that I was keeping cool, but Lucy kept coming up to the third floor and saying, "*Boy* it's hot up here." And the reason she was coming up was to ask if she could please turn the air-conditioning off, because the floors below were now so cold that icicles had formed on the bathroom faucets. There followed a period of acute marital stress. If you put one spouse in a refrigerator and the other in an oven, this results.

I called in the experts. They ranged from people like the guy in those "Hey, Vern" commercials to refugee German rocket scientists. The former said, "Whutcha do is, block off yer intaykes on the second floor, but not so's ya brayke the whole system 'cause then you're gonna hafta replayce the whole *thang*." The latter said, "You haf an imbalance in ze zyztem. You require a new zyztem, ezzentially," which they said they would be able to install for five thousand dollars.

Five thousand dollars being five thousand dollars, I called in more experts. They advised putting in a separate "unit." That meant gouging a large hole in the roof. (The attic office had no windows and forty-five-degree-angle sloping walls.) It also meant rewiring the whole house for reasons I still don't understand and the certain prospect of rain getting in.

I had a brainstorm: rearrange the entire floor plan of my office so that my chair was directly underneath the register. It worked! As long as I sat bolt upright in my chair, I was enveloped in the slender shaft of cool air, leaving only my forearms, extended toward the keyboard, to glisten and bead with sweat. There were drawbacks. If I wanted to turn on my printer, which writers tend to do from time to time, it meant getting down on my hands and knees and crawling under my desk to reach it. But it seemed a small inconvenience.

More serious were the muscle cramps. Within a week I couldn't get out of the bed in the morning owing to the spasms that ran from my neck to my waist. Lucy was not as sympathetic as usual because of her now-chronic rheumatism from living in the refrigerated downstairs. I went to a doctor, who prescribed ibuprofen and Flexeril, which helped with the muscle spasms but had a tendency to put me to sleep. This did not do much for my prose style. Assignment editors stopped calling. I began drinking heavily. Water, I mean. I thought I could air-condition myself internally by drinking continually from a pitcher of ice water, but all this really did was make trips downstairs necessary at the rate of approximately one every ten minutes.

Faced with being divorced by a pre-pneumonic wife, addiction to muscle relaxers and the demise of my writing career, I wondered if the time hadn't come to spend that five thousand dollars on ze new zyztem. However, a chance encounter with my next-door neighbor architect promised a brilliant solution to the problem: convert the low-lying, shaded garage into an office. Of course! Why hadn't I seen it?

I'll call my architect friend Hobart, because he is a fine man and I don't want to do anything to impede his career. Hobart said it could be done for $25,000. A lot of money, sure—five times more than a new zyztem—but I'd end up cool and with three times the space. "Let's do it," I said. (The same words, now that I think of it, Gary Gilmore said on his way to the firing squad.) Hobart drew up five thousand dollars' worth of blueprints and put it out for bids. The bid came in at $57,000.

I swallowed a few extra muscle relaxers and asked myself how such a thing could be. Then I remembered the Law of Rusher's Gap. Named for its formulator, author and columnist William A. Rusher, it goes like this: Say you want to convert your garage into an office and they tell you it's going to cost $25,000. Now you know, in your heart of hearts, it's going to cost $40,000, right? Well, Rusher's Gap is the difference between $40,000 and what it *actually* ends up costing.

Hobart and I and the contractors entered into negotiations. We drew up new plans for enlarging the existing office, etc., etc. Looking back, I wonder if we couldn't have brought about peace in Central America if we'd spent as much time and effort on that problem instead. The negotiations broke down when the contractor came in with a bid so astronomical only Copernicus could have made sense of it. But it wasn't the money that did it. It was the asterisk at the bottom of the contract that said, "Does not include new A/C *if required.*" (Italics mine.)

I wrote out a good-bye check to Hobart, whose total bill had come to just under $10,000, and said to Lucy, "We've tried the liberal solution and hurled large sums of money at the problem. It still won't go away, so why don't we?" I said, "Let's go someplace really cold for the summer, like Maine." Lucy agreed, and we rented a bungalow in the woods in Maine. There was moss on the roof and it was so dark we had to turn on the lights at 10:00 A.M. Perfect, I said. Perfect.

The temperature hit ninety and stayed there. The radio said it was the hottest summer in Maine's history, at least in living history, and people in Maine live forever. Most of them remember the Spanish-American War and none of the ones I spoke to could remember a hotter summer. When we got back to D.C. in mid-September it was still in the high eighties.

One day while I was inspecting the joists in the basement to see if they were strong enough to hang myself from, it struck me how very . . . cool the basement was. I thought, Aha . . . I wouldn't even need to have to put in air-conditioning. It's cold enough down here to keep hamburger fresh, why not me? It is a little dark and damp and it does tend to flood when it rains, but so does Venice, and what's a little arthritis?

So now I've solved my problem of keeping cool during the D.C. summers. My new basement office is nearing completion. We found a wonderful contractor who said it could be done for $40,000 and it looks like it's only going to end up costing $105,000 by the time the paint dries. A lot of money, you say? Well, yes. Yes it is a lot of money. It's twenty-one times what a new zyztem would have cost. But this is how it works in Washington. How do you think the deficit got so big? It's not so bad as long as you take enough of these muscle relaxers. Here, have one. See? Nothing to it. You just take out your checkbook and write zeros. It's got so I hardly notice. And when I go down to the basement and stand there and look out the new windows and see the heat waves vibrating off the pavement outside and I feel how nice and cool it is, I think how comfortable President Garfield would have been down here. Yes. I think he might even have pulled through. I'm going to go drink some more water now. The doctors say it's important for me not to have stress and to drink a lot of water.

—Architectural Digest, 1989

Hot Hot Hot

As I sat down to write this, on a train, a young woman walked past wearing an above-the-knee pleated skirt, ivory stockings, bone-colored pumps, a blue double-breasted jacket, a strand of pearls, gold earrings, and blond hair pulled back with a barrette. I think she got on in Philadelphia.

She looked like she got on in Philadelphia. Grace Kelly, who must figure prominently in any discussion of what twentieth-century man finds sexy in twentieth-century woman, was from Philadelphia. There's that scene in *Rear Window* where she sweeps into Jimmy Stewart's Greenwich Village apartment wearing that long Edith Head skirt—I don't even remember seeing her legs in that scene, only the dress, and that face. Fast-forward to Sharon Stone uncrossing and crossing her gams in *Basic Instinct*. Two hot blonds in the latest fashions. What's to compare? In sex, as in architecture, less is more. I remember something else about that scene: Jimmy Stewart being annoyed at her. What acting that must have taken.

Before that lovely woman walked by on the train, I'd planned to write a heavy-breathing encomium to the miniskirt, which I've always thought of as the twentieth century's most brilliant achievement, grateful as I am for antibiotics, automatic teller machines, and passenger-side air bags.

But things have changed since Mary Quant first raised hemlines and male heart rates back in the mid-sixties. In those happy Beatle days, the miniskirt had an innocence and a larkiness to it that seem lost in our Age of Less Innocence, with its crotch-grabbing singers and in-your-face jeans and well-oiled glutei maximi. I have a theory—I am nothing if not a deep thinker—that once all those gorgeous, mile-long legs were revealed, the next logical step was to adorn them with sexy black stockings and garters! Panty hose (for my money, one of the century's worst inventions) made the mini possible, but in doing that paved the way for seventies kink, which in turn led to some rather harder-core stuff. Remember Liza Minnelli in *Cabaret* in 1972, all got up in black stockings and garters and the Berlin S & M bit? Charlotte Rampling two years later in the positively wicked *Night Porter*?

Once that hemline went north, Pandora started opening boutiques with names like the Pleasure Chest, serving all your latex needs. It's been a while now since Cole Porter sang, "In olden days a glimpse of stocking/Was looked on as something shocking." What lyric would be left to him in an era of butt floss bathing suits?

I'm constantly begging my wife to buy more miniskirts to show off her (lovely) legs. I was a very happy camper when, about the mid-seventies, the fashion industry glommed on to the fact that men were desperate for lacy underthings. The *Victoria's Secret* catalog, which in the eighties replaced *Playboy* and *Penthouse* as the reading matter of choice, has long been a regular arrival in our home. And lest I start sounding high-and-mighty about butt floss, I'll point out that a good linear foot of my bookshelf space is devoted to back issues of *Sports Illustrated* swimsuit issues showing off the Vargas girls of today: Cheryl, Paulina, Kim, Kathy . . . Alexis . . . Elle . . . Ashley. . . . No point, either, in pretending that I'm immune to the glories of Lycra and high heels. Not long ago, while I was walking down Fifth Avenue in New York, a young woman cling-wrapped in what looked like Azzedine Alaïa went clickety-clicking by on three-inch Manolo Blahnik heels. This apparition left me wailing at the moon, and it was only eleven in the morning. She was wearing dark sunglasses. On top of an outfit like that, sunglasses add a cool edge of mystery that makes it hurt even more.

Best come clean on the boots, too. Why did that silly-but-irresistible Nancy Sinatra song "These Boots Are Made for Walkin'" twang such chords when it came out? What is it about women's boots? The modern boot phenomenon, started in 1963 with Courrèges's quite innocent white kid boots, and before the end of the decade Grès was designing those wet-look, thigh-high, black-patent-shiny "wading boots." From

Pert Miss to Mistress Pert in six years flat, followed by all those Helmut Newton spreads in the seventies showing half-clad amazons strolling through Mad Ludwig's gardens in jodhpurs with riding crops. Maybe the fascination with boots isn't such a mystery after all. I've always suspected that the success of the movie *Pretty Woman* had more to do with that poster of Julia Roberts in thigh-high boots than with the movie itself. Just another theory I'll be presenting in a paper before the Academy of Arts and Sciences next month.

On balance, the only complaint I have against Pandora is that she's enabled the whole unfortunate Madonna business, which, thankfully, now seems to be going away. Otherwise the post-sixties gave men rather a lot to get all het up about.

Yet once the old endocrine glands calm down, more . . . shall we say . . . platonic images of feminine beauty do come to mind. One of the most arresting images of a woman that I have seen—aside from the first time I clapped eyes on my wife-to-be—was of a lady in a long evening gown. Only her shoulders and arms were on display, and her impossibly long neck, opulently chokered with pearls. It was at some opera premiere in Washington, D.C., in the eighties. I've forgotten almost everything about the night, even Placido Domingo's singing, except for that epiphanous lady standing there in the lobby, exquisite and unapproachable, something between a Klimt and a John Singer Sargent.

"Who *is* that?" I hissed to my wife, who herself was struck. The answer was Vicomtesse Jacqueline de Ribes.

Later I came across the famous Richard Avedon photograph of her, taken some years before. It was the same pose. She hadn't moved an inch in all those years, or gained a year of age. Here was a woman whose natural beauty and poise and clothes had bestowed something like immortality. Would that be possible in a miniskirt?

Perhaps. Marilyn Monroe's single most immortal pose had her in panties and an up-blown skirt, standing over a subway grate in 1955's *The Seven Year Itch*. Tom Ewell, amiably ogling nearby, stood in for Everyman. This was fashion as peekaboo, a transitional moment between the demure fifties and the "Why Don't We Do It in the Road?" sixties. She and Ewell never actually consummate their affair; and at the end he runs off to catch the train to join the wife and kiddies on vacation.

Marilyn wore clothes the way the Vargas girls wore them—as things for the beholder to peel away, or see through. But with rather less of Vargas's felicity. That image of her backstage with JFK and Bobby Kennedy at the president's 1962 birthday party at Madison Square Garden, wearing a five-thousand-dollar flesh-colored, rhinestone-embroidered dress that she literally had to be sewn into, is both risible and haunting. Risible because Rubenesque blonds probably ought not to squeeze themselves into sausage casings, even for the president of the United States; haunting because she died soon afterward. Like so many beautiful women, she was at her sexiest in a simple, sleeveless summer dress. Or in whatever they happened to be wearing around the house. For my money, Elizabeth Taylor has never been as radiant as she was in *Giant* (1956), stepping through heifer pies in jeans and a plain shirt.

Born in the fifties, stuck in the fifties. Stop me before I start praising Doris Day. As a matter of fact . . . why not? There was something ineffably sexy about that chaste tomato (as long as she wasn't singing "Que Será, Será"), and I think it must have been the clothes. She and Marilyn had sort of the same body—more or less—sort of the same hair. But Doris did not hang around on top of subway gratings. She dressed like Mom. Marilyn dressed like Aunt Marilyn, Mom's sister, the one she wouldn't let you go spend the weekend in New York with.

The most romantic movie of that decade was also the one in which clothes played the largest part—*Sabrina* (1954). *Pygmalion,* set on the North Shore of Long Island, to the tune of "Isn't It Romantic?" Audrey Hepburn as the chauffeur's daughter who falls in love with the boss's two sons, first William Holden, then Humphrey Bogart. First we see her as a pretty but dreary young girl in a ponytail and a jumper with a long-sleeved black T-shirt. She's sent off to Paris to learn to cook and is taken under the wing of a seventy-four-year-old French baron who sends her back to America a woman—with gamine-short hair and, to judge from what follows, about ten steamer trunks full of Givenchy.

When we see her next, she's standing on the Long Island Railroad platform looking drop-dead in a jewel-necked double-breasted suit, a turban—a turban!—big earrings, and with a French poodle with a diamond collar. Before you could catch your breath, she was gliding across a moonlit tennis court—in a straight-skirt ball gown with an embroidered overskirt. Then it's off for a day's boating with Bogie, for which she wore the shortest of short pants and a man's madras shirt with an upturned collar. Ahoy, my heart. Then to Bogie's Manhattan skyscraper office (30 Broad Street) for their big date at the Persian Room, in a black boat-neck sleeveless cocktail dress with a V back, accessorized with a hilarious sort of *Swan Lake* ballerina hat and elbow-length black gloves. Givenchy transformed a skinny tomboy into the most beautiful woman in the world. By contrast, Cecil Beaton's subsequent voluminous wardrobing for her *My Fair Lady* seems a matter of, as the emperor puts it to Mozart in *Amadeus*, "too many notes." Givenchy, whose clothes enabled Edith Head to take the Oscar for *Sabrina*, went on to name his new Italian fabrics after the film. Hepburn said of her *Sabrina* wardrobe, "My dearest wish . . . was that Billy [Wilder] would allow me to keep them. I could not have afforded a whole Givenchy wardrobe at the time, although I did own a coat I had bought with the fee from *Roman Holiday*." Givenchy was such an indivisible part of Audrey Hepburn that twelve years after *Sabrina*, when she was making *How to Steal a Million* with Peter O'Toole, the following lines (quoted here from memory since it doesn't seem to exist on video) were added to the script as an inside joke:

H: Why do I have to dress like a washerwoman?
O'T: Well, for one thing it will give Givenchy the night off.

But to look back on the first half of the century . . .

I've always been a sucker for Dior's New Look of 1947, with its belted suits, shirtwaist collars, pleats, and longer skirts. What a relief it must have been to women who'd been through those long, improvising years of the war. Finally there was some decent material available, and the time to be creative with it. Frivolity is not esteemed when soldiers are being killed on beaches.

The New Look coincided with the beginning of the Cold War. Though there's no direct connection between wearing fan pleats and containing communism, politics and fashion did play off each other during the following forty-two years, until the Berlin Wall was sledgehammered down. Remember the pajama suits that briefly became the rage after Nixon opened China in 1972? A definite improvement over the short-lived Nehru jacket. After a thoroughly depressing decade of Vietnam and Watergate and Iranian hostage taking, America elected a good old-fashioned, unapologetic cold warrior to the presidency, which made everyone feel confident, or at least better, and after Nancy Reagan wore Adolfo to the inaugural, signaling a definite end to the Rosalynn Carter era, it wasn't long before ladies were dressing to the nines in puffy taffeta evening dresses and coming to the office in very sharp "power" suits. The Chanel suit came back, too, making people wonder why it had ever gone away in the first place; and the Pretty Young Things filled the tables at Mortimer's, mostly in black velvet minis and shifts, as the masters of the universe snapped their suspenders and tightened the knots of their yellow ties. The masters of the universe were ridiculous, especially now that we know the secret of their success—insider trading—but the ladies of the eighties, when we finally beat the Evil Empire, were a pleasure to behold. I'll take them over the grunge-clad, nose-bolted ladies that followed any day. Maybe I'm just terminally Republican, but I've never understood the point of paying a lot of money for clothes with holes in them or why beautiful women would want to clump around in combat boots looking like heroin addicts who haven't washed their hair in two weeks. *So* glad that's over.

The forties: Aside from Dior, the decade seems to recede in a sepia haze of Andrews Sisters hair, gabardine, and painted-on stocking seams.

The thirties: the Age of Slink. All those languid starlets, languishing liquidly in the back of their limousines. Alluring, in a vampish sort of way, but I always wondered if they had any energy left for the really fun stuff after so many cigarettes and martinis.

The twenties: more energetic. Whole lot of whoopee going on back then, flappers flapping, drunk on bathtub gin, ladies holding on to their brimless cloche hats as they indulged in the new sport of motoring.

No need to dwell on the suffragette teens. The higher hemlines must have come as a relief to a generation of men reduced to fantasizing about what their wives' ankles looked like.

Which brings us to the double-aughts, or whatever those zero-zero years are called, the Edwardian era of high collars, massive, corseted monobosoms, and below-the-ankle skirts. Yet there was something ineffably majestic to those haughty ladies of the boulevards with their S-curved silhouettes and tiny waists that still give rumor to stories of rib-removing operations.

I love the shirts and neckties they wore. As I finish this, on a plane as we begin our "final descent" (why *do* they put it so alarmingly?), the flight attendants are walking up and down, wearing very smart single-breasted jackets, shirts, and ties. I can't put my finger on it—or maybe I don't want to—but there is something irresistible about this look. Marlene Dietrich, Julie Andrews, Diane Keaton, Maggie Smith, and Helena Bonham Carter in *A Room with a View.* A good friend of mine has just proposed to a woman who dresses in menswear to killer effect. I'm very happy for him.

One night recently in Los Angeles, my friend Alison took me to a new place called House of Blues, where in order to get to the bar on the third floor you have to talk your way through more roped-off checkpoints than you ever did in Cold War Berlin, manned by muscle-boy bouncers wearing telephone-operator headsets (for heaven's sake). Eventually we achieved the sanctum sanctorum, there to encounter such luminosities as Andrew Dice Clay and Jim Belushi. But it was not to them that my eyes were drawn, for everywhere you turned were beauties—and I mean beauties; hey, it's L.A.—turned out in the latest Ter et Bantine and Isaac Mizrahi jackets, with microshort skirts. It took a great deal of concentrated effort to pretend to be more interested in Mr. Clay's repartee than in the three-alarm pin-striped pulchritude sitting on the next couch over. Took imagination, too, to see the Edwardian palimpsest behind that cardiac-arresting modern version. But it was clear enough: The century had come full circle, and I was a long way from Philadelphia.

—Vogue, 1994

Explosions in My Skull

The first one went off a month after I turned nineteen. I was on the FDR Drive at 106th Street in Manhattan, inching along in traffic when I became aware of a dull pain behind my left eye that within a few minutes turned into a burning sensation. Over the next eleven years, the pattern would repeat itself without variation hundreds of times: the ache, followed by the burning, followed by mounting pressure. Back on the FDR, I soon began to moan out loud and twist in my seat. I remember stomping on the floorboard, massaging my temples. Tears flowed from my left eye. On a scale of one to ten, I'd put the pain at nine. (By comparison, I once had a live cigarette shoved into my eyeball and had to wait fifteen hours to get to a doctor. I'd rank that pain—which was memorable—at six.)

After three-quarters of an hour, the pain suddenly vanished. *What the hell was that about?* I wondered.

It happened again the next day, and again, and again, totaling as many as ten one-hour headaches in a single day, every day for a period lasting anywhere from a couple of days to 6 months. I was diagnosed as having cluster headaches, a variety of vascular headache in which the blood vessels inside the head constrict and then dilate.

At first the doctors I saw pretty much shrugged and prescribed various vasoconstrictive drugs, as well as painkillers. But the relief they provided was minimal. By the time the Percodan or Fiorinal did their work, the headache would have abated, only to return in a few hours, just as the painkiller was wearing off. I could not have been a very stimulating conversationalist during that time of my life.

Frustrated, I turned to alternative medicine, which promised not only relief, but even a cure. I spent two months of mornings in the lab of one alternative guru while his assistants squirted extracts of corn, dust mites and chocolate under my tongue and logged my reactions. I ended up with my very own allergy serum and a supply of disposable hypodermics. Every Friday morning for weeks I shot myself in the bottom. The headaches got fiercer; the guru got richer.

I had tests: regular X rays, tomographic X rays, electroencephalograms, a CT scan. Friends, relatives and coworkers all had suggestions: a clinic in Switzerland, biofeedback, psychoanalysis, homeopathy, more gurus.

I read deeply on the subject. There was consolation in finding out that some of the great writers had had migraines (if not clusters). Lewis Carroll is said to have gotten the idea for *Alice in Wonderland* during the hallucinatory aura that preceded one of his migraines. Alexander Pope would call for steaming pots of coffee in the middle of the night so that he could inhale the vapors. (I'll say this for my headaches: I've never since wished that I had been born in the romantic past. Give me the latter twentieth century with its abundant pharmacopoeia any day.)

It was my father who, after witnessing a particularly bad spell of my attacks, finally found Dr. Frank Petito, a Manhattan neurologist. I think of him the way some people think of Elvis or Mother Teresa.

Dr. Petito did two things. First he prescribed, in addition to the vasoconstrictors, Elavil (amitriptyline), an antidepressant with sedative effects. I chafed at the notion of being tranquilized until he explained that there was something in Elavil—they didn't know what, exactly—that blocked headaches. Instead of getting ten a day, Dr. Petito said, I might get only two. Then he told me to stop smoking. "If you quit," he said, "you probably won't have these in five years. There's a higher correspondence between smoking and cluster headaches than there is between smoking and lung cancer." This was news. "There's no data yet to support the idea that stopping smoking stops clusters," he went on, "but I believe it, and several experts agree." I was left to wonder why none of the half-dozen or so doctors I had been to before had told me this. I guess they were no Frank Petitos.

So I gave up smoking. More or less.

The Elavil worked wonders. Two headaches a day definitely beat ten. But they did remain a fact of life. By then I was working in the White House as a speechwriter, a job that can have its stressful moments. I remember one day trying to bang out an arrival statement aboard Air Force Two—my drugs were in the cargo hold, an error never again to be repeated—and pleading with then Vice President Bush's doctor to shoot me up with morphine, or something, so I could finish the speech. The most he would offer was Tylenol with codeine. It was a mark of what an analgesic snob I had become that I spurned his wimpy white tablets.

A few days later, back in Washington, I found myself laid out on an acupuncturist's table, my skull bristling with 20 needles. ("It won't do you any harm," Dr. Petito had said, "but I've seen no evidence to suggest that it will do you any good.") I went through the mandatory ten treatments, each one increasingly painful since they insert needles into the exact same spot.

The headaches never came back. I tease Dr. Petito about Western Med being aced by a Chinese lady with needles, but nice as it would be to think of myself as living proof of a medical breakthrough, the truth is that Dr. Petito was probably as responsible as Dr. Wong. The headaches disappeared almost exactly five years after I more or less stopped smoking. They had lasted eleven years, about a quarter of my life at the time. I don't miss them much.

—*American Health,* 1994

The Passion of
Saint Matt

For Christians, Palm Sunday is an important day, marking the entry of
Christ into Jerusalem for the Passover, and the start of the holiest week
of the liturgical year. Priest and congregation read aloud the Passion of
Saint Matthew, beginning with the betrayal of Judas Iscariot and ending
in the laying of Christ in the sepulcher. It is the most dramatic stretch of
prose in the English language.

I consider myself a reasonably reconstructed, post-Vatican II Catholic,
which is to say that while I suspect Latin is the language He prefers—an
AT&T connection, if you will, to the scratchy MCI or Sprint of the new
liturgy—my knees don't jerk in the pews every Sunday when the priest
tells me to shake hands with the person next to me.

Now, any Catholic who is not totally tone-deaf knows that the relevant
ecclesiastical committees have been hard at work turning the beautiful
sinewy prose of the Douai-Reims Bible into Formica-flat American.
(The Douai and King James are for practical purposes identical.) Since
1965, we have become accustomed to this. But last Sunday's rendition of
the Passion, taken from the New American Bible, was so lifeless, so devoid of passion that one despairs over the harrowing of the language at the
hands of the church's liturgical bureaucrats.

Consider:

King James Version: ". . . the spirit indeed is willing, but the flesh is
weak."

New American Bible: ". . . The spirit is willing but nature is weak."

What—pray—is wrong with the classical metonymy, "flesh"? "Nature" here sounds like ersatz Emerson.

In the King James Version, Jesus begs his Father, "If this cup may not pass away from me, except I drink it, thy will be done."

Last Sunday that was reduced to: "If this cannot pass me by without my drinking it, your will be done."

Bad enough to eliminate one of Christianity's great metaphors, the cup of sorrow, but to leave the sentence as they have offends basic English usage. "Drinking" what? "This"?

In King James, Peter "smote off the ear" of the high priest's servant. In the New American Bible, he is "slashed," making it sound as though he had been mugged.

Jesus rebukes Peter with a phrase that has survived the ages: "All they that take the sword, shall perish with the sword." That is now: "Those who use the sword are sooner or later destroyed by it."

"Art Thou the King of the Jews?" demanded Pontius Pilate. "And Jesus said unto him, 'Thou sayest.' "

"As you say." Jesus' artful answer to his executioner is thus reduced to a shrug: *Yeah, whatever.*

King James's scholars tell us that Golgotha, the site of the crucifixion, meant "the place of a skull." The writers of the New American Bible make it sound like an Aaron Spelling TV show—"Skull Place." Okay, okay. But why have they gone to such lengths as changing words that even the least sensitive parishioner could not possibly have mistaken in meaning? "Wine mixed with gall" becomes "wine flavored with gall," as if the other choices were cherry and vanilla. It was the particular charity of a group of wealthy women of Jerusalem to see that the condemned were offered wine mixed with a grain of frankincense to dull the excruciating pain of crucifixion. When Jesus, in His death agony, cried out to his Father, a bystander soaked a sponge in "vinegar . . . and gave him to drink." In the New American Bible, he is offered "cheap wine." Chablis? Thunderbird?

At the moment of death, "Behold, the veil of the temple was rent in twain from the top to the bottom; and the earth did quake and the rocks rent; and the graves were opened; and many bodies of the saints which slept arose."

Whatever your religious belief, that is prose to raise the hairs on your arm. Does this do it for you?: "Suddenly the curtain of the sanctuary was torn in two from top to bottom. The earth quaked, boulders split, tombs opened. Many bodies of saints who had fallen asleep were raised."

The chief priest and pharisees tell Pilate that Jesus was "a deceiver" and beg him to make "the sepulcher sure, sealing the stone and setting a watch." Here the New American Bible sounds like an FBI report. They ask Pilate to put the tomb "under surveillance."

All this is deplorable, but not contemptible. But what are we to make of the fact that the two thieves between whom Christ was nailed have suddenly been transformed into "insurgents"? Ronald Knox, the great translator of the New Testament, was satisfied with "thieves"; even the very contemporary Good News New Testament (Fourth Edition) only goes so far as to call them "bandits." When the modern ear hears "insurgents," the mind thinks of Vietcong, mujahedin, contras, Shining Path, Kurds, a half-dozen jumbled and bloody acronyms. What's next? *And they crucified Him between two freedom fighters. . . .*

The new edition of the New American Bible will be out soon. In this version, all references to gender will be expunged. The Son of God will shed all that sexist baggage and emerge as the Child of God. The Sermon on the Mount will no longer offend the National Organization for Women, Greenpeace or the Physicians for Social Responsibility. We will have arrived at the scriptural equivalent of "You can call me Ishmael, if you're comfortable with that"; of solar panels at the cathedral of Chartres; of Bach's "Saint Matthew Passion" performed by the Mantovani Strings. It will be accessible to all, and meaningful to no one. To use the old phrase, in the fullness of time they will have my Saviour sounding like a Valley Girl. I am wroth.

—The Washington Post, 1987

My Own
Private Sunday School

□

"Dad?" My daughter, Caitlin, six, asked me one day when she was about five, "What's God?" I broke out in a sweat. This was the Big One, existentially speaking: *Where do we come from? Where are we going? Will we have to change planes in Atlanta?*

I suppose in this day and age I should be grateful she didn't ask, "Dad, what's a condom?" Still, her question made me feel I had failed, big time, as a father. I'd already filled in about twenty nursery school applications. I'd already started to put money away for her college education. I'd already bought her her first computer so she'd be able to get a job in 2000-something. Clearly, it was time to get cracking on the spiritual side of things.

And yet, how to proceed? A practicing Roman Catholic for almost forty years, I'd recently crossed over into the agnostic camp—which I think of as the "just-the-facts-ma'am" school of philosophy—so I wasn't quite sure how to answer "What's God?" I did want Caitlin to grow up open to God and spirituality. Which isn't to say that I hope she'll run off with the first Jehovah's Witness who bangs on the door. Quite the contrary: I want her to be able to look that Jehovah's Witness right in the eye and say, "You've *got* to be kidding."

What she needed, in other words, was a firm grounding in the Judeo-Christian heritage. Besides, I'd rather she knew something of Abraham and Moses and Jesus than of Barney and Lambchop and Thomas the Tank Engine. She already *knows* about them.

I went out and bought a beginner's Bible. The stories are nicely told, and the illustrations are friendly. Everyone looks clean and presentable; no one looks too scruffy, even Goliath, though you probably wouldn't

invite him to dinner. It's not called a whale in the text. The chapter is titled "Inside a Fish," which to me doesn't have the same oomph as
"Jonah and the Whale." The chapter about the Roman discovering
Jesus' empty tomb is titled "Surprise!"—which is sort of cute, even if it
does make a pretty crucial New Testament event sound a bit like a panel
from *Where's Waldo?* And Cain and Abel are left out, which is probably
for the best, because Caitlin often expresses the desire to murder her
two-year-old brother, Conor. No good could come of her learning how
common fratricide always has been.

"OK," I said to Caitlin one Sunday morning. "Today we are going to
read the Bible."

"Actually," she said, "I'm busy." That is, watching *The Rescuers Down
Under* for the eight hundredth time. I did what any other loving-but-
firm father would have done. I asked her if we could read the Bible after
her video was finished.

Boy, if she only knew what her dad's new-found agnosticism was
sparing her. Sunday Mass, confession, Communion, confirmation, holy
days of obligation, Lent, four years of boarding school with Benedictine
monks, trudging up to Mass at 6:15 A.M. in winter, in the dark . . . I'll
say this for a Catholic upbringing: great memories.

In fact, the Bible was an easy sell on Caitlin. She gobbled it up. One
morning she insisted on reading the entire New Testament. We were
halfway through Jesus' ministry when I asked, "How about a video?"
Anyway, she got a firm grounding in her Judeo-Christian heritage. For
example, she now knows that God is present in everything. And I do
mean everything.

> CAITLIN (*pointing to her foot*): Is God in my toe?
> DAD: Well, basically. The point is, he's in you. And in Mommy,
>   and in Conor . . .
> CAITLIN (*suddenly alarmed*): God is in *Conor?*

A few hours later: "Is God in Conor even when he does something *really*
bad, like putting the firewood log in the toilet?"

(Confidential to agnostic parents: Expect a barrage of questions intended to provoke you, such as "Is God in bubble gum?" The good news
is that eventually your kids will tire of provoking you—by which time
you are on Prozac.)

She now was ready to explore even more complicated moral and philosophical questions.

> CAITLIN (*sweetly*): Dad?
> DAD: Yeah, honey?
> CAITLIN: Does everyone die?
> DAD: Say, how 'bout a Flintstones pop-up ice cream bar?
> CAITLIN: But Dad, *am I going to die?*
> DAD: Well, uh, I guess everyone dies. I mean, it's part
>   of . . . what's your favorite part in *The Rescuers Down Under?*
> CAITLIN: But what happens *after* you die?

You can postpone this moment, but you can't avoid it. Ultimately, the important thing is to remain true to your convictions. If you lie, they'll pick up on it and never trust you again. Which is why, as an agnostic dad—difficult as it was—I looked her right in the eye and said, "You go straight to heaven."

—*USA Weekend,* 1994

Mr. Robertson's
Millennium

□

As *annus mirabilis* 2000 approaches, we'd best start to deal with it: there will be Elijahs on every street corner, cable channel and Web site urging us to repent, repent, for the end is at hand. There's just something about an impending millennium that brings out the gloom and doom.

The year 999 was a boom year for monasteries. Penitents flocked in, hysterically bearing jewels, coins and earthly possessions by the oxcartful, hoping to cadge a little last-minute grace before Judgment Day. The year 1999 may turn out to be a similarly good one for the coffers of fundamentalist Christian churches—especially if Pat Robertson's apocalyptic novel, *The End of the Age,* is any indication of what the faithful think is going to happen when the ball atop the Times Square tower plunges into triple zeros.

Mr. Robertson is, of course, no ordinary street-corner Elijah. He is a graduate of the Yale Law School and chairman of both the Christian Broadcasting Network and International Family Entertainment (the Family Channel). He has his own daily television show, *The 700 Club,* and is the author of nine previous books. In 1988, he ran for president in the Republican primaries, giving the distinctly non-fire-breathing Episcopalian George Bush a brief case of the heebie-jeebies during the Iowa caucuses and establishing the Christian right as an electoral force to be reckoned with. So when he ventures forth into pop-fictional eschatology, attention must be paid—if only for the pleasure of hearing a president of the United States tell the nation in a televised address, "We are the world," and to watch as an advertising executive is transformed into an angel.

It's hard to define *The End of the Age* exactly. It's sort of a cross between *Seven Days in May* and *The Omen,* as written by someone with the
prose style of a Hallmark Cards copywriter. The good guys—a born-
again advertising executive and his wife, a black pro basketball player and
a Hispanic television technician, all led by one Pastor Jack, a descendant
of the eighteenth-century American preacher Jonathan Edwards—tend
to sound like a bunch of Stepford wives who have wandered onto the set
of *The 700 Club,* eerily polite and constantly telling one another to
please turn to the Book of Revelation:

" 'That's right, Manuel. Every bit of it is in the Bible. As a matter of
fact, whole books have been written about a diabolical world dictator
called the Antichrist. He got that name because he will try to perform
for Satan what Christ performed for God.'

" 'Wow, I hope he fails,' Cathy said."

The bad guys tend to sound like the villains in a Charlie Chan movie.
In fact, they sound as if they were being simultaneously translated from
some sinister Indo-Iranian tongue:

"Panchal, sorry to wake you. Get your people ready. Tonight the gods
have given America into our hands."

That "sorry to wake you" is one of the many unintentionally hilarious moments that relieve the general tedium. For all the apocalyptic py-
rotechnics, the book leaves the eyeballs as glazed as a Christmas ham. But
just when you start wondering what's on C-SPAN, there will be a reason to go on:

"The Antichrist raged within his palace. . . . The final battle was coming. He would march on Jerusalem at the head of his armies. 'Then,' he
said to Joyce Cumberland Wong, 'I will win! At last I will have my revenge!' "

The book begins with a bang in the form of a 300-billion-pound me-
teor that lands in the Pacific Ocean with the force of five thousand nuclear bombs, setting off a three-thousand-foot tsunami, earthquakes,
fires, nuclear plant meltdowns, volcano eruptions, ash in the atmosphere,
floods and food shortages. All in all, a rather bad hair day for old Mother
Earth, sending the Antichrist ouching toward Bethlehem to be born.
Meanwhile, at 1600 Pennsylvania Avenue, things are a bit sticky:

"Well, here's the story," the secretary of defense explains to his top
general over lime-and-sodas while the world burns. "As you know, we

had one President commit suicide. The next was killed by a snakebite, and then the man who left the cobra on the President's desk was murdered. They say he committed suicide, but don't you believe it."

At this point, if I were the general, I'd have asked for some Scotch to go with my soda, but in evangelical literature the good guys don't drink.

"Now," the secretary continues, "we've got this ex–campus radical in the White House, and if you heard the speech tonight, you know he's got some mighty big plans."

That would be the aforementioned "We are the world" speech, and yes, President Mark Beaulieu (read "mark of the beast") does indeed have some big plans: a one-world government with its own currency and a police force in United Nations–ish uniforms, a grand new $25 billion world headquarters palace in Babylon with some positively kinky special effects, computer-tattoo ID markings for everyone, drugs and orgies for schoolchildren, vintage wines for the grown-ups.

Your basic liberal agenda, right down to the Chardonnay. President Mark of the Beast's cabinet would certainly provide for some memorable nomination hearings:

"For Secretary of Education, the President had selected a Buddhist monk who shaved his head and dressed in a saffron robe and sandals. For Secretary of Agriculture, he asked for a shepherd from Nevada who lived alone in the hills and spoke broken English. The man's only known 'credential' was that he had once played jai alai in Las Vegas. For Secretary of Energy, he named a Lebanese Shiite Muslim who was a member of the terrorist group, Hezbollah, and ran a filling station in Dearborn, Mich.

"For drug czar, he picked a man who had spent his life crusading for the legalization of all narcotics. For Secretary of State, a professor of Eastern religions from Harvard University"—a Yale man just can't help himself—"who had close ties to Shoko Asahara, the leader of the Japanese cult of Shiva worshipers known as Aum Shinri Kyo, or Supreme Truth. They had been linked with a poisonous gas attack in a Tokyo subway in 1995. And he chose for Attorney General a militant black feminist attorney who advocated abolishing the death penalty and closing all prisons."

I'll bet not one of them paid Social Security tax on the nanny.

The End of the Age is to Dante what Sterno is to *The Inferno*. When you have a hard time keeping a straight face while reading a novel about the death of a billion human beings, something is probably amiss.

But lest we be too smug, bear in mind two recent events. In March 1989, a large asteroid passed within 450,000 miles of Earth. Had it landed in an ocean, according to scientists quite genuinely rattled by 1989FC's sudden appearance, it would have created three-hundred-foot tidal waves. If you think 450,000 miles is a country mile, consider that Earth had been in the asteroid's path just six hours earlier.

Then there was Hurricane Gloria. In September 1985, this violent storm was working its way up the Atlantic, headed for Virginia Beach, Virginia, headquarters of the Christian Broadcasting Network, with murderous force. Mr. Robertson went on the air and prayed, commanding the storm to stay at sea. It did—and came ashore at Fire Island, demolishing the summer house of Calvin Klein.

—*The New York Times*, 1996

Remembrance of
Mansíons Past

□

I was lucky, in an age in which houses seem to be getting smaller and smaller, to have grown up around some of the big ones. I think it's because I had the run of such places when I was very young that I still tend to look on stately manses with affection but something less than awe. Thus I found myself in an immense, nineteenth-century former Rothschild *hôtel* in Paris a few years ago, tossing a Frisbee in the state dining room—a modest Louis XV affair full of *boiserie* and crystal, slightly less large than a basketball court. To me such houses have purposes their builders might not have foreseen: outside ledges to crawl along while horrified nannies threatened from fifty feet below; marble floors for bicycle riding and roller skating; laundry chutes for physics experiments with medicine balls.

When I finally read *Brideshead Revisited* I found myself on familiar ground: the ache for a vanished house in which one's happiest days were spent. I wonder if psychologists have got around to classifying a Brideshead Syndrome, or does that fall too squarely into the problems-of-the-idle-rich category?

But like many relics of grander days, great houses are subject to peculiar ravishings. The Georgian-style house my mother grew up in, on a beautiful estate in Vancouver, British Columbia, was sold after my grandfather's death in 1965. Some years later, I found myself in a movie theater watching Ann-Margret and Jack Nicholson in *Carnal Knowledge* rutting away in the same gardens where I used to play with my Teddy Bear. Not long afterward the new owner sold Shannon, as it was called, to developers. The house was carved up into apartments, and where there had been lavender beds, roses, riots of sunflowers and cypress stands you will now find one hundred and ninety condominium units.

We buried my father's mother not long ago, next to grandfather, by the hickory tree in the Quaker cemetery, in South Carolina. Camden was not yet in its spring glory, when the dogwood and azalea explode in white and pink. I remember it was always around then that I would come down from the north, sometimes calling her from on the road to announce my impending arrival with a carload of disreputable-looking college friends. "Oh, darling," Mimi would always say, however inwardly alarmed at the prospect of our invasion, "how long can you stay?" Soon the car would turn up the white gravel driveway that slopes up over the terraced hill, tires crunching past pines and magnolia toward the house, its balcony purple and drowsy with great boughs of wisteria. The day of the funeral we drove there for one last look. The new owner had kindly called to give his permission, but we drove through furtively, like trespassers.

My grandfather had bought the house in the thirties after a turbulent career in revolutionary Mexico. It was forlorn then, sitting atop a blasted hill bitterly fought over during the wars of independence and secession. The house, Kamschatka, meaning "far off and lonely place," had been named after the Russian province. When it was built in the 1850s, the house stood a full two miles from town, a long way by carriage. Legend has it that the slaves buried the silver to keep the Yankee soldiers from getting it, and that it is still there somewhere. Mary Chesnut, author of the famous Civil War diary, lived there. Her husband, James, had built the house for her so that she could entertain on a grander scale, and though we don't know exactly what it looked like at the time of its building, even in its pristine state it could not have been as beautiful as my grandfather would make it almost a century later. What imagination he had. Even Tara, post-Sherman, looked grander than Kamschatka when he and Mimi first saw it.

How odd to find such vision in a man who had grown up the son of a Texas sheriff in the 1880s. He brought in over a half-dozen Italian land-scapers and transformed the parched barren hill into a paradise of flowers and greenery, and added brick walls, patios, walkways and arbors, Palladian cottages and stables.

He loved water and built fountains—not nearly as grandiose as Brideshead's, but more southern and languorous. You could hear the one out front from the bedrooms; its splash gave a sense of the most profound tranquillity. One night my cousin Billy caught an enormous catfish down at the pond and brought it back in a bucket and put it in the fountain with the goldfish. The trauma of it all must have given the poor thing an appetite. The next morning there were no flashes of orange in the weedy murk, only a fat, digesting, bewhiskered catfish.

There was a ghost. (I know, I know, but hear me out.) Several times he woke up people who until then quite definitely did not believe in ghosts. He was said to be a cavalry officer who had promised to return from the war. Unable to keep his promise in life, here he was, keeping it in death. One night one of the guests was awakened by the sound of boots and spurs clumping up and down the hall. He came out of the bedroom and stared into the darkness. Then he looked up and suddenly there was the ghost, standing at the head of the stairs, his uniformed figure silhouetted in the moonlight. It never occurred to anyone that they should be afraid of him.

I remember the big, candlelit dinners when I was very young and allowed to stay up: Ella and Jeff bringing in great silver salvers of freshly shot roast squab and quail, the room perfumed with magnolia blossoms, forsythia, hibiscus and oleander.

On the wall in the dining room was the one valuable painting in the house, a dark oil of Andrew Jackson. If you looked closely, you could see the scar on his chin from when he was a boy and a British soldier had struck him for refusing to polish his boots. You had to really look for it, since Old Hickory had a lined face. But my grandmother liked that scar—it appealed to her innate American pride. So we'd keep on looking, poring over the great South Carolinian's face until she found it—there! "I think that's just a wrinkle, Mimi." "Oh. You know, darling, I think you're right."

I hope the condominium units will never come to Kamschatka. I could handle it if they made a movie there, even one with nude frolics in the fountain with Billy's catfish; but condos would probably drive even the ghost away. Meantime, I hear the new owner has filled it with children and noise, which is how it should be for great houses that live on after their builders have gone.

—*Architectural Digest*, 1985

Sergeant Pepcid's
Lonely Hearts Club Band

I sensed there was something wrong right after the opening of Sunday night's *The Beatles Anthology: Part One* when the announcer's voice boomed that the evening was being brought to us by something called Pepcid AC. The AC stands for Acid Controller. You take Pepcid in anticipation of getting indigestion. The other two main sponsors of our collective walk down Penny Lane were a credit card designed by Ringo, and Ford Taurus wagon.

The next two hours contained forty-seven-odd commercials, not counting promos for the local TV news team that's On Our Side. One ad for every two-and-a-half minutes of Beatles nostalgia, a hard day's night indeed, considering that the only thing we learned that we didn't already know was that Ringo was miserably hung-over when they shot his solo scene in the movie of that name, walking along the canal kicking bits of debris and muttering to himself angstfully. Ringo's commentary made it clear that he was describing one of the immortal moments in modern cinema. (Ten bucks to any aging boomer who actually makes it all the way through *A Hard Day's Night*.) *On Wednesday in Part Two, George reveals that he had turista during the beach scene in* Help!

Grateful as I was for Ringo's now-it-can-be-told revelations—I already knew that the Beatles started in Liverpool, did gigs in Hamburg, and came to America in 1964 and went on the Ed Sullivan Show—the fact is his new credit card is much more interesting.

About halfway through I found I had stopped paying attention to the Anthology, despite the breathless alerts that an original Beatles song, "Free as a Bird," was upcoming: "Stay tuned for the world premiere of the new Beatles song." Instead I was fixating on the commercials. It was the ads that fascinated, for they showed us what boomers truly care about most—ourselves.

Twenty-five years ago, when the Beatles broke up, the only acid my generation cared about came in windowpane, blotter, or Orange Sunshine. Now we have this yuppie Prufrock leaning over his wife's shoulder as she prepares lasagna with spicy sausages, fretting that this will bring on esophageal Hiroshima. But he can rest easy—she has bought him acid controller. He can eat all the spicy sausages he wants! Now on to the day Paul and John first met . . .

What more is there to be said of Ringo's credit card? For the past twenty-five years one has followed dear Ringo's career, uttering, "Pingo, Ringo, Ringo," then, "Say it ain't so," and finally, *"Duude."* And yet you still can't bring yourself to dislike him. He is what he always was—Ringo. Even the name was never quite on the level. He has become the Kato Kaelin of the Beatles. Where will he turn up next? In the Hawaiian sunshine, on a real estate infomercial? On the 900-number Psychic Hotline? *I felt this vibration in me head and I knew we were gonna be really big.* Stay tuned.

"We're in our fifties now," said the woman in the Ikea ad to her couch potato husband. "That hurts," he replied, following up with a snappy rejoinder about the sound of one hand clapping. Zen and the art of Some Assembly Required?

Then there was Fran Dresher, nasal sex kitten of the '90s, jimmying her thighs into Hanes's Smooth Illusions. "It's like liposuction without the sur-ge-ry." Followed immediately by low-fat Tostitos Chips. *Bet you can't eat just the whole bag.* Doubtless the next Beatles Anthology will be entirely brought to us by Olestra, the new fat substitute recently okayed by the FDA.

For aching boomers there was Tylenol Flu. *What? They're giving your hospitalized father Advil? But don't you know it's got ibuprofen! Get him out of there, man, now!* Message (as Bush's speech texts used to say): You have a cold and your parents are croaking. I was surprised not to see any Jacoby and Meyers law offices ads: Are you quite sure that Dad has made out his will?

Kodak was a major presence. The Grim Reaper is upon us! The memories must be preserved! *And this time we've figured out how to keep them from turning green after a few decades.* Notice how all those pictures of you when you were a Cub Scout now make you look like something from *The X Files?*

Cars had barely been equipped with seat belts when the Beatles were playing Shea Stadium. Now we must have not only dual air bags in our Volvos, but also side-impact air bags. Yes, I agree, I must have them too, even if this means karmically aligning myself with crash-test dummies. If James Dean's silver Porsche had been equipped with air bags, he'd now be alive and endorsing nicotine patches.

"Tonight," said the announcer between news of Ringo's appearance tomorrow on *Good Morning America* and Ford Taurus "Making the Dream Come True"—what are we talking about here? a station wagon—in tones denoting The Second Coming, "you're just minutes away from when the Beatles reunite." Best of all, the Anthology is "coming to stores December 1. You haven't heard everything yet!"

There was more? Mercedes, Xerox, Pizza Hut, "Home of the Stuffed Crust," Arizona Jeans, "More attitude than latitude" (whatever that means), Motorola Pagers "You jumped fast enough to make Pavlov proud!"

Finally the great moment had arrived, after—literally—a countdown. 0:59 . . . 0:58 . . . 0:57 . . . Then there they were, sitting around a table, George, Ringo, Paul. Paul said, "We didn't see how to do a reunion without John, but then we figured out a way." He winked, and "Free as a Bird"—available December 1!—began. It was good to hear John's voice again, but as the music played, you wondered how it all was playing with the man who wrote, "The way things are going, they're going to crucify me." Was he turning revolutions number nine? Had he reached, in anticipation, for the Pepcid AC?

—*The Washington Post,* 1995

Bugging Out

A quarter-century or so ago, I saw a rather earnest movie done in the form of a documentary and narrated by a fictional scientist who has been drummed out of the scientific community for tiresomely asserting that insects are taking over the world. It wasn't just that the little buggers would outlast anything humans threw at them and dance on our graves. No, no, this entomological Cassandra begged us to understand, in the sort of language we now get courtesy of Mark from Michigan—*it is all part of the plan.*

It sounded perfectly plausible to me, but then I was eighteen and stoned. Successive assaults by the multitudinous cockroaches in my college dorm only heightened my sense of impending doom. Still, in time I ceased gibbering about the coming Armageddon and got a life.

But now, each summer, after a few days in our decomposing mossy rental on the Maine coast whose plumbing was last repaired during Roosevelt's second term, I find myself, like that chimp contemplating the human skull, considering my position in the chain of being. I find myself, too, on about the fifth trip into town to the hardware store, cozying up to the proprietor. "Rufus," I say, "they've been guzzling that stuff you sold me like it was strawberry milkshake. I'm a regular customer. Surely you have something *special* under that counter? DDT? Napalm? Sarin? Just between us. No need for the EPA to know anything. Heh heh."

I know it's tricky, revealing one's insecticide wet dreams in the magazine that published *Silent Spring*—and, what's more, on a typewriter just up the road from E. B. White's old barn, home to the most famous spider in history. But there it is.

Each summer in our cabin, where—true fact—some years ago a woman died of complications from a spider bite, my wife, my children, my dog (in his capacity as larval troop carrier), and I are intimately reacquainted with the insect kingdom: flies, mosquitoes, midges, gnats, moths, earwigs, beetles, weevils, wasps, plant hoppers, assassin bugs (that is an actual type), back swimmers, thrips, lice, stone flies, crickets, termites, damselflies, dragonflies, horseflies, ticks, mites, millipedes, and centipedes.

This summer brought us friendship with yet another glory of creation: carpenter ants. My first clue that the spring had not been a silent one came when I walked into the room that serves as our living, eating, and sleeping quarters to find a significant pile of extremely unpleasant matter heaped on the floor. Naturally, this drew my eye to the ceiling beam above. Where, exactly, I mused, did this revolting, excreting winged horde fit in the ultimate scheme of things? Did He who made the Lamb make them? The British scientist J.B.S. Haldane, asked what a lifetime of study had taught him about the nature of God, replied, "An inordinate fondness for beetles." You could call this point of view bugnosticism.

Yet now I see—writing this, enfolded in citronella, my face sticky with Repel—that they also serve who only creep and crawl. These unlovely arthropods show us our true selves. There is the Zen monk who removes his sandals lest he step on an ant. And there is me, shaken by my wife out of a rum-deep sleep at 2:00 A.M., handed a flyswatter, and told to kill—kill!—the mosquito that is freaking out the kids. In summer, I see my place in the ultimate scheme of things: groggy in a bathrobe, snarling and swearing, ridiculous, fencing with the vanguard of Apocalypse.

—*The New Yorker*, 1995

"Washington Writer"

□

Writing brought me to Washington. I was sitting at my desk at *Esquire* magazine in New York, eating my New York bagel, musing New York thoughts—rent control, the newest twenty hot restaurants that had opened that day, and whether I could get a reservation—when the phone rang. It was a desperate vice presidential press secretary calling from—cool!—Air Force Two. He needed a speechwriter, needed one fast, needed one cheap.

What the hey, I said to myself philosophically. Could be an interesting gig. I've always thought of writing as a journeyman's trade; perhaps the way a studio musician might think of his own craft. Here was a chance to work on a new album with George Bush. (*Voodoo Economics Lounge?*) Do it for a year, go back to the Apple with neat Secret Service stories.

That was fifteen years ago. Here I still am, with every intention of staying, despite having spent the last forty-eight hours in inane Sisyphean battle with minor functionaries of the D.C. government over—oh never mind. I like it here.

I wrote my first novel. It had the words "White House" in the title, and that somehow fixed me, if not pigeonholed me, as a "Washington novelist." At first I was quite delighted with this appelation. Me, a "Washington novelist." I don't think we're in New York anymore, Toto.

I wrote a second novel that didn't have "White House" or "Washington" or "Potomac" or "Power and Principle" or any other denotative code words in the title. There was a disappointed sound from the gallery when it came out (despite good reviews). *It's very nice and all, but frankly we were rather expecting another Washington book. . . .*

I wrote a third novel. It didn't have D.C. buzzwords in the title, but it was certainly a "Washington novel." (Main character: a K Street tobacco spokesman. Washington enough for you?) The gallery expressed satisfaction: *Now* that's *more like it.* Once again I was, in the reviews, a "Washington novelist," or just "Washington writer." "Washington satirist" followed. I guess whatever my feelings about the Department of Public Works, this effectively rules out fleeing to the burbs. "Bethesda novelist," "Chevy Chase satirist" just doesn't have the same oomph. There's this, too: if you live somewhere where renewing your car registration is automatic and painless, you won't be inspired to write satire. Efficient government—local and federal—would only wreck my career.

Washington was my writer's capital, as Melville put it in a more aqueous context, my Harvard, my Yale. I was quite innocent when I arrived here with my houseplants, Hermes typewriter and *Bartlett's Familiar Quotations.* I'd seen a bit of the world; rather a lot of it, actually. But oh what a brave new world was Washington, that had such people in't! A few weeks after I arrived that suffocating July, 1981, I soon found myself in the White House mess, that is, the Navy-run dining room in the basement, listening to two (grown) speechwriters arguing furiously over who had had more "face time"—face time! oh brave neologisms!—in the "Oval" with "POTUS." (The first term is synecdoche, of course; the second an acronym for President of the United States.) All this I watched in fascination and in wonder. Here was a ritual that had been acted and reenacted since the first royal court was established thousands of years ago in the palmly deserts of the Fertile Crescent, when the first Rosencrantz and Guildenstern squabbled over who had spent more time sucking up to Assurbanipal.

I don't think my two messmates were familiar with Alexander Pope's "Epitaph for one who would not be buried in Westminster Abbey":

> *Heroes and kings! your distance keep,*
> *In peace let me poor poet sleep,*
> *Who never flattered folks like you:*
> *Let Horace blush, and Vergil too.*

The little episode was my first inkling that I had found my proper place in the universe. There's a Spanish word my father taught me early on:

querencia. Literally "favored spot." It's used in bullfighting. When the bull enters the ring, the matador watches very intently as the bull seeks out the spot where it feels safe. Once he finds it, he will continue as the anger and pain increase, to return to it. The matador must therefore take care not to put himself between the bull and his *querencia,* for once he has set his charge for this—to put in a Washington way—safe house, he will keep going, no matter what stands in his path. He will not be tempted by a proffered cape. Woe to the matador who has misjudged the invisible spot in the sand. At any rate, I had found my *querencia.* Or, as these things happen, it had found me.

I was surprised to find myself so contentedly situated. I was a New Yorker, and New Yorkers—for the most part—are programmed to disdain Washington as a third-rate burg with not enough first-rate restaurants. Of course, Reagan changed that, for a time. The Eastern Shuttle was crammed with **boldfaced** names from "Suzy Says." There was a touch of mink about the place for a while until the new tenants, a Greenwich Episcopalian and his what-you-see-is-what-you-get wife moved in and the ethos changed from Rodeo Drive to—go figure— Country Western. But all that was merely ebb and tide. It was permanent Washington, with its solemn absurdities, its motorcades of vanity, its noisy earnestness, its pomp and mitigating circumstance, its serene solipcism—to say nothing of its perfectly good, even terrific restaurants—that held me here.

Otherwise I suppose, I would have given the houseplants to the lady next door, dropped off *Bartlett's* at the Vassar book sale, and caught the last shuttle back to New York.

I'm still perplexed about this elusive thing, the "Washington writer." Is Charles McCarry a "Washington novelist" because he has written about spooks? Larry McMurtry spent a quarter century here—though he did keep a place in West Archer, Texas—but managed never to become a "Washington writer." *Lonesome Dove* isn't about Strobe Talbott at the disarmament table. Is Anonymous a "Washington writer"? Apparently not, as one hears he's just bought a new house in Pelham, New York. It would be a stretcher to call my British chum Christopher Hitchens a "Washington writer," though he has certainly created the most interesting, or as we used to say in foreign policy speeches, "vibrant" Washington literary salons going, with a Vermouth splash of Hollywood glam, owing to his *Vanity Fair* gig. Very casual. Martin Amis, Salman Rushdie, Julian Barnes, Kevin Costner's coming. Barbra Streisand may drop by. Come early and have a drink, shall we say *vers sept heures?* Doesn't *sound* like a "Washington writer," does he? What about Edmund and Sylvia Morris, the Nick and Nora of biography (Reagan–Clare Boothe Luce). Are they "Washington writers"? Nah. Too exotic. But they're here, thank heavens.

Was Gore Vidal typed as a "Washington writer" after *The City and the Pillar?* He seems more of a Washington writer now, in his umpteenth decade as a resident of Ravello, Italy, than he did after that first shockeroo of a novel appeared. He writes oftener and oftener these days about Washington. *Nostalgie de la boue?* An aspect of his narcissism? It was here, after all, that he grew up and first fell in love, with, now he tells us, a Saint Alban's schoolmate. Perhaps in the end, you don't have to live here at all to be a "Washington writer." Perhaps—how does it go?—Washington is a moveable beast.

—*The Washington Post,* 1996

Wish I'd Said That

I was on a jury recently, and got to say something I thought I'd never get to say. It was during the preliminary process known as *voir dire,* French for "Interminable process that makes you regret ever having registered to vote."

The judge was asking us a series of questions to determine our suitability to serve. He asked if any of us knew anyone in the intelligence agencies. Not wanting to share the particulars of my answer with a packed courtroom, I meekly stuck my hand in the air and asked, "Your honor, may I approach the bench?"

"Approach," he said. I approached, feeling very puffed up and important.

The next day I recounted my thrill to my friend Geoff Norman, who happened to serve with Special Forces in Vietnam. He shared my excitement: "It's like the first time I got to say, 'Cover me.'" This rather put my big rhetorical moment in perspective.

For most of us, life is less dramatic than the movies. Few of us will get to deliver the really cool lines, like "Charge!" or "Sponge, clamp, sutures," or "I'd like to thank the Academy."

I suppose that most men, at some point in their lives, have imagined themselves saying, "Take her down to periscope depth." Or even, "Fire torpedo tubes number one and two." Who among us hasn't found some excuse to say out loud, "Set your phasers on stun"—even if we were only holding a water pistol?

Space is the final verbal frontier. A lot of really studly things get said in space, starting with, ". . . three, two, one, ignition, liftoff." But with my math SATs, there was never a chance I'd be the one pronouncing those words. Or, "Fire secondary stage booster." Or, "The Eagle has landed." Sometimes, when I land at the airport, I call my wife and say that, but from that to the taxi stand is downhill.

I have gotten to say some of the big lines. Once, as I poured out the ashes of a friend, I said, "We now commit his body to the deep, in the hope of eternal resurrection, when the sea shall give up her dead." I've said, from the top of a ship's mast after crossing an ocean, "Land ho!" Melodramatic I admit, but it sounded better than, "Yo, Spain!" A few times at sea, I've uttered those goose-bumply syllables, "Thar she blows!" I've said, on my knees, "Will you marry me?" A few years later, I said until I was hoarse, "It's a girl!" A few years after that, "It's a boy!" So I've been lucky. I've gotten to say the best of it.

A friend of mine tells the story about the magistrate in Scotland. The town drunk was hauled in before him for the umpteenth time. The magistrate looked down on him and said, "You have been found guilty of the crime of public drunkenness. It is the sentence of this court that you be taken from here to the place of execution and there hanged by the neck until you are dead. And may God Almighty have mercy upon your soul."

The drunk fainted. As they were reviving him, the bailiff looked up quizzically at the judge. The judge shrugged and said, "I've just always wanted to say that."

I know exactly how he felt.

Index